SUCK *and* **BLOW**

SUCK and BLOW

And Other Stories
I'm Not Supposed to Tell

JOHN POPPER

WITH

DEAN BUDNICK

DA CAPO PRESS

A Member of the Perseus Books Group

Editorial production by Lori Hobkirk at the Book Factory
Design by Cynthia Young at Sagecraft
Set in 11.5 point Minion Pro

Cataloging-in-Publication data for this book is
available from the Library of Congress.
ISBN: 978-0-306-82404-3 (hardcover)
ISBN: 978-0-306-82405-0 (e-book)

Published by Da Capo Press
A Member of the Perseus Books Group
www.dacapopress.com

Da Capo Press books are available at special discounts for bulk purchases in the
U.S. by corporations, institutions, and other organizations. For more information,
please contact the Special Markets Department at the Perseus Books Group,
2300 Chestnut Street, Suite 200, Philadelphia, PA 19103, or call (800) 810-4145,
ext. 5000, or e-mail special.markets@perseusbooks.com.

All photos are courtesy of John Popper, except for the following:
10 is from Patrick Stevens; 23, 25, and 32 are from AJ Genovesi;
13, 15, and 17 are from Andrew Schuman.

10 9 8 7 6 5 4 3 2 1

For Eloise,
Welcome! This is only the beginning;
the Afterword is all about you. I'll see you there . . .

Jordan, I love you . . .

CONTENTS

1

APPLYING MYSELF

As I sat in the dean's office, my moment of sweet vindication was at hand.

The New School for Jazz and Contemporary Music was going to open its doors in the fall of 1986, and I was angling to be among its first students.

The problem was that after five years of high school (that's right, five—I delivered an encore performance of my junior year), my grades were mostly F's, with a few D's sprinkled in.

Around eighth grade I had made a vow not to do any homework. It just seemed pointless to me. After-school time was *me* time. When my parents and teachers told me to apply myself, I reasoned that by not doing any homework, I was being true to my nature and, therefore, *was* applying myself. I kind of felt like Einstein because he would do his work, then rip it up and start from scratch—I just took a modern approach by not doing any work at all. I also found that if I set expectations really low—if I kept getting F's and then every once in a while get a D, everybody would pat me on the back for it.

But as the dean looked at my transcript and began shaking his head, saying, "I don't know, John . . . . . . ," it didn't seem like a pat was forthcoming.

I had graduated from high school a month earlier and was out of options.

The Manhattan School of Music had seemed like a possibility. I had just finished a two-week summer program there, but then they sent me thirty-two bars of Bach that I would need to learn for an audition. Since I really don't know how to read music, that was out.

It was at the Manhattan School summer program where I met Arnie Lawrence, who was among the founding faculty of the New School. He was the one who had encouraged me to apply.

The only other plan I had was to make my way to Chicago, harmonica in hand, and find Sugar Blue. I would challenge him to a duel, and if I lost, then in some twisted variation of Ralph Macchio in *Crossroads*, I would sell my clothes and become his apprentice. If I won, then I would sit on his throne as the King of the Blues.

My family thought this was stupid.

I really had no plan at all.

But as I sat across from the dean, the one thing I did have was my harmonica.

I pulled it out of my pocket and he asked me to play. I threw everything I had into the solo and, as I brought it to a rousing, climatic close, he sighed, "Okay, we'll let you in."

The dean had completely proven my philosophy.

If hadn't had my harmonica in my pocket, I wouldn't have gotten into the New School. But if I'd gotten good grades *and* had a harmonica in my pocket, then all of that work would have been completely redundant.

That's the important thing to remember: if I had gotten A's in high school, it would have been a waste of all that valuable time.

So kids, if you aspire to a job someday where you'll tour the world, receive a check for a million dollars, receive the adulation of a million fans, and find yourself in the White House greeting presidents, then stop doing your homework.

2

BLINDING THEM
WITH SCIENCE

I always sat way too close to the TV.

This not only impacted my vision—I've got the glasses to prove it—but also impacted my *vision*: I had certain expectations of the world.

After absorbing so many scripted stories from my particular vantage point, I sought to experience one of those dramatic moments when time stopped and E.T. took the bicycle into the sky.

As it turned out, that actually happened to me—when I was a junior in high school (for the first time)—and I've felt the repercussions ever since.

My high school in Stamford, Connecticut, was particularly abusive to people who didn't fit in, and they decided they were going to break me. I hadn't mastered showering—I was a once-a-week guy—and I'd make weird noises humming to myself because I was usually the only company I kept. It was pretty easy for me to be pegged as a weirdo. I was big and didn't play football, and if you were big and didn't play football, that was two strikes against you. They even tied me to the bleachers once.

I remained fairly antisocial for a while after we moved to Princeton, New Jersey, when I was sixteen. That's where I would eat pencils for money—the key is you bite the eraser off first and swallow it like a pill, and by then everyone is just grossed out. I didn't really have a normal sense of social interaction with people. I lived in my imagination.

But it was in Princeton where my moment arrived.

I was the third-string trumpet player in the beginner band. I had landed there after I did really well on an untimed SAT in the special ed class where they had placed me after the move from Stamford. I had shitty grades, and they were going to send me to a school for the learning disabled, but then they tested me and discovered that I had college-level reading and comprehension skills.

They decided they needed to somehow connect me with school. The remedial teacher saw me playing harmonica in the parking lot, so she sent me to the high school band teacher, who explained, "We don't really have harmonica here. We play big band jazz. Is there any other instrument you'd like to play?" I said, "I dunno—trumpet?" because he had one there and it looked shiny. So he said, "Great," gave me a trumpet, and kicked me out of his office.

They sent me to the trumpet teacher, who gave me homework—it was a complicated instrument and you have to learn the rudiments—but homework was something I had given up back in eighth grade. Needless to say, I did not flourish at the trumpet.

I was resigned to playing third-chair trumpet and having my trumpet teacher yell at me and wag his finger until this one day in the JV band when we were playing Thomas Dolby's "She Blinded Me with Science." It was our first opportunity to really get to solo, and the band teacher went around the room pointing to different people. I did my crappy trumpet solo—I could barely play the damn thing—but also had the three harmonicas in the trumpet case and, luckily, had one in the right key. So I held it up and he said, "Yeah, sure, give it a try."

It was one of those Excalibur moments. I started playing, and suddenly the whole room stopped. I can remember somebody in the saxophone section saying, "He's so good." The next day I was in the first-string band playing harmonica, and I never had to touch a trumpet again. They even brought in the principal to watch me.

It was like the moment in *The Natural* when Robert Redford gets his hand on a baseball bat. It was a defining moment, and right away almost everyone in school knew my name—"Hey Popper! You're that harmonica dude!" Basically it's been that way ever since and I've developed a comfort level with people knowing about me and what I do. Over the years I've realized that they'll sometimes claim to know things about me that aren't even true.

So here's my version of the story, admittedly told from the perspective of a guy who sat way too close to the TV.

For another indication of what this time of my life was like, I'll jump ahead a year to a moment when I went with a friend from the jazz band to see Wynton Marsalis in Red Bank, New Jersey. We were hanging outside, having a cigarette, when we realized the dressing room window was open and there was Wynton with his group. I had my harmonica in my pocket—that's the great thing about a harmonica: you can just have it in your pocket. I whispered, "Should I play?" And my friend said, "No, don't do it."

But I couldn't control myself, so I played a little bit. Then we heard, "Yo, play that blues, man." It was Wynton. So I just went off—by then I had a standard going-off thing that I would do at high school assemblies. I went off and then heard "Holy shit!"—and that was my hero Wynton Marsalis saying that.

He invited us into the dressing room and signed my harmonica case. I was on cloud nine and still have that harmonica case.

That's something I can't stress enough: before I played the harmonica, I had no social skills. Actually I'm not sure I have social skills now, but at least the harmonica acts as a substitute. It's amazing how people don't give a damn about you if you lack social skills.

I wasn't the one who got it the worst in my high school, though. There was this whole cast of people who no one saw, at least not in Princeton. I was scary—"Don't mess with him—he's weird and doesn't comb his hair." I think I had this desire to fit in but no way to do it. So the contrast with suddenly being known by everybody was all the more striking.

It was during my middle school days when I first became a performer. I've always called those years my Vietnam experience because that's when I was really picked on—hunted for meat, I used to say.

I attended the Harvey School in Katonah, New York. It was a boarding school, but I would a drive half hour each day from Stamford, Connecticut. We had to wear a tie and jacket and call teachers "Sir." When a student did something wrong, he would get demerits, and when he had enough, he would have to run laps. In the winter when it was too cold to run, we had to write "How sharper than a serpent's tooth it is to have a thankless child" ten times. So we'd tape ten pens together and write them that way. Demerit pens, we called them. (The quote is from *King Lear*. I looked it up. I don't think I knew that at the time.)

They had a mandatory sports program, and I did not want to get naked in the locker room. So I would hide in the woods with the other mutants, like the three-foot-tall kid with the giant head and the kid with the really thick glasses. I was the fat guy. We were like the kids in *Lord of the Flies*, so I guess I was Piggy. We hid in the woods and tried making wine with some berries we found. It was horrible.

The head of the athletics department was a full-blooded Hungarian, Mr. Gobel. He called me a half-breed because my dad was Hungarian—he was raised there before he escaped the country in 1951—and my mom's a WASP who can trace her roots back to the First Families of Virginia, back to Thomas Jefferson and Patrick Henry. Mr. Gobel decided he was going to make a man out of me, but I was no good at soccer and didn't want to wrestle, so I cried. The guy under him, who was the JV wrestling coach, took pity on me and made me the wrestling manager. This meant I had a little clipboard and didn't have to change my clothes in front of the other kids.

School was from eight in the morning until five at night, and practice was from three to five in the afternoon. I had to sit there and help the coach out. At the end of each practice I had to walk out onto the mats and tell a joke. If they didn't think the joke was funny, they got to kick my ass until I got off the mat. So what I learned to do was to tell a joke and run. That's how I began learning the rudimentary aspects of captivating a crowd. I looked at an audience as an angry mob of people bent on trying to kill me—I think that was an actual vaudeville tradition. If you walk up to a tiger and look at it in the eye, it'll do what you want, but if you blink, it'll eat you. There really is that element when you're on stage—you start out performing for self-preservation, and then you get better at it and eventually you want to share yourself. I think most people who perform want to share themselves, but it's also probably a defense mechanism on some level.

I wanted to be comedian. In Stamford I met Tom Brown, who was into *Saturday Night Live*. He got *me* into *SNL*—I think comedy was an important refuge for a lot of fat or antisocial kids. I had finally found something I could imagine doing with my life: performing.

After middle school I attended Stamford Catholic High School, where we participated in the Green and Gold Show. It was some sort of talent show, and Tom and I did sound effects. We were horrible, but I became addicted to that moment when the lights came up. It was the first time I was ever on stage, and that was when I decided I really wanted to be a comedian.

But all of that changed because of *Saturday Night Live*. After I saw the Blues Brothers I suddenly wanted to play the harmonica like Dan Aykroyd's Elwood Blues.

I always had some connection to music. I can remember learning that I had perfect pitch when I was a kid singing in church. My sister's violin teacher told my parents to encourage my musical development, so they gave me a cello, in part because my great grand uncle David Popper was a world-famous cellist (I found out later in life that I'm also related to the philosopher Karl Popper). But I had a shitty bowing hand and it's hard; you've got to practice—it doesn't give you gratification right away. So I looked good with it but I never practiced and never learned to read the notes. Eventually I abandoned the violin. The next step was piano lessons at age eight, but again I didn't read music, although it was certainly a better experience than the cello. Then my parents had me take up the tuba—that's a classic: give the fat kid a tuba. It was a baritone horn, so they took a little bit of pity on me, but the same thing happened. I never learned to read music and didn't practice.

When I was eleven I took guitar lessons. It started out promising—I had learned one of Vivaldi's fugues by ear. I could play it with my thumb and two fingers—my index and middle fingers on my left hand and my thumb on my right hand. That was encouraging, and I fooled the guitar teacher for weeks when I played "Love Me Tender." I was pretending to read the music but was really playing it by ear. Then one day I played the rhythm slightly differently, and he realized

I had fooled him and kicked me out, telling my parents, "I can't do anything with this guy." Now that, to me, was the biggest mistake—if you have a kid who's fooling you, that means he's gifted, so work with him. But this, along with my academic career, just reinforced my authority issues. I can't stand anybody telling me what to do.

I received a harmonica for my fourteenth birthday but I didn't really play it for nearly two years. The day I got it I could play "Oh! Susanna" and "High Noon (Do Not Forsake Me)." But I put it away until I saw the Blues Brothers, when I realized, *Oh, that's what you can do with a harmonica!*

Then, just as I started getting going with the harp, we moved to Princeton, New Jersey. (By the way, either harmonica or harp is fine by me. I often call it a harp because it's less syllables; Mississippi saxophone also works, but that's long. Some people say mouth organ, but that sounds a bit NSFW.) Moving to Princeton was like being in a Spielberg movie: it was a pristine, beautiful bubble amid the rank highways of Central Jersey, where the sports teams were terrible but the studio band would win award and after award in every jazz competition from there to the Berklee College of Music. The musicians were the hot shits, and the lead trumpet in the jazz band was kind of like the quarterback. It was in Princeton where I would meet the other guys in Blues Traveler.

We moved because my father had taken a job as the vice president of the pharmaceutical company Squibb (which became Bristol-Myers Squibb in 1989). He moved there to pursue his American dream with his wife and seven children.

My father grew up in Hungary, and while he was teenager the Nazis and Russians were fighting over Budapest. There was rape and murder and all manner of bloodshed. Families lost everything. As my dad and his sister, my aunt Eva, were fond of saying, "You don't want to remember these things. You went through them and they happened and you try your best to forget them." As I got older and he told me a few stories, I realized there are American problems and there are old-world problems, and the two are very different.

He has plenty of stories from this time, and my family is working with him on a book about his experiences, so I'll leave those to him.

He came to America, where Aunt Eva put him up and took care of him. She died in 2014, but she led a remarkable life—hung out with Salvador Dali and fought with Zsa Zsa Gabor, because you can't have two beautiful Hungarian women in a room together. Lest you think I'm prone to exaggeration, here is her obituary:

A brilliant, witty, international beauty, born in Budapest, Hungary. She was married for 20 years to US Airforce Officer and diplomat Karel Pusta. Later, she enjoyed 20 happy years with Paul Kovi, owner of the famed Four Seasons restaurants. She has lived in Paris, Washington D.C., New York, California and Budapest.

She worked as a Hungarian broadcaster for Radio Free Europe, a prominent event planner for Hilton Hotels, and Fashion Editor at East/West Network, a publisher of Travel Magazines. She was active in the American Hungarian Foundation and in 2007 won the Officer's Cross Order of Merit of the Republic of Hungary for her diplomatic efforts to improve Hungarian/American relations. Her friendships included luminaries such as Salvador Dali, Pablo Picasso, Oleg Cassini, and David Niven to name a few.

Aunt Eva was a part of this glamorous, jet-set kind of crowd, and among the people she knew was András Simonyi, the Hungarian ambassador. She had him come to a Blues Traveler show in 2005, and he invited me to the ambassador's house in Washington, where I sampled various delicacies. He also plays guitar, so I brought him on stage with us at the 9:30 Club for a couple of tunes. "Who the hell is he?" the band asked. I told them it was the Hungarian ambassador, but they were skeptical. To this day he's one of our most oddly accredited sit-ins.

Aunt Eva helped my dad acclimate to his new country, and soon he enrolled at George Washington University. That's where he met my mom. While they were dating he went off to Fort Lewis in Washington State. He joined the Army to get his citizenship as quickly as possible. He wanted to marry her but didn't want her to wonder whether he was marrying her for citizenship, so he decided to become a citizen before he proposed. He worked his butt off for that.

He finally became an American citizen, they were married, and he started working toward that American dream. He was a computer systems designer when I came along in 1967. He worked at a bank, U.S. Trust, then an ad agency, J. Walter Thompson, and eventually at Squibb.

His version of the American dream was to have seven kids. He was a Catholic, and that was a very Catholic thing to do. My mom's a Presbyterian, so I guess she just went along with it. Her father was a Navy admiral, and his father a Navy admiral before him, who, I am told, helped design the Panama Canal.

My mom had seven kids in rapid succession. She basically spent thirteen years of her life having children. She was a baby machine. Then when I was around eight or nine, she went to Fordham Law School in New York City. As soon as she became a lawyer she turned into a different person. She lost weight, the color returned to her cheeks, and she started getting excited about stuff again. It was exactly the right prescription.

It also allowed the three younger ones to be on our own without as much supervision. I remember the four older kids weren't allowed to say, "Shut up," but by the time our parents got to us, they were so worn down that we could swear all over the place.

My dad didn't want Hungarian kids in America; he wanted American kids, so he never taught us to speak Hungarian. I know the words for "May you be butt-fucked by a horse," but that's about it, and it does you no good in a cab. (I was in Budapest, and I so wanted to show the driver I could speak Hungarian, but where was that going to get me?)

My brother Tom lives in Hungary—I can't tell whether that makes him a renegade or a prodigal son—where he's the editor of a newspaper. He says that the way my dad speaks Hungarian is like ancient Shakespearean Hungarian.

We were in Egypt once, and this guy in a thick Egyptian accent asked my dad where he was from. My dad, in his thick Hungarian accent, said, "I am an American." And the guy, in his thick Egyptian accent, asked, "No, where are you *really* from?" And my dad answered in his thick Hungarian accent: "I am an American." They went back and forth like that for a while.

Once he was an American, that was it.

When I was a kid I'd wake up and he'd be singing, "I'd love to be an Oscar Mayer weiner . . . . . . " horribly out of tune and making up the words but bellowing at the top of his lungs. He loved the sound of that song. I think it was because he'd had to learn English, and in Hungarian the W sound is substituted with a V sound, so singing that for him was liberating. (When my little brother was five they went around the class asking what words began with the letter V, and my brother said, "vindshield viper.") He told me that he used to fall asleep with his lips in a pucker to help him with words like "you"—speaking Hungarian doesn't require much puckering.

Every now and then I try to imagine what it was like for him—to leave behind everything you know and go to this whole new place with all of these different rules and learn a completely different language. Then, if you keep driving through the smoke, you're going to get a life that you wouldn't otherwise have been able to get.

I think that's why I've always enjoyed the Marx Brothers because I can appreciate their perspective. It's immigrant humor. It's anti-authoritarian and subversive, and that's part of the American story. It was also my attitude in school.

I admired Groucho, but I *was* Harpo. Harpo was a free spirit. Groucho was more pragmatic; he accepted that we have to talk our way around situations, which is basically an intellectual approach to being Harpo. Whenever I saw Harpo my eyes lit up. I wanted to be that guy. After all, who doesn't want to pull a swordfish out of his pants?

3

WHIPLASHED

When the film *Whiplash* came out in the fall of 2014, I heard from a friend that the character of the perfectionist teacher/band leader, for which J. K. Simmons would go on to win the Academy Award for Best Actor, was based on my high school band teacher Anthony Biancosino. So I went to see the film, and the real giveaway was that the beginner band is called the Nassau Band and the competition band is the Studio Band. Those are unique to Princeton because Nassau Street was the main street in Princeton. Eventually I read an article that said that the writer/director, Damien Chazelle, did indeed attend Princeton High School. Although it was two decades later, Mr. B was still there and, like Miles Teller's character in the film, Damien was a drummer in the band.

Mr. Biancosino did a lot of good things for people, and I never saw him slap anyone, but he was a serious perfectionist about the drums. Just like in the movie, he would kick someone off the drum kit and put him on this really bad, out-of-tune conga drum. He would put a drummer on, kick a drummer off, put a drummer on, kick a drummer off. When I was there all the drummers went through that, particularly because they were rock drummers and he wanted a big-band drummer. The drummers' love of Led Zeppelin's John Bonham was unacceptable to Mr. Biancosino, but if you were a high school drummer in the eighties, you loved John Bonham. At some point he'd get so frustrated that he'd play the drums himself, and he was terrible at it.

He really did love the kids, though, and wanted us to succeed as a top-notch band, which we did, and we had the trophies to prove it. I still have a couple of my own; they're in my office at home: Best Soloist trophy from 1985 Carteret Jazz Festival and the Verona Jazz Festival Outstanding Soloist Award.

The songbook, though, was an advanced repertoire compared to most other high school bands. Chan Kinchla, my future guitarist, was on the Princeton High School football team and remembers being mortified by this. At halftime the other team would have a marching band parade show, then we'd bring out a little stage and play Glenn Miller. Seeing our big band come out at halftime was not a source of pride or inspiration for the squad.

We played these aggressive competitive-style jazz songs with super-challenging time signatures, crazy-ass solos, and ridiculous horn parts. They were all written by some asshole at a music college somewhere who saw a business in creating weird things for high school bands who wanted to participate in the competition circuit.

But even though Mr. B certainly could be intense, particularly when it came to the drummers, I escaped all of that. We'd play "Whiplash," which Hank Levy wrote in 7/4, or "Chain Reaction," which was in 13/8, and everyone else had to learn these very precise parts. But not me. I was free to make up what I wanted because there weren't any harmonica parts written. There was no one to tell me if I was doing it wrong; there was no harmonica authority. There was a trumpet authority, there was a trombone authority, there were authorities for all the other instruments, but I had this great autonomy.

I was an attraction, and Mr. B would just point to me for a solo, and that's all I had to do. I would watch my band leader yell at everybody else while I would just sit there. On the rare occasion when he did yell at me, it would be something vague like, "Could you make it a little more peppy?" or, more commonly, "Don't be such a smartass." That's when I would excel; I would soar when they just left me alone. The key lesson was that there are times when you should fear authority, but you certainly don't have to listen to it.

I took a clean, unused plunger to make a homemade harmonica amplifier and plugged it into a bass amp. I cut a larger hole into the end of the plunger where the stick normally goes in and wedged a tape recorder microphone into the contraption.

Then Mr. B put a few more rock songs into the repertoire within the confines he deemed acceptable. We did the *Ghostbusters* theme and "Lapti Nek," the song they play in Jabba the Hutt's palace in *Return of the Jedi*, which was a funk in E-flat, so I could jam on that. My harmonica was a selling point for letting him do this, and instantly I went from being a weird mutant into being the big man on campus.

When you start out so antisocial, it's a pretty lonely existence. I'd already made my peace with all of that. So to turn it around within the time I was in high school seemed to me like it was out of a movie. I felt like Molly Ringwald.

That band was the first team I ever belonged to. At first they didn't know what to make of me—they thought I was an antisocial belligerent—but eventually we became friends. The first girl I ever fell in love with was the alto sax player. I would have a crush on her forever and write tons of songs about her.

But although that whole experience transformed me in many ways, the one thing it didn't change was my attitude toward schoolwork.

It began all the way back in first grade when we were supposed to practice our writing. We were told to write something like "Today is Thursday" in the morning, and it would take me all day, so already I was pigeonholed. There were the Lippincott kids who would learn how to read stories and the SRA kids who were the morons. It was all about people deciding who you were and where they thought you belonged. They tested me and decided I was disgraphic, a form of dyslexia.

So for many years I would do my best—or my interpretation of my best—and at the end of the year they would advance me to the next grade. By the time I got to middle school, where there was more of a blind emphasis on grades, my parents started to take notice.

That was when my dad bought me my first shotgun. It was a single-shot Iver Johnson, and my dad told me we had made a sacred oath, and in exchange I would get good grades. He wanted to buy me the shotgun, and I really wanted the shotgun, but I was certain I was flunking and didn't know how to tell him—I thought this was news best told by a report card. So he purchased it on the promise that I would get good grades. What I was thinking the whole time was, *He's going to find out my grades suck and I'm not going get the shotgun.* But he bought it and unveiled it—"Here's your shotgun because you got good grades!" Then he took a look at my report card and gave the shotgun to my little brother. Eventually I got my first shotgun, but it took years.

History repeated itself in the spring of 1983 when we moved to Princeton. We moved on my sixteenth birthday, and although the driving age in Connecticut was sixteen, it was seventeen in New Jersey. My parents felt terrible about this, so I used this guilt to get myself a moped—it was legal for me to ride it by myself even though I couldn't drive a car for another year. I had wanted a mini-bike since I was a kid, so I thought, *This is crazy—I get a moped. New Jersey's wonderful!*

But it was all on the condition that my grades improve. So I thought, *Oh no, here we go again.* I brought home my report card, and suddenly my little brother got to ride the moped. He was too young to ride it on the road but was allowed to ride it in the yard, and of course, he crashed it the first day. He didn't really hurt it, but when I finally had my chance in the fall, the little basket was already bent.

The new school year always came with optimism, at least for my parents, but nothing much changed for me. I had, by now, made my own sacred vow not to do any homework.

What I found was that I did okay, especially in English and history, when I listened to everybody talk the next day. I would take in the class discussion, and when that ran dry I would be interesting or distracting. The teacher might ask, "Does anybody know the theme behind the *Godfather*?" and I would sing it, and that would crack the class up. I'd be the funny guy, and it would also take the teacher out of his lesson, slowing everybody down and catching me up. Then if I really didn't know what else to say, I would challenge everyone else, and as long as I could interject something interesting, the teacher would get caught up in it as well. So we'd still have a nice conversation and we'd all learn something; it just might not be something from the lesson plan.

My only problem was that in science and math class this approach didn't work at all. I can still remember one of the questions in chemistry: "What is the definition of work?" There was some sort of equation involving energy times something, but I wrote, "Work is the accomplishment of doing something." I thought that was a perfectly acceptable answer, but the teacher didn't agree.

I would be so behind that I didn't even want to be in front. My parents would get me a tutor, so I'd make friends with the tutor and then the tutor would do my work for me. If I were behind in English, I'd work on it with my mom and give dictation, which was great.

I also learned another neat trick about education, which is if you keep getting F's, they eventually become meaningless. The teachers would say, "He's not being taught right" or "He's not properly motivated." Then they'd give me some sort of catch-up make-up test, and I'd get my mom to do it when I was young or my smart tutor when I was in high school, and that worked just like a dream.

Another riff on that same idea is if you get a detention then skip that detention. They'll give you another detention and then you skip that one. Eventually you get so many detentions that you can't be there to do all these detentions and then you're free.

Going to school with two working parents and a working moped gave me another kind of freedom as well. In the morning I would go to band practice, and then around second period I would disappear on my moped. I would cruise by the supermarket, grab some canned ravioli and some Pop-Tarts, go home, and watch my videotape of *Letterman* from the night before. It was a great way to spend my time. Little did I know I was doing career research.

During my junior year, we were only allowed to have eighteen absences, and I had fifty-five. If you just keep skipping, eventually they have to work something out with you. You don't go straight to being flunked out unless they genuinely don't care about you. That's the thing: they cared about me enough not to kick me out of school, but they still didn't know what to do with me.

There had been a contract I signed with the help of my guidance counselor that was supposedly with the superintendent. I promised I would work really hard so I would pass. But my guidance counselor had a baby, and her replacement hadn't quite understood that this contract was supposed to be taken seriously. The new guidance counselor thought I had committed to trying harder, but what I had actually agreed to was that if I had any more absences, I would be expelled from school. This gave me carte blanche for some time to skip classes, apologize, get detentions, and then skip those detentions. It worked for quite a while.

But finally there was a meeting with all of my teachers, my mom, and the principal. What was I to do when I was finally confronted by all of these people I had been lying to, who had now gathered in the same room? My first instinct was to identify the factions. Half of them wanted to punish me and half wanted to punish the system. Well, how was I supposed to feel when I was getting these mixed messages? I started them on arguing with each other. The only person who got what I was doing was my history teacher. He was looking over at me, shaking his head, laughing, and the next day he said to me, "I saw you in that meeting. You're going to do just fine in this world."

Eventually it all caught up with me—sort of. They gave me the choice to work really, really hard and graduate with my original class or, as I heard it, I could relax and repeat junior year. This wasn't much of a choice for me. My parents were against it, but I said, "Wait, did you say I could relax?"—again, missing the point. It's all about figuring out what motivates a kid, because if you're going to be motivated *for* a kid, all you're going to be doing is striking a stubborn mule. You'll hurt your hand and nothing will happen except that you'll ensure that the homework will remain undone.

Eventually they decided to let me graduate. I got so good at one weird little thing that the school let me out with less than the required credits. You needed a hundred credits to graduate, and my bass player Bobby did it with ninety-eight. That's pretty good, but I did it with ninety-four. That became a badge of honor.

Their attitude was, "Let's just let him out of here." They wouldn't have done that if I were headed to bank robbery or petty crime, but they knew that I was smart and that there was no way I was going to independently pass a chemistry test. So what were they supposed to do? Make me sit there until I was thirty-five? I remember when I got my diploma there was the largest round of applause, and it was mostly from the teachers. I think I kind of broke them down, and it was, strangely, effortless, primarily because I knew of no other way to get through it.

What I'm best at is avoiding work, and I worked very hard at it.

4

TOO MANY NOTES

After we moved to Princeton I began spending hours in the basement with the harmonica. I was happy to do that because I never saw it as work as long as no one was telling me what to do.

It started in Stamford when my friend Tom Brown introduced me to *Saturday Night Live*, which led to me discovering the Blues Brothers. My first goal was to play like Dan Aykroyd. I remember somebody said that Dan Aykroyd sounded like Paul Butterfield, so I went to get a Paul Butterfield album at the Princeton Record Exchange—it was the double album, *Live*. Shortly after I took it home, I loved it so much that I attempted to kiss the album, dropped it, and, in the process, broke it. But I had the other disc, so I played "Drifting and Drifting" every morning. I woke up and I learned the solo to the live "Drifting and Drifting," note for note.

Paul Butterfield was doing Elmore James and John Lee Hooker tunes, which got me fascinated with those guys. But when I heard Jimi Hendrix do "Voodoo Chile," both the full one and "Slight Return," *that's* when I knew what I wanted to do for a living. That was when I stopped wanting to be a comedian—because there was a sound Hendrix was getting that I'd never heard before and I *had* to make that sound happen on the harmonica.

With my lips I could do anything. My fingers sucked; I could never make my fingers do what I wanted to do on the cello or the piano or the guitar. But my face could always generate the sound I was after. I felt a link to Hendrix in that way because he really seemed to be able to get any sound *he* wanted. When you hear a Hendrix solo, you feel that he was only limited by his ears.

I first *really* listened to Hendrix at my friend Steve's apartment on 16th Street between 7th and 8th Avenues in Chelsea. I'd known him since first grade, and he had moved from Stamford into this little shit-box apartment with his mom. We'd smoke pot and then play Hendrix and Santana records—about fifteen years later when I inducted Carlos into the Rock and Roll Hall of Fame, I described first listening to "Oye Como Va" and seeing God.

Around the time when I was still playing trumpet in the beginner band, Steve and I started a rock group with Zach Throne, who also lived in the city (and would later become a professional musician). We'd hang out at Zach's father's apartment. Zach's dad was a character actor, Malachi Throne, who was in the unaired *Star Trek* pilot, which later became part of the episode called "The Menagerie." That was his big claim to fame, at least in our minds, so we called ourselves Menagerie. We later changed it to Beggerman Thief. It was a saxophone, a guitar, and a harmonica, but all we really did was smoke pot and fantasize about the limousine we'd have someday.

I'd get on the bus from Princeton, and I remember bringing the trumpet case one time—back when I was still playing in the beginner band—and putting it on the escalator at the Port Authority. It wedged in there, stopping the whole escalator, and the case broke. I then had to carry around the trumpet case tied together with a belt. So that really wasn't going so well.

However, I was really progressing on the harmonica. I spent months in my basement with the TV at half volume and me at full volume. I would just go through the rudiments and was applying what I'd hear in band class—that's a fifth, that's a third—and was really getting it. Then I was trying to sound like Eddie Van Halen's "Eruption." I kept trying to do these intervals faster and faster. I would spend hours at it each day, and it never felt like work; it felt like play, which was interesting to me.

My sister started to hide the harmonica because I was driving everyone nuts. I learned to do three notes because of the "Eruption" finger tapping, and then I learned a sextuplet phrase. In my head I would say, "The O'Shaughnessy Cage"—that was the phonetic pattern—and once I learned to play that fast, I just changed my position with that same pattern and started moving around and keeping it to triplets or sextuplets as I needed. I developed this technique over the course of a year and a half.

This was long before I was learning to play full melodies, but it was a beginning, and that was already more than anyone had figured out how to do on a blues harp. I'd already discovered something truly unique, and I was only seventeen years old. I kept it up, and pretty soon not only would I be as fast as anybody; I would also have my own sound. That should be the goal on any instrument—to make a sound that's just like you.

The caliber of blues harmonica in New York during this era was terrible. In Chicago, however, you had Sugar Blue. I saw him when I was in high school and drank five gin and tonics and still walked away sober. He was the first guy I saw go up on those high notes, so I went home and started working on those. The problem with Sugar back then was that he was on drugs, so he was hit or miss. But when he was on, he was an amazing player.

A couple of years later, when I started playing out in New York, I began to run into these traditionalists who thought the harmonica had to keep the vocabulary established in the 1940s. They thought it should sound the way James Cotton played it because he was the last guy to play with Muddy Waters. For them, that was as far as the harmonica could go, and anything more was blasphemy.

They would hear me play and then would tell me things that were straight out of the movie *Amadeus*. They told me I used too many notes. I wanted to ask them which notes I should lose. Or they would say, "You've got to learn about tone, son." Or they'd give me an antiquated saying or colloquialism to shut me down or get me in line behind them. Their initial reaction to me was one of fear.

So at these jam sessions I would be as nice as I could until we got on stage, where I would then beat the shit out of them. They didn't know what to do with me. Almost immediately my approach was completely different, and I smacked the cowboy shit out of them. When the song was over I would be completely oblivious—"I don't even know what happened"—and they would just stare at me like there was a weird light around me. I let them look at me that way because every time I listened to them, they were trying to stop me. I'd run into that before in high school—if there's any kind of unique approach, the first reaction is to shut you down, and I've never encountered that more than in the harmonica-playing community.

I remember Robert Bonfiglio, who plays classical harmonica with symphony orchestras, called my parents and warned them, "People will try to stop him." I thought he was nuts, but he actually kind of called it. We met on a gig, a Chuck Wagon commercial my teacher got me when I was a student at the New School. For some reason, he was playing the jaw harp and I was playing the harmonica, even though he could have played the harmonica, and he invited me to the Harmonica Club. They would meet on Wednesday and talk about "harmonica issues" and "harmonica rights," and I noticed that he would twitch a little whenever he said harmonica. I just knew, *Don't ever go to this place. Whatever you do, never go there.* I sensed rituals involving a paddle and hood.

I also got a feel for the politics of the scene, and I knew that if I was outside of it, they'd have to like me because they couldn't dismiss me—in fact, they would need me. So I wouldn't go to the harmonica clinics and talk about harmonica rights. They invited me to speak once and I sent them a stripper instead. I took that one out of the Bill Graham playbook.

Bill Graham was once called into a meeting by other promoters and because he liked the mafia sense of it, in the middle of the meeting he had a bunch of guys run in wearing suits and hats and carrying violin cases. They swarmed into the meeting and asked him, "Boss, are you okay?" Bill waved his hand, said, "It's alright," and they left. I loved his theatrics, but the best I could do was muster up a stripper. Where Bill wanted to be a mafia don, I elected to be the Joker.

I wanted to look at my instrument like you would a trombone or an electric guitar. There was no trombone club. Nobody was meeting to discuss electric guitar issues. There shouldn't be clubs for specific instruments like they're factions. I don't want to feel like a persecuted lost tribe of the music world. The harmonica is an instrument, not a religion.

The other thing I eventually learned was not to turn everything into a duel. I can hurt a lot of people, but I've done that, and again, it's just like treating the harmonica like it's part of that lost tribe. If you go around always trying to outplay other people, you'll be a chophound and that's all you'll ever be.

Jason Ricci is an awesome harp player. He's someone who plays very differently from me, and I love that, but people always want to compare the two of us or put him in opposition to me. He's that *other* harp player. There's this harmonica documentary, *Pocket Full of Soul*, where because of that dueling culture, people want him to talk about me. You can tell he's sick of it but has to acknowledge me, so it's a big pain in the butt.

One time when I was still in high school Blues Traveler was invited to back George Jr., who was playing the Princeton reunion with Pinetop Perkins. He had this harmonica player Bill Dicey with him, and Bill gave me the whole too-many-notes-you-got-to-learn-about-tone speech.

Cut to a few years later in New York City around 1990. Blues Traveler had become a big deal, and I was a hotshot in New York City. We were in the Nightingale Bar in the East Village, and somebody came in and said, "Bill Dicey is playing next door at the Dan Lynch Blues Bar." Well, I'm remembering the whole little speech he gave me, so I said, "Oh *is* he?"

So I walked next door to sit in with him, and no one could have turned me away. He saw me, and I could detect the worried look come over his face. I asked him whether I could sit in, and he said somewhat meekly, "Okay, okay, the second set." I'm sure he could see the look on my face, which was, *Ho ho ho, let's have some fun!* Because by then my style was quite acceptable. In fact, it could be said that people were freaking out over it and really loved it. And he was trying his best—I could heard his game go up—but in the end he was very ordinary, a standard blues harp player from the 1980s.

He was doing his thing, and I was sitting there, waiting for my turn to kill him, because at that point I was very good at assassinating people in jam sessions. I was like a professional killer. I approached it like a mafia hit man: "Hello, I will be murdering you tonight." Then I'd put the gun to your neck, right behind the temple, and pull the trigger. I'd leave the body somewhere convenient, walk away, and get a good night's sleep. It was that kind of playing.

But as I was sitting there, I looked around, and the whole crowd was loving what they were hearing. They were rocking out because that was all the music they'd heard, this standard blues kind of show. So I started thinking that once I hurt this guy, I was going to leave, and they would say to themselves, "Well, he's not really as good as I thought." I'd done that before. I'd played with people, and the audience was wowed, and then they'd feel the letdown, especially if I wanted them to feel the letdown. So I started thinking about the people in the audience—how they weren't going to have as much fun and it was really going to deflate the whole show—and I just left.

I walked back to Nightingale's, and my band was waiting, asking, "Did you hurt him?" I said no and explained why. Bob Sheehan said, "I'm proud of you." I remember that as the first time I didn't act like the harp player who always had to go and protect his turf, like I'm the king-shit harp player here. I'm glad I broke the cycle.

I've been fortunate to play with some amazing harp players over the years—like Lee Oskar, and he's good, he's got enough accolades, he's confident, and all that—but when you get two harp players together, there's still this impulse to duel.

I was always looking for Sugar Blue in Chicago, and when I finally met him—we had an interview for *Musician* magazine—I purposely left my harmonicas someplace else. I didn't bring them because I didn't want to be known as that harmonica player who always had to duel.

I'll occasionally relapse, though. I've known Galactic for twenty years, and I was recently doing a song with them and saw Ben Ellman play harmonica for the first time. So I took him aside and asked, "How come I've never heard you play before? You sound so different from me and you're really good."

He told me, "Well, I did play for you once. You were sitting in front of the stage at this little club where we were playing, and I kept inviting you up. You shook me off, but I kept asking. Eventually you agreed, and you proceeded to destroy me on the harmonica, then you handed me the mic and said, 'Don't ever do that again.'" After I heard this I thought, *Wow, I'm such a badass but also kind of a dick.*

I will bust Ivan Neville for what happened in 2006 at Warren Haynes's Christmas Jam. Ivan was doing the musical directing, and I was there along with Mickey Raphael from Willie Nelson's band and Taylor Hicks from *American Idol*, who is a perfectly nice guy. Ivan saw the three of us and had this devilish idea. He said, "You know, we could do a three-way harmonica jam with you and Mickey and Taylor Hicks." And as he said the name "Taylor Hicks," he gave me a look like, *You know what to do, John. You know exactly what to do.* So I responded, "Yeah, we could," like, *Don't worry, boss, I'm on it. I got this.* I went to Mickey and explained, "Our job, which we will deny, is to hurt this man. We're going to do a three-way trade-off. Play as hard and as elaborately as you can."

Poor Taylor did not know what hit him. Mickey would take a solo, then I would take one, pushing each other as hard as we could. Then Taylor would come on and honk as hard as he could, and one of these things was not like the other. It was a Taylor Hicks torture session. He was trapped and could not get out of it.

In October of 1995 I learned that James Cotton wanted to sit in with Blues Traveler. Back when I was a senior in high school, James Cotton played a set of his own at the Princeton Reunion. I snuck in to watch him do his harmonica thing, and after he was done I sat down next to him. I already knew I played weird. I'd never heard anybody who played like me. So I asked, "Mr. Cotton, can you let me know what you think of this?" I played as hard as I could, my Eddie Van Halen-est, and he looked at me and asked, "You got any pot?" I said, "No." So he told me, "Then I don't want to talk to you."

That would have been a great story except three months earlier a friend of mine in high school, Chris Gross, who would later become known as Chris Barron when he was in the Spin Doctors, had gone to a James Cotton show. Chris told me that the same thing happened. He tried to speak with James Cotton, who then asked him if he had any pot. Chris said no, and James Cotton said, "Then I don't want to talk to you." So it turned out James Cotton had given me his stock thing.

Then in 1995 Blues Traveler was in Memphis, and James Cotton wanted to come out and play with us. He had been in Muddy Waters's band from the mid-fifties through the late sixties. He plays a style he helped cultivate, but in my opinion it's really Little Walter's style. Little Walter was definitely an innovator. He was the first one to put the microphone to the harmonica, and when he left the band, James Cotton was forced to play an imprint of Little Walter. So James Cotton had some shoes to fill, and he maintained the expectations of the harp in an electric blues setting that had been there since the forties.

But one thing I knew in 1995 is that I could house James Cotton. I remember what happened in Princeton, and I said to myself, "He may be nearly seventy, but I'm going to hurt this old man." And the fun part was he went up there and was as James Cotton-y as James Cotton could be. The crowd loved it, and I didn't want to hurt him. We had a great time together. And that's the thing: you have to be honest. That's what works and that's exactly what he did. I had waited years for the chance to hurt James Cotton, but I couldn't hurt him with all my power because he was James Cotton.

One of the players I love playing with is Charlie Musselwhite. I've always had harmonica players trying to outdo me somehow or show me their chops because I have this overpowering way of playing that they think requires a response. And Charlie Musselwhite was the first guy who still just played like himself. He had plenty of chops that were so tasty that I wouldn't attempt to do them, and we would play *together*. It was so easy and really fun.

But when it comes to less technically proficient players, what I've come to accept over the years is that if somebody picks up a harmonica and they're playing what I happen think is lousy but the audience doesn't seem to mind, then I shouldn't let it bother me.

I recently saw my first Bruce Springsteen concert, and he's a terrible harmonica player. But am I really going to go, "No, no, sorry, everyone—that's no good." He's rocking the house with that crappy harmonica. I think it's really an eye-of-the-beholder situation. Are people enjoying it? That to me is what determines what's good and bad. There is a technical aspect that I could become anal about and fixated on. I do think you have to look at it like a technician, but what I think is important about a musician like Neil Young, for instance, is that the harmonica he's playing serves a purpose.

The guys in my band do a great impression of me trying to enjoy Neil Young's harmonica playing. I'm making this expression as if to say, *Oooh, you almost got it.* But the fact is he's doing something that's effective.

I know what I can make a harmonica do, but if that's your only objective, you're not going to connect with people. Then again, if you're a total slob on the harmonica, you won't be able to do anything people notice. You really have to balance that out, which requires awareness.

Where I try to draw a line is Alanis Morissette. I can hear her *breaking* the harmonica when she puts it in her mouth. There's a track she did, "Hand in My Pocket," and I can hear the reeds breaking during the harmonica solo. They're not meant to be blown that hard, and I'm arguably the only person who hears it every time that song is played. It's like, "For a solo we're going to smash this violin against the window"—that's the sound I hear when I hear that song.

I think it was Bob Dylan who lowered the expectation of what a harmonica is supposed to do. Dylan never captured my imagination on the harmonica for a second; he was just somebody breathing in and out—he taught a generation to just breathe in and out on the harmonica. But I think that was a fair price we paid for Dylan's songwriting contributions, which opened up everybody's head.

I think he was looking at the harmonica the way Woody Guthrie did, which was that anybody can pick up a harmonica; it was sort of like a mouth zither or an autoharp, and it's a very vox populi kind of instrument. That's the way you would play if you bought a harmonica and were singing to your family in your house before there was popular music on the radio. Dylan not only informalized the performance; he made it more intimate. I think we owe that to him.

Dylan did it for the entire world, and one of his points was, "I don't have to be a meticulous technical musician. I can always be of the people and have a human experience with my music." In his songwriting you can hear the brilliance, but in the harmonica not so much. But he's using it to sell that point.

I can use speed to catch everyone's attention, but what I really learned from all the bebop players is that what's important is a melodic phrase and that leads to scales. You want to expand your vocabulary, and that means you want some discipline on your instrument that takes you far away from Dylan's approach to it.

You need to open yourself up to melody. That way you're actually saying something with all that vocabulary. If you got nothing to offer but chops, you're just reading the dictionary really fast.

5

BUCKING THE ESTABLISHMENT

While I was still in the JV/Nassau Band at Princeton High School, Mr. Biancosino kept telling us that we should form groups of our own together outside of school. He loved to lecture us. Mr. B was a great guy but kind of nuts.

So in the fall of 1983 I approached the drummer for the Nassau Band and asked him whether he wanted to get together and rehearse. He was a freshman, only thirteen years old, but he was up for it. His name was Brendan Hill, and that was the beginning of Blues Traveler.

We called ourselves The Establishment and played in Brendan's parents' basement—you always go where the drum set is. Along with Brendan, we had his brother Sebastian on bass and this guy Levi on guitar. We would play Police and Tears for Fears covers, the Euro-punk-sounding shit that was going around in the eighties, and I kept asking when we could play a song with a harmonica in it. So to appease me, we'd do a twelve-bar blues, and it was terrible. Still, this was the first time I was in an actual band that would actually rehearse, and that part of it was cool.

The Establishment never played anywhere other than the Hills' basement, although we talked about having gigs. I kept challenging us to try something new, and Brendan agreed, but we took a lot of wrong turns to get there. Mr. B was impressing upon us to be good players, and his bands were very jazz oriented, so at one point I thought it would be great to have Sebastian's girlfriend sing. We gave that a go and did "Greensleeves," for God's sake. Brendan was ready to hang himself. It was terrible.

Then at some point Sebastian and Brendan agreed to try something else. I think they got into the energy of what I was now doing with the varsity/Studio band and liked the harmonica. So that spring we got rid of Levi and began writing our own songs.

I decided we should call ourselves Blues Band. My thinking was that this is going to be what we are—we're going to play blues.

To some degree I think the name was sparked by the fact that my older sister Emily and I had always talked about forming a band. When we were little kids my younger brother, Ted, got a Bugs Bunny drum kit, so we decided to call ourselves the Bugs Bunny Band. Emily would be the manager, and she promised us ten candy bars a month. We never received our full allotment of candy bars, but then again, we never played a gig. It was in this spirit that my sister and I toyed with the idea of the $1.98 Blues Band. I think that's what put the name Blues Band in my head. Of course, I may have been influenced by the Blues Brothers there as well.

The problem with Blues Band was that the Blues Brothers had Matt "Guitar" Murphy and Steve "The Colonel" Cropper. We didn't. We replaced Levi with the only guitarist we could find, and he was horrible. David had been in the Nassau Band, but eventually he came to Studio Band because Princeton was literally out of guitarists. At the beginning of one song he had to do a simple trill, and he just couldn't do it. He'd mess it up in the middle, and it would almost be adorable if it weren't so annoying. He was there when we needed a guitarist—there was a real dry spell—but like Mr. B, I was really hard on him. Eventually we replaced him with someone we'll call Mr. Y, who wasn't very good either. There was just an amazing shortage of guitarists at the time.

In early 1985, the winter of my second junior year, we expanded to a five piece with a new vocalist. Chris Gross was the guy I knew in English class, and we hit it off pretty much right away. We were sixteen or seventeen, and all we did was talk about songwriting.

I can still remember this song he wrote about working at Thomas Sweet, the ice cream place on Nassau Street.

> Scooping at Thomas Sweet
> don't ya know I'm pretty neat
> Scooping at Thomas sweet
> where the work is hard and the pay is beat
> I work all night to the broad daylight
> Let's scoop, scoop, scoop on

We'd go off into the Herrontown Woods in Princeton and smoke pot and write songs, and he was really my songwriting counterpart. The lyrics I was writing—and I still have this problem—took too long to get there. But Chris could really get to the hook really quickly and really cleverly. Sometimes he would get a little wordy and I would be a little more to the point, but that was the counterbalance we had.

I think it was inevitable that he would play with my band, so we asked him.

The problem was that we were way too rigid for him. We had band uniforms—we decided on blue jeans, a white shirt, and a thin black tie. It was, again, a little homage to the Blues Brothers. I was also borrowing from Studio Band, where we had uniforms.

Chris hated the uniforms. He would wear his tie around his head while he sang the Thomas Sweet song with us and a couple of other songs he wrote. Another problem was that in the middle of the set he would jump off stage with that characteristic Chris Barron leap and start dancing with a girl he liked. Also, he wouldn't show up to band meetings, and we were so rigid about rules and stuff that everyone agreed I had to fire him.

A few years ago I said to him, "Man, we were so uptight back then," and he responded, "You know, I've been waiting for decades for you to say that." Even with all that happened in the Spin Doctors, he wanted me to acknowledge that we were too uptight when he joined Blues Band. And yes, we were. It was true.

After Brendan's brother graduated from high school in 1985, my friend Felicia, who played violin in the orchestra, became our bass player. She was the little sister of our friend Ben and was well on her way to Yale, but she agreed to do us a favor, thinking it would be kind of fun. She gave it hell, and we all liked her, but she really was not a good bass player. She took a bass solo in our demo that . . . well . . . let me just say that every bass solo Felicia played was a testimony to her friendship and loyalty to us.

Both Felicia and Brendan agreed we needed to get rid of Mr. Y. Whenever he would start to solo, he would drool uncontrollably, and I can't stress this enough—*uncontrollably*, because there was no method to his drooling. The drool would come of its own volition and wouldn't stop until well after he was done. It was an odd nervous tic, and I've never seen anything like it before or since. He would start going, and Felicia couldn't stop laughing. Brendan had seen this guy Chan Kinchla playing in the practice booth at school and said we had to get him. So Brendan asked him, and when Chan showed up, he was pretty sloppy. But he was also the first guitarist we had who actually could make a phrase, a confident loud phrase, and when he'd do his spiel he'd keep going. That became the final lineup for Blues Band—Brendan, Chan, Felicia, and myself.

When we replaced Mr. Y with Chan, having found a real guitar player so we could become the band that we now are, Mr. Y became so despondent that he decided to kill himself. He ate an entire box of Clorox bleach powder, figuring he would die after beating Chan in a guitar duel at the Spring Fling that we were playing at our high school. So he came up to us in his cool Stevie Ray Vaughan hat and said, "Mind if I sit in?" We were late setting up our gear so we said, "No, we're really busy." So because he couldn't sit in, he had to go throw up the Clorox he ate, so we inadvertently saved his life. We ignored him into a suicidal state and then we ignored him back to life.

We played a few actual gigs as Blues Band. Some of them were in school or at parties, but our first professional gig was at John and Peter's in New Hope, Pennsylvania. We got $200 and six people showed up. Those six people were our parents. It wasn't even our friends—it was our parents. My parents couldn't make it because they were working, but the other six parents were there. I have a tape of the show, and you can hear them all laughing. They were the only ones in the room as we played.

Chan was the first person in the band I couldn't physically intimidate, and there were plenty of alpha-male moments when he would just be contradictory, but he could play. It became so much more fun with him—he was a real student of Jimmy Page. He came in, and at first he had no control, but because we all had way too much control, that was the perfect balance.

As soon as he started ripping I immediately began thinking, *How am I going to control this guy?* because I was such a control freak. The good news is that when it came to the music, he was starved for information—all he wanted to do was play better. He never wanted to slack when it came to playing music. He did like drinking beer, though, and he kept bringing it to rehearsal and eventually got us all in trouble with Brendan's mom.

All of our parents were really helpful, although Brendan's parents bore the brunt of having the band there because that's just how it is for the drummer's parents. Brendan was born in London of Irish parents, and his mom and dad had all these tea cups and china sets because they really took their tea time seriously. Everything would rattle when we were playing because we were under their kitchen. The basement was also surrounded by pipes covered in asbestos, and I kept smacking my head into them. I still wonder whether I can get some workman's comp out of that.

I should also mention that my parents would let everyone in our house drink because none of us did it very much. So our liquor closet was always open, and when Brendan and Chan discovered this, it became a feeding frenzy. I remember one time Chan took a fifth of Jack Daniel's and drank it. My dad eventually noticed it was missing and came to me to ask what happened. I told him I didn't know, and he insisted that Chan get him another bottle of Jack Daniel's. This was how my dad thought, even though Chan was seventeen.

But then I came downstairs one day and found our cleaning lady's brother passed out on the floor in our basement next to many bottles of booze. I thought he was dead. As a result, because now my father couldn't prove that Chan had been responsible for the missing Jack Daniel's, he had to go out and buy Chan a bottle. To this day this is one of Chan's favorite moments of vindication: when my fifty-something-year-old dad had to buy him some whiskey . . . even though Chan had pilfered it in the first place. I remember another night Chan showed up at my house completely drunk. He kept saying, "Let's call our album *Felicia's Hairy Butthole*," because he was drunk and wanted to be disruptive. He was with Brendan, and I told them to meet me at the bowling alley because my mom was in the other room. But I had no intention of meeting them. As it turned out they hitched a ride to the bowling alley and were stuck out on Route 1. So they called me late at night, and I was so mad at them when I picked them up to take them home, I said, "I don't want to hear one word out of either of you motherfuckers," and Chan goes, "John . . . " To this day he claims he was going to apologize, but I slammed on the breaks, did a total high school skid out, and I yelled, "That's it! Get out of my car!" Brendan said, "But I didn't do anything!" And he didn't. He had just followed Chan because he wanted to go bowling, but I left them there on the highway and went home.

There was also an incident when Chan was thwacking the back of my head while I was driving. So I pulled over the car and said, "I am not leaving unless you get out of the car or promise you will not hit me if I'm driving." Then after a long bit of arguing, we were philosophizing and he said, "John, I promise I won't hit you unless you're driving," and I said "Okay." So I drove away and then he started taunting me, "Ha ha, I said *unless*." So I pulled over again and went to look for a road sign to get him out of my car with (the thought process was still forming, but I likely would have used the sign to scoop or poke him out of the car, much like getting a grizzly to rear up on its hindquarters in order to spear a vital area and perhaps land a decisive blow. The key with a larger, stronger opponent is never to swing wide; they will always catch the implement and likely hit you with it). Eventually he apologized, but when it came to the music, he was always serious.

There was this moment early on when Chan, Brendan, and I got really stoned and played in the basement for what seemed like twenty minutes, but in actuality three hours had gone by and we taped it all on Brendan's sister's Fisher Price tape recorder. That was the first time we got high and really let loose.

Then we went across the street where we could smoke cigarettes because we had to hide all of this from Brendan's mom. And while we were listening to it, this black cat walked up to us and hung out with us. So we called it the Black Cat Jam, and that's where our mascot of the black cat came from. A lot of our early songs came out of that jam too—"Sweet Talking Hippie," "But Anyway," and "Mulling It Over." I wrote a poem about it called "Black Cat Blues," and we recorded a version of it later with a really slow pocket because we'd already plumbed the grooves we had from the original jam by that point.

Around this time we began sneaking into Princeton University to play frat parties and eating clubs. One time this college kid came up to me and said, "I know what you're thinking—rich white kid exploiting your music." I didn't want to tell him that my dad was VP at Squibb and I lived up the street and that I think I'm Caucasian as well. So instead I said, "I hear you man," because that's what he wanted—you just learn what role to play.

But I would never suggest I was anything but a white kid from the suburbs. One thing I've always felt is essential is to keep it true. I wasn't going try to talk about the blues in some stereotypical way, like I was James Cotton in some juke joint in the 1950s. I will never know what that experience was like. I can't fathom what James Cotton went through, all anyone can know is their own experience.

I think that's also why I came to value songwriting, which became important. If I just went for chops I think I would have gone the way of Joe Satriani where people know my quantity and think, *Okay he does that*, and it would pretty much be my only function. This way I can be more than a harmonica meme.

They say that Paul Butterfield, who was one of the best ever in my estimation, died on a bar stool trying to convince someone he was Paul Butterfield. That is the fate of a harmonica player—no matter how good you are, you're a harmonica player. The way around that is to write songs, and because I'm a songwriter, I don't ever have to just be a harmonica player. But being a songwriter allows me to put that harmonica in weird places, and that allows me to surprise and to think in terms of melodies.

During my senior year the space shuttle *Challenger* crashed. I wrote a song about it for my English class called "Ain't That Life." Picture a seventeen-year-old telling you about life. All of my songs went about ten verses too long, and this one had a very sappy bridge:

> A newborn kitten freezes
> While two young lovers part
> And maybe right here some sucker
> Could be taking this song to heart

It was a bit juvenile, but they had me come in and sing it for the PTA. I could smell that they didn't know how to talk to the kids about the space shuttle disaster. I was really good at honing in on stuff like that. People were traumatized, and the teachers really wanted to connect with students. I loved it when teachers wanted to connect with students—they were easy prey. I didn't have to do any homework senior year; I just got an A for writing a song about the space shuttle blowing up.

Later, at the New School, I had to take one English class, and again I didn't do any work, then I busted out this space shuttle song around Christmas and passed. I remember thinking it was good because everyone I sang it for thought it was so deep and moving. But then I tried it out in New York to some girl in her twenties, and she laughed in the middle of it. I remember thinking all of the demoralizing things a young man would feel at that point, but at heart I was like, *Yeah, she's right.* I knew it was lame. To be fair, it was a high school assignment gone awry that I had milked for two years, but it had finally hit the ceiling in that moment. I was humiliated but also thought, *This is why I came to New York. It's time to put away the stupid bullshit you can get away with and do something real.*

Back in high school I also wrote a song called "Honesty and Love" for Sarah, the first alto sax in the Studio Band. That one I submitted to my creative writing class because if you're going to write a song, it might as well be homework too. But my teacher kept telling me to revise it—she asked me to knock out about half the verses. I remember thinking, *How dare you! Which verses?* At the time I thought she was so full of herself. She seemed like one of these small-minded people who thought everything she said was brilliant, but I have to admit she was right about one thing: revise, revise, revise. In my mind everything I wrote was gold, but the thing is, if you revise properly, you're bringing the gold out that's being worn into the ground by your inability to shut the hell up.

I wrote "And So It Goes" on a Casiotone with the electric rhythm section and the drum-fill button. I stole the bass line and timed out the fills that Brendan would have to do later. My voice hadn't even changed yet, but it was about my "wisdom." We worked that one for a couple of decades, so I guess I owe Casio a royalty.

There was another one I would pluck out on the piano, this really annoying, poorly executed Bach homage. I used two fingers and the sustain pedal so it sounded all echoey. It had nice songwriter form, but I was ripping off so many pop songs from the seventies, Carpenters kind of songs that were prevalent in the suburbs. I remember it was the first time that girls would talk to me because I was the weird kid. One of them said, "You know, when I heard you play that song, that's when I realized there was more to you." She didn't want to have sex with me or anything, of course, but we became friends.

So even if Blues Band had some cheesy, formulaically written original songs, at least we had original songs. We had ambition, we had confidence, and soon we had a new bass player and a new name.

When I went off to the New School in the fall of 1986, the rest of the band was still in Princeton High School. We decided to keep the band going and I'd come back to rehearse and do laundry. One of these times I heard a rumor that we'd fired Felicia and that this major Deadhead Bob Sheehan was now our bassist. I had met him a couple of times—he kept showing up with his bass—and we let him sit in with us at a school homecoming dance.

The rumor kept circulating, and eventually Felicia said, "You know, I don't really want to do this anyway." She stepped aside happily and Bobby was in the band—it was kind of like he talked himself in. He knew we were the best band around for what he wanted to do.

Now, I can't confirm or deny that Bob Sheehan started that rumor, and we will indeed never know how it came to be known that Blues Band had fired their bassist and replaced her with the King of the Deadheads Bob Sheehan, but I do find it interesting.

What happened next was we took a lot more acid, smoked a lot more pot, and sounded better, at least to us. We needed an acid test, and we did one of those in New York City. It had rust-colored-carpeted walls—imagine tripping balls in a room with rust-colored-carpeted walls.

My friend Steve came to play and trip with us on the saxophone, so picture five absolute maniacs throbbing on one chord over and over again with occasional flurries of individual expression. This must have gone on for five or six hours at top volume, and I suffer to think what people must have thought when they walked by. The rust-colored carpet kept everything in a Van Gogh painting, while we took the Black Cat Jam—that one-chord vamp with lots of pockets in it—and brought it to a new echelon of throb.

I would recommend to any jamming band that they trip some serious balls once, maybe twice. I think it's useful a couple of times. Is it useful all that time? That depends on you.

We were locked in an overcrowded, very furry room, and there was nothing but the music. In that era the band would play two-chord songs—we'd get a groove and beat it to death. But when you're tripping, it's amazing how stuff comes out of nowhere and starts to connect to other stuff. If there's anything I remember from that jam, it was how we would segue into other parts of the jam and into a melody. When you play in a band where you've had this sort of acid test, you connect in these ways and can always recall that connection. Something really important happened to us that day. I still have the tape somewhere.

There were two kinds of musicians coming out of Princeton High School, the kind Mr. B loved and the kind he hated. Brendan and I were in Studio Band, which Mr. B cared about, despite the abuse Brendan got from him. He saw good things for us, and we shared a lot of favoritism in Studio Band. But as far as Mr. B was concerned, Chan and Bobby were potheads, and Mr. B put anyone he didn't need in a practice booth with their instrument. He didn't give them any attention, and the way Chan tells it to this day, that was the best thing he could have done for him. I think that's true because Chan needed to woodshed.

Our music program rejected Chan and Bobby, so they did not have the musical rudiments beaten into their heads, while the program loved Brendan and me, so we did have those rudiments beaten into our heads. It was a good combination because Chan and Bob brought a sense of "Do what you want to do because it sounds good," and Brendan and I brought a sense of "Here's a section within a structure, and here's where it has to go." It was the combination of those two approaches that made it good.

I would also say that Bob Sheehan was the band's first promoter. He knew how to get the word out, and that was a major contribution to Blues Traveler. We didn't even have a name for it. If there's a thing I regret, it's not being able to value this skill and acknowledge it at the time because even he didn't know he was doing it—it's just the way he was. Suddenly there would be a bunch of people there. It was because he could make friends like diving into water.

This is a description of Bobby taking a midterm exam: as soon as the teacher walks out the door, he says, "Okay, smart guy, you give all the answers, and you, you're the lookout." Then he would get the whole classroom organized so that everyone is going to get a good grade and does it in a way with the smart guy, the lookouts, and the people writing it all down that would make it fun. There was a lot of Huck Finn in him. Bob Sheehan is eternally Huck Finn.

After we finally put him in the band, Bobby said, "We need a cool name like Blues Entity, because when we play right we become this extra entity." *Ghostbusters* was on cable around that time, and there's a scene in which Gozer announces, "The Traveler has come!" So we became Blues Traveler.

6

THE DARK ART
OF HARMONIES

I first met Arnie Lawrence at a Manhattan School of Music summer session after my senior year of high school. He really opened up my head.

"Just play something," he told me.

"What do you want me to play?"

"Just play anything."

No one had ever asked me to do that before. It's a small thing, but it's a really important thing to just "play anything."

He also had this great exercise with me, a trombonist, and a saxophone player. There's a joke—a woman's away, no one's home except for her parrot, and a plumber, who the woman had called, stops by. He knocks on the door and the parrot says, "Who is it?" And the plumber responds, "It's the plumber." The parrot repeats, "Who is it?" And the plumber answers, "It's the plumber." Then the parrot asks again, "Who is it?" And the plumber yells, "It's the plumber!" This happens a few more times, and the plumber eventually gets so upset that he has a heart attack and dies. Then the lady comes home, sees this dead guy on her doorstep and asks, "Who is that?" and the parrot says, "It's the plumber."

Arnie had us play the joke over and over again with everybody taking different turns being the parrot, being the plumber, being the lady, while a pocket evolved behind it. And it became a song. It was a really neat exercise, and we would often do things like that.

His approach was very ethereal, and Arnie was the first teacher other people took seriously who I could actually relate to. He was starting the New School for Jazz and Contemporary Music the next fall on 13th Street and 6th Avenue in Greenwich Village. And after the Manhattan School of Music sent me the thirty-two bars of Bach that I would have to learn, it became pretty clear that the New School was my best bet. And after I sat down and played for the dean, I was in.

When I went to the New School the first year, it felt very unofficial. It was 120 handpicked students in a room with the finest jazz musicians in New York. There were no rules or curriculum, so we'd invariably just play, and that's where I learned the most.

The second year had some of that, but they needed a formal curriculum, and suddenly you had new classes where you were going to learn to read music. I wanted no part of it. The way I am with school is the more you offer me that I don't want, the less I will attend. So I would just show up for the classes that interested me.

I remember one time I didn't go to school for about three months because I was so busy with Blues Traveler. Then I came back and they said, "We're flying you to San Diego tomorrow to represent the New School, not to compete but as an exhibition." I was the harp wunderkind that everyone was talking about, so I was a selling point for the school.

But unlike high school, the focus really wasn't on competition. What I liked about the New School is they didn't make you feel like a student; they made you feel like you were already gigging, and getting used to that feeling was the best lesson they thought me. You had to figure out stuff on your own.

Arnie Lawrence was the perfect guy for that. He was a straight bebopper who made his bones playing for the *Tonight Show* in the sixties—he was first alto in that band with Doc Severinsen. He played with everyone from Count Basie to the Brecker Brothers to the Rolling Stones to James Brown, and he was born to teach.

In high school Mr. B's focus was on being fast and loud rather than whatever we might be thinking about. But Arnie would expound on ideas that would stay in your head. He could talk about music the way you imagined Gandalf talked about magic or the way Yoda talked about the Force. He was like Yoda to me. He would challenge you in spiritual ways. I told everyone back home that he was teaching me the dark art of harmonies.

He had this great line, "The blues is the sound a baby makes when it cries for the first time because after you know you'll get picked up, then it's all show business." And getting that first cry is what the blues is to me. If you can remember why you cry even though you know you'll be picked up, I think that's a good exercise for everybody. It's not about just sitting there and doing primal screams; it's a much deeper thing than that. Life by its very nature kind of hurts, and that's not a bad thing—it's just the experience of living. I think the objective of anybody playing music should be to take that, express it through sound, and share it with others.

He called our little group the Dummies, and it had me and Eric Schenkman in it. The other bebop guys looked down on us because we didn't know *Giant Steps* and the fake book or the real book because we came from a rock-and-roll background. Luckily Arnie recognized rock as a primal endeavor, and there was a time when bebop used to be one too. Part of what made Charlie Parker great was that he was trying to go score smack. He had to play well because he had to hustle in order to get enough to eat and some drugs, which—for a while at least—can really motivate a person. But by the mid-eighties that was something missing in bebop.

Bebop was being put in a jar like a museum piece. Everybody was trying to play Charlie Parker's solos note for note and write them down, which I thought was the dumbest thing ever. That's not what he was trying to do. He couldn't play King Oliver's solos note for note—he would vary them. And I think by the time the eighties rolled around, bebop had been so celebrated as this music of the streets that it was no longer the music of the streets. It was kind of this doomed trap because even if you want to show people what's cool about that music, once you've turned it into an effective class, you've put it in a jar and deprived it of oxygen so it's no longer a living thing anymore.

You don't want art forms to die; what you want is for art forms to breathe. And usually it's the ones that aren't considered fully art forms that get to do the most breathing. And that's why Arnie called our little group the Dummies and told us to wear the name as a badge of pride. We did so because we knew the jazz students were missing something.

There's that old joke: How many jazz students does it take to screw in a light bulb? Three: one to screw it in and two to go, "Ooh, yeah, uh-huh, yeah!" They always had to make the noises at the right time to show they were "getting it." They were so hell-bent on trying to keep something the way it was, but I happen to think you do a better job of keeping something the way it was by having something new struggle to get out and speak in slang because it's honest that way. If there's an adjective that music or any art form has to be, it's *true*. If you don't mean it, it won't come out of your horn. Charlie Parker said that, and I've learned that more by not trying to sound like Charlie Parker than I ever would if I'd tried to sound like Charlie Parker.

I don't need to know who was the house band at the Savoy Ballroom in 1936. I'm glad they were there. I'd love to be exposed to the music and to know where it came from, but there's a point when it does me no good. What I'm looking for is a sound, and the only way to find a sound is to play.

By the second year the New School had to get a curriculum going or they wouldn't get accredited, and I was getting busier playing gigs with Blues Traveler, who by then were in town and going to their various colleges, in theory. I was just rehearsing and playing and skipping more and more school. By year three I was skipping almost all of my classes.

I was the only harmonica player at the New School—it was a small class—and one time they brought Toots Thielemans in to teach me. Arnie knew Toots, and a year earlier he got me to call him on the phone. Toots said, "I don't put too much stock in the blues harp, but keep on puffing." A bit of a blow-off, but he actually relented the next year and came in to personally teach me. We had this seminar series every Friday, called the Peep Your Hole Card Series, where some musician would come in, and this time they brought the world's most legendary harmonica player. But I blew it off because we'd had a gig the night before and I slept in—"Ahh, seminar, they always have a seminar. Why do I have to get up at nine in the morning?" And on Monday everyone was like, "Ohh, man . . . " He told me to keep on puffing and then I blew him off, so in my mind we're kind of even. But, yes, I regret it.

During my first year, while the rest of my band was still in high school, I lived at the Y on 34th Street. I would come home on weekends and bring some laundry, just jumping on the bus down at the Port Authority, which was right near the Y. We would rehearse on the weekends and then I'd go back to the city, learn about more complicated music, and bring it back to the band.

My mom gave me forty bucks a week, and somehow I made that work—largely because I had access to the NYU cafeteria through some deal the New School had worked out. I wasn't big on throwing things away, and eventually there was a sea of trash in my room. I remember stealing an entire pineapple one time and smuggling it under my coat, thinking, "This is the size of a small turkey—I can go home and eat this for weeks." But I had no refrigeration, so it turned brown and rotted. Then I would get some chicken from Kenny Rogers Roasters, and the bones would sit there and accumulate. I got mice. Eventually the Y management had to come talk to me about the odor.

They threw me out because of the smell. The day I was leaving I finally put it all into trash bags and tossed it out the window because there were mountains of trash below me. Little did I know there was a guy below there working. I made his day a little stinkier.

The very first thing I did when I got to New York outside the New School was look for open-mic jam sessions because I figured that's where I could go and shine. I was like a killer with a smile on my face. I'd be really nice and sweet and innocent, and then I'd get on stage and hurt any other harp player who was there, along with most of the guitar players.

There was one at Abilene's on 21st and 2nd—now it's a KFC—which was an extension of those old-school cutting sessions, although no one actually got cut these days. You'd be cut from the jam but not on your physical person. A woman named Lyvette ran it, and she was a bit down on her luck but had been one of Wilson Pickett's background singers in the 1960s. She called me Poppy because she said I had a voice like a girl. Sitting in the crowd one night was Joan Osborne, who'd started hanging out there maybe a year or two earlier.

Joan told me about Nightingale's and about Jono Manson. I never would have met Jono Manson if it weren't for Joan. Through her I discovered Jono, the Sweetones, the Worms, and the whole Nightingale's scene. So Joan was pivotal; she was the right person to bump into.

Joan was putting a band together with Jerry Dugger, who was Jono's bass player; Mark Horn, the drummer from the Blue Chieftains; and Johnny Allen, who was playing the guitar. She called the band Ain't Mozart and invited me to play as well. We would do standards. Occasionally she would put in a song of her own and was a really good songwriter—her hit song "One of Us" was written by one of the Hooters, but I think if she'd put in more of her own songs, she would have been recognized earlier.

Johnny Allen would hire me to sit in with him at Mondo Cane, and that's where I met the Mondo Cane crew, and they ended up hiring us a lot.

The Blues Traveler guys would come in on some weekends. I remember one time they came to see me with Johnny Allen at Mondo Cane and a fight broke out—somebody in the crowd was drunk. They'd call the crowd on Bleecker Street the bridge-and-tunnel crowd because that was how they'd come over from Jersey. They'd go to see music around Bleecker and MacDougal, and the Mondo Cane was in that area.

So a fight broke out, and Johnny threw his guitar behind him, jumped into the crowd, and started punching this guy. Meanwhile Bobby, who just came in as my guest with Chan and Brendan, seized this moment because he was dying to get on stage. So he jumped on stage and said, "No problem, folks, it's all just part of the show." Nobody had invited him, but he was a pig in shit—he was so happy, and I loved him for that. Then I looked back and the drummer, this older guy who had worked with Jimi Hendrix back when Hendrix first came to New York in the mid-sixties—I was in awe of that—just kept drumming away like it was another day at the office. How could I not want to do this for a living after that kind of night?

During my second year at the New School I think I was in the Spin Doctors for a day and a half. We had a class project with me, Brendan (who was going to Rutgers but was also a part-time student at the New School), Eric Schenkman, and Billy and Robert Buscaglia, two brothers who were heavy-metal guys and came to the New School together to learn some chops. We were the core of the Dummies—the rock-and-roll guys—and we called this band the Trucking Company. We wound up writing a really cool tune, "Hard to Exist," around a figure that another guy, Abe Fogle wrote, that later became a song shared by Blues Traveler and the Spin Doctors.

It was a cool band, but I wasn't sure what was going to happen when Brendan and I had Blues Traveler gigs. They could find another drummer, but what were they doing to do about a lead singer? So I figured my friend Chris was dying to have a band—at that time all he was doing was serenading girls over at the music store in Princeton. I thought that way we could share the front-man duties and not worry if Blues Traveler and the Trucking Company book gigs on the very same night.

But then Chris was a little condescending to Eric with some advice and squished Eric's hat while patting him on the head. Eric was very quiet about it, and at the end of the night he said to Chris, "If you ever touch my hat again, I'll kill you." That's when I realized my little experiment had gone woefully awry. Within a day Eric had gotten the Buscaglia brothers to want to reject Chris. But a short while later Chris found Eric on his own and they talked about it, made friends, and formed the Spin Doctors.

Apparently Chris was really great at misbehavior followed by reconciliation. I attribute this to Chris's incredible survival instincts and his knack for breaking rules, whether they be hat or tie.

The New School offered me a perfect place to go and hide when I was out of money. But once we were able to pay our rent from our gig money, I called my parents and said, "I love you and I want to thank you for the opportunity and I'm quitting school."

I walked in that day, and the question the school had for me was, "Are you learning more out there or in here?" And that was the last question I needed to answer. Clearly I was learning more out there. It was what I wanted to do, it was why I was going to music school, and I was able to live off that, so it could be my job. I think the school's attitude was as long as I wasn't quitting school to be a taxi driver, that they didn't need to teach me, I could go off and make a living.

My parents, of course, freaked out. They told me not to do anything until they called the school. I don't know who spoke with them—it was probably Arnie Lawrence—but then they called me back and said, "We'll support you in whatever you need to do." They said I convinced them when I said, "I'll never forgive myself if I don't try." But after they called the school, they were much calmer. I don't know who spoke with them, but I think they told my parents that "This is what a musician's supposed to do, and he's doing it." I think that in a situation like this it's clear to everybody except your parents.

I remember when the Spin Doctors got their gold record. I was so envious because I wanted to show my parents a gold record—in our line of work it's the only official vindication you get from a certified agency that says, "Yes, these guys know what they're doing." Until then your parents wonder, *How is he going to make a living? Is he going to sell enough records? Is he going to have enough gigs?* And the first real accreditation you get when you go off with your band and play is a statement of record sales. And when we got our first gold record, I sent one right away to my parents.

It took a while for my parents to appreciate that the music scene operates under an altogether different set of rules from what they were used to. Chico Hamilton at the New School once said about me: "This cat, the groove always ends up landing in his pocket." But then he looked me in the eyes and added, "You are one of those guys who's always late and will always be late."

I think I've proven him right on both counts. I remember there was some show I was supposed to do at the New School. My parents came in for it and I was late. The gig was starting already, and I had this sack of laundry I had done in New Jersey. I showed up right in time for my solo, and Arnie Lawrence's take was, "Yup, right on time." My parents told me afterward that they would have killed me but that Arnie's position was that I was right on time. I put my laundry down, played the show, picked up my laundry, and left. When you pull that off and everybody's so happy to see you, all is forgiven. And I've learned to live life being forgiven.

A few years later there was one night in Providence when I miscalculated the drive from Quakertown, so the guys had to go on stage and explain that I wasn't there yet but that we'd start as soon I arrived. I should mention that I was about two and a half hours late. I thought it was four hours from Quakertown to Providence, but it was six. I had forgotten that you have to drive the whole length of Connecticut. I thought, "I'll just swing by!" Nope. The audience booed them and they had never been booed before, so when I finally showed up, they were pretty pissed off.

I've been late a handful of times, but generally I show up at the last minute. My attitude is to simply just wake up and play, and that sometimes gets me into trouble.

After I left the New School I'd continue to play with a lot of the same guys. In the early nineties we had this group called Wasabi with Arnie Lawrence and members of Blues Traveler, Spin Doctors, this great band called The Authority, and whoever was around. The whole point of it was not to rehearse. It was an improvising band, and we knew to stretch out a jam for fifteen hours on the key of E because we had mastered the dark arts.

7

SLOW CHANGE

By the spring of 1987 we were officially Blues Traveler with Bobby in the band. We'd play keg parties all around Jersey whenever I'd come home, and it was very clear that the plan was for everybody to move to New York the following year.

After high school all of our parents said we'd have to get jobs or go to college. I remember my father sat me down in our living room and said, "Son, do you see all this? It's mine." His point was that I needed to find a job or go to school. We all had similar situations in which our parents were willing to pay for college. So we decided to use that time to blow off school while we figured out how to get the band working. We had four years to make it happen. There was a ticking clock.

Chan's father was a psychology professor at Princeton and helped get him into NYU, so Chan would have some excuse to be in New York. Brendan got into Rutgers, and they had some sort of New York program; he also was accepted into the New School on some level. Bobby enrolled at Long Island University, the Brooklyn campus. Chan called it LI-No because he never showed up there. But because the New School had amps and gear and practice rooms, that was where we basically went to go rehearse, and we'd rehearse all the time. Once we'd get gigs it was a beautiful balance of Nightingale's teaching us how to sell beer and get people dancing and then the New School showing us the finer attributes of the dark arts of harmonies.

We had this death-or-victory tribal mentality. It was a reckless thing we were trying to do, but we were reacting like it was normal. The New School helped make it normal because we went to a college to learn how to go out and take huge risks, but they don't tell you about that—when they were talking about risks they were talking more about the aesthetics.

There was a long dry spell of actual gigs. Every week we would go to the open-mic night at Abilene's and do it as a band. Eventually they gave us a gig.

I remember I was on cloud nine because we had been doing these open-mic nights forever. I felt like, *I'm the King of New York—I finally work here!* But then I made the mistake of walking down the wrong street on my way back to the Y. There was this crazy gang of kids who had these boxes of crescent rolls—maybe they'd knocked over a deli— and they were whipping them at everything and knocking out street-lights. I was already committed to walking down the block and figured that if I ran, they'd chase me. One of them called out, "Hey man, don't he look like Benny Hill?" I laughed, and they threw a box of crescent rolls in front of me. Then they started winging them at me, and I walked away with baked goods flying at my head. That took me down a peg or two. I didn't feel like I was the king of New York so much as I just worked there.

As it turned out, I didn't even work there very long, at least not right away. When we finally played at Abilene's, it ended up being somewhat anticlimactic because they never had us back. The lady who owned it was a big Elvis Presley fan and couldn't stand the way we did "Hound Dog." So after playing our funk version of "Hound Dog," we were done at Abilene's.

Then we tried playing an open-mic night at Dan Lynch on 2nd Avenue near 13th Street and were kicked out. The amps were at ten and we played "Slow Change," which has a 7/4 part. They were hosting a traditional blues jam, as they did every Sunday, and they stopped us because of the time signature—"You guys can just leave." We didn't know what had happened. We didn't realize you could get kicked out of an open-mic jam session.

So we walked out and right next door to Dan Lynch was Nightingale's, where Joan had first brought me after an Ain't Mozart rehearsal. We went in there, and that's where we started hanging out. Nightingale's never turned us away and never minded what we played because they weren't about "traditional blues." Jono Manson, who led the house band and was the king daddy, took us under his wing and taught us how to work a bar.

Tom Hosier was the manager at Nightingale's. He was awesome to us as well. The fact that Tom liked us ran counter to everything he liked in music. He couldn't stand jam bands, and he couldn't stand loud bands or psychedelic bands. But we were the exception to that rule. Tom always seemed like he was in an annoyed mood, but that just added to the ambience of Nightingale's.

I was a wide-eyed kid, and I remember asking him about Woodstock because he had told me he'd been there as a teenager. In the eighties being at Woodstock was this huge badge of honor, and I wanted to know what it was like.

He told me, "It rained for three days and we were living in our own filth. You want to know what it was like? Jimi Hendrix played and I didn't even care."

I remember Tom made me a bouncer one night because I needed the fifty bucks. Matt Dillon came to the door and it was five dollars to get in. He ponied up the five dollars for himself and then came back to me, "Listen I'm with some friends and I was wondering . . . "

I said, "Look, you're Matt Dillon. You can get them in if you want to. Just ask."

So he did. "Can you get my friends in?"

I said, "Sure, you're Matt Dillon . . . " I just kept saying "Matt Dillon" over and over. I let all his friends in, and does he call? No . . .

Many years later we were at a table read for the *Simpsons*. I believe they were considering having us on the show, but it didn't happen. The actors all play multiple roles, and because Harry Shearer is both Mr. Burns and Smithers, it was surreal watching him argue with himself. While we were there, though, I spoke with Hank Azaria, who apparently had been a Nightingale's regular and a big fan of Blues Traveler during that era.

Before that point most of our gigs had been New Jersey keg parties. But we had to leave Jersey because the cops could tell when we were warming up that there would soon be underage drinking going on.

Some of our New York City friends tried to help us by throwing parties and hosting gigs in nontraditional places. We tried it at a performance space on 18th Street, and there was also a night when we came up to the roof of somebody's brownstone in midtown Manhattan. It was a gorgeous evening, and we were told we could play there all night. People brought kegs and lots of weed and LSD. We were about to start, everyone was tripping, and then Chan broke a string. Do you know what it's like restringing your guitar when you're really tripping your face off? There's no way to understand what "in tune" means.

There were two hundred people on this rooftop waiting for Chan to tune the string, and they were really starting to get into the tuning process as a song in its own right. Eventually he did it, and when we finally played our first song, there was this amazing release of energy. But then an old lady came out and said, "You've got to stop. It's too late—you can't make any more noise." She shut the whole thing down.

So there we were, two hundred of us on a rooftop, tripping balls and with nothing to do. As I remember, a keg got thrown off the roof and landed on somebody's Volkswagen Rabbit. This was when our old friends were coming in from New Jersey and merging with our new friends from college. It was an attempt on our part to try to get something going before we could land legitimate gigs.

But then starting with Monday night at Nightingale's, we began to build our scene in New York. The way we brought people in was by handing out fliers that promised free nitrous, mushroom tea, and joints. What gave us an edge was that we knew a lot of people who were young and new to the city, just like us. They came to see us because even though we were still rough—there was an energy to what we were doing. So Monday at Nightingale's quickly became a mob scene where everyone was stoned to the gills.

This was the era just after the repeal of New York's cabaret laws. Before that time in New York, if you did not have a cabaret license, you were not allowed to have more than three musicians on stage at your place. The bass player usually had a long table and would sit at the bar—sometimes he'd be in a closet. So Jono had two bands: Joey Miserable and the Worms, which was a great band with horns, and a trio version called the Sweetones.

When we got there, they had just repealed the law, and it helped us immensely because there was a lot of work for bands. Eventually we would play five or six nights a week, all over the city.

I had the knowledge to lead and Bobby had the balls to lead. He was fearless. He would get to know a scene quickly, and soon he would be running it. Chan was this sexpot who was ready to take it all on, and Brendan was the quiet one. I was the weird one, but when I stuck with Bobby I felt fearless. I was more theoretical, saying, "We could do this . . . " and then he'd be like, "Fuck it, man, we're gonna do two of those. Stop thinking small."

I was going to the New School and learning about the aesthetics of music and philosophy from these jazz legends, and then at night I'd play with Jono and learn how to sell drinks and get people dancing. Together, those two schools helped develop the way we played as musicians. Once you learn an art form and how to go out and peddle that art form, it never lets you down, much like a magical power.

I can remember watching the Worms with Jono, and it seemed like the whole floor was made of rubber. Everybody was just bouncing up and down. Then when the song stops, you have a few seconds and want to keep the momentum, but you want to pace it and do it right where everyone's happy and getting the right kind of hammered and having fun. You learn these things through experience. It's the right balance; and it's sort of like hosting a party. And if you do it right, the crowd gives you the energy back, so your energy and their energy augment, where one plus one equals three and it keeps reverberating back and forth. We drive them and they drive us, which pushes them, which pushes us, and it's sort of like a combustion engine. If you have all the balances of the combustibles right, it lasts for a long time as long as you don't flood your engine.

The goal is to make what Miles Davis called social music. Bill Graham called it pelvic music—music you can move your pelvis to. It's social interaction music; it's music people live their lives to. Bebop was a great social music because when you went to a club to hear Dizzie play, you were slowly sipping your gin and tonics with your girlfriend and it got you into the mood and into the moment and you were a part of it. You were participating just by being there, and that to me is my favorite kind of music.

There's such a beautiful mishmash of American culture that happens in a bar, in real time, in real music. Suddenly nobody's white, nobody's black—we're all just here, and that is a great feeling. I think music can do that when it's allowed to.

Most places where bands play also sell alcohol, and as people start drinking, they get a little looser and want to dance. If they're too stiff, they don't quite want to make fools of themselves, which is what they're supposed to do. And what you learn very early on is that the people paying you to play there want you to sell booze, which actually helps your show and makes it more fun for everyone. I always say we work 'em from the front and the bartenders work 'em from the back.

Jono and a couple of the older guys explained that if the bar has a good night, they'll hire you back, and if the crowd you draw doesn't tip so well, they won't. It's important to remind people to tip their bartenders; to this day I always mention that. You should make friends with the bartenders—they are your pals.

The lessons of the New School and their artistic applications made for a great combination with the practical realities we learned while having actual gigs at Nightingale's. If you combine the two, then you've got something special. If you just play dance music, then you might as well play covers, and if you just play super-ethereal, aesthetic, virtuoso music, you're going to bore the shit out of everybody. It's gotta be some kind of balance, where people's feet are moving so they subconsciously respond, and then they're free to get into it on a conscious level.

Jono taught me how to read a crowd. You can't ask everybody how they're doing—there's that great scene in *Buckaroo Banzai* when he says, "Wait a minute, somebody's not having a good time." It would be great if I could stop and focus in on everybody's problems, but over time you get good at reading the rumble of the room. We started as a family and we remained a family, and that was also an advantage—we truly could rely on each other in way that was instinctual. When you join a band with other people, they have to think about their interests and you have to think about yours, but we were literally living in the same house. That was a huge advantage when it came to decision making because our interests were aligned.

The first apartment we moved into together as a band was 354 Bergen Street in Brooklyn. We lived there from the early summer of 1988 through 1989. It still says Blues Traveler on the sidewalk where Chan and Brendan wrote it in the cement. We were on the top floor and had a beautiful view—we could see the Twin Towers. We were just a train ride away from lower Manhattan, and the neighborhood wasn't as dire as our next apartment, where people were smoking crack in the hallways and vestibule. This was an alcohol neighborhood turning into a heroin neighborhood, and the good thing about alcoholics and heroin addicts is that they're slower and in many ways harmless, whereas the crack guys hit you and run before you even see them.

In our crack neighborhood we would pack our van trailer after doing a gig, and if we didn't park it in some place that was absolutely secure, people would come and unscrew all the sheet metal from the trailer. Then we'd come outside and find some wheels and screws on the ground. You know it's a crazy neighborhood when they're stealing the steel from your trailer.

The other problem with living in a crack neighborhood was that the guys had to try the crack because they'd done all the drugs in Princeton. Crack had been demonized in our suburban mindset, but Chan and Bob seemed pretty fearless about jumping in and trying it. There was a brief point when I went right there with them.

One of the four times I smoked crack led to an incident in which I almost got razored in a crack house in Brooklyn. Crack seems like a social drug, but everyone is actually sitting there silently waiting for their turn to smoke, listening to the clicking sound of the gas stove kicking over because you need that flame to heat up the stem of the crack.

When you smoke crack it feels good, but just as cocaine seduces you into thinking that everything is a brilliant idea, crack makes you think you're down for anything. I was leaving after our big crack session and wanted to grab a bag of weed for the next day. So I went down to Myrtle Avenue at two in the morning, which, when you're on crack, seems like standard routine.

Now the thing we all knew about Myrtle Avenue is that if you gave somebody your five bucks, they'd say, "Wait here," and then you'd never see them again. So up comes this guy who looks like Mike Tyson and asks me what I want. I explain that I want a nickel bag and he says, "Give me the money. I'll be right back." I tell him, "I can't leave the money with you. I'll go with you." That's my solution: I'll follow him.

So he takes me into this very scary project, which starts looking worse and worse, but I'm not deviating from my plan. When you're on crack, that's all you have to worry about: don't deviate from your plan. We go up to the second floor and he says, "Okay, now you've got to give me the money and I'll get you the weed." My response is, "No, I won't part with the money."

This is how I learned a very valuable lesson. When you're in a run-down project trying to score some weed from a Mike Tyson guy while you're on crack, you shouldn't say the word *no*. When I did, his face changed from a Mike Tyson face into an angry Mike Tyson face, and he pulled out a six-inch razor blade. Suddenly I'm very aware that the mood has changed and that this is not a cooperative market experience.

He said, "I think you're going to give me your five dollars—what do you think?" I said, "I think here's my five dollars." But that didn't stop the aggression, because when you're turned into the victim, you're encouraging a robbery, so he started patting me down. I remember weakly saying, "What are you doing? Stop it."

This whole time I was carrying on my shoulder a lunchbox tied together with a bandana, which held my harmonicas and my Shure 58 microphone. When he said, "What's that?" it snapped me out of my victim mentality. It was clear to me he wanted my five bucks more than I could ever want my five bucks, but it was also clear that I wanted my lunchbox full of my harps more than he could ever want it. That's when I turned on him—"You're not going to get it, so walk!"

That actually stopped him, which left me a little stunned, but he said, "You better not be downstairs." Then he left and I thought, "I'm on the second floor, how can I not go downstairs to leave?" This had me perplexed. I was afraid to leave, but eventually I sucked it up and decided he meant, "Don't be downstairs hanging around." When I finally left I could hear him in the background with his friends saying, "Hey man, I got your weed," and they were all laughing. So I walked out of there with my harmonicas and my life, realizing that crack is a little whack.

I also remember various episodes during this time when people would disappear into the Brooklyn night and then come in at four in the morning kicking me awake for eight dollars. That period lasted for about half a year, from 1988 to 1989.

This was the era that established me as the teetotaler of the band, at least comparatively. Brendan drank a lot with the guys, but he didn't party the way they did. But I became the sheriff of drug consumption. If something was done in front of me, I would throw a huge tantrum. That being said, I certainly partied with the guys at certain points, just to such a lesser degree that it didn't really seem to count. However, I was eating constantly, and that really became my drug of choice. Instead of going out, my big party was staying in with food and television.

Still, the drugs were a fun part of that time, and I heartily recommend them except for all the damage they do.

That second Blues Traveler apartment was at 282 Washington Avenue near Bed-Stuy. It was a former convent with beautiful inlaid wood. Brendan called it a place we could grow into, although shortly after we moved in, he moved to Park Slope with his girlfriend, so this place to grow in was him depositing us into a nice arrangement. But by then we were touring, so we'd be there less and less often.

This was where Dave Precheur, our tour manager, lived with us. Once a week we received a per diem. He would place a twenty-dollar bill in each of our folders in his filing cabinet. His room was his office, so we'd all barge in there. It was a fucked-up Partridge Family.

Cockroaches chased us out of our first place. It was as if one day the roaches came to us and said, "Look, you guys have been really nice, but you've got to find somewhere else to live." I always carried an air pistol when I went to the bathroom because there were huge roaches everywhere. I remember naming one roach in the bathroom Blue Thunder because he looked like the helicopter in that film and was so magnificent. He was too tough for the air pistol, but finally we got him. New York back then was just a thin layer of crust on top of a seething civilization of roaches.

It didn't help matters that nobody ever threw anything away. Chris Barron moved in with us and said he used to live off the Cheez Doodles he found lying around my room. So along with the cockroaches, we eventually got mice.

One time I was on my way out to a gig and was walking through the kitchen when I heard some scratching. It was a mouse, stuck in the lone garbage can that did not have trash in it—that garbage can was probably the only place in the whole apartment that wasn't covered with trash. The mouse was climbing on the garage around it and fell into an empty garbage can. Now I had to dispatch this mouse, so I loaded my air pistol with actual pellets, not just air for dispatching roaches when I was crapping. I calmly shot the mouse, who ran around in circles and then died. I started to walk away when I again heard scratching and thought, "Oh my God, it's not dead." I came back, and there was another mouse over the dead mouse's body. Clearly it was his girlfriend.

So I shot the second mouse and winged it, but my air pistol was now out of CO_2, so I had to go find another cartridge while this thing was screeching *eep eep eeep* and running around in circles.

I loaded up and killed that mouse. By now I was getting late for a gig, but I heard more scratching, so I went back and there were two more mice. Apparently it was a double-date.

What Chan likes to point out is: "Yeah, it's great, you killed them, but I had to carry them out to the trash." Well, as far as I'm concerned, I'd done my part.

From Bergen Street we went to Washington Street, and from there we'd eventually each find our own places. By the mid-nineties Bobby was in Manhattan, where he lived on the same penthouse floor as Tom Cruise on Astor Place. Bobby thought he had tried to be nice but Tom Cruise had shunned him: *Oooh, get away from me, you creepy-looking hippie.* So Bobby liked to fuck with him whenever he could—"Oooh, you're Tom Cruise, Mr. *Days of Thunder.*" They were separated by a wall, and before we would go on tour for three months, Bobby would do things like throw his trash over the other side. Then he'd say, "Wait a minute," and would turn the volume up to ten on his stereo and direct it at Tom Cruise's place. So he terrorized Tom Cruise for while, but I never got in on that.

Back when we were still living together we maintained a communal approach to our funds. Through the New School I'd already met enough people so I could get a job playing a harmonica on commercial jingles. I think my first was a Volvo commercial where I did half a bar of down-home harmonica. What they learned was that I couldn't read music but that I had a good ear and could figure it out. So they learned to point at me, I'd play half a second of a harmonica fill, and then I'd get five hundred bucks. The money would go into a shoebox that the band would save for recording—unless somebody got wasted and spent it on drugs or booze, and then I got some serious moral vindication, at least.

At that time we were really communist about everything because if one of us couldn't afford the rent, there was no band. So all of our money went into a pot, and then we would get what we needed out of it because generally we were all earning the same. The guys would do that too—if they would do a gig moving furniture or something, the money would go to that.

Having said that, I am prepared to admit that there was one night at Nightingale's, back when harmonicas cost ten or twenty bucks, when this old guy came up to me and said, "I'll give you fifty bucks for one of those." I looked around, made sure my band guys weren't looking, and put that cash right into my back pocket.

The decision to pool our funds also applied to our publishing money, which we decided to split. I suppose I was the major decision maker there because I was writing a lot of the material, but Chan wrote as well. Bobby and Brendan also wrote a little bit. To be fair, the whole band wrote parts of many more songs than what appeared on the writing credits.

Still, at some point it became a factory in which I was the guy who would write stuff and then we all would split the money. That started to annoy me, but back then we were an impoverished family. Brendan wouldn't have been able to eat, and we wouldn't otherwise have had a band in which I could experiment. I wasn't a professional writer where I could say, "Okay, I've got your stuff." It would be this long, agonizing process, and they would put up with me. Eventually we sold the publishing, and now we don't share because I'm only doing that once.

I did it with these guys then because this was our big dream company and we were living together, so it seemed like a tribal-family thing. I wanted it to stop when we had kids, but after Bobby died and amidst all of the hullabaloo, it seemed simpler to keep sharing the publishing. But by 2003 we started changing it. I'd always wanted people to know who wrote which song but I also think maybe it's good to be paid that way.

We ended running up a huge debt and had an issue with an accountant, who unbeknownst to us, had run up a huge debt. In order to pay the debt, selling the publishing worked really nicely. As it turned out, Chan and I, who wrote a lot of the material, wound up running up the biggest debt, so it kind of evened out. Nothing really evens things out like going into debt together.

About ten years ago I ran into Chico Hamilton, who was one of my teachers at the New School, and he said, "How's that communal thing going where you split all the money?" He then explained, "When there's a communal system, one guy does all the work."

I asked him, "Where the fuck was that advice ten years ago when I could have used it?"

8

SWEATGLANDS

It was an exciting, Wild West kind of time.

It was also a pretty smelly time—we didn't shower a lot.

We were a cool underground thing for a while. Looking back, it didn't take long for that next step, but I remember thinking, *God, when is it going to happen?*

One thing that New York really showed us in the late eighties is you have to have a mission when you're there. You have to be working for something. It's very hard to live in New York and just kick it, sort of relax, and do nothing—that takes a special breed called an actual New Yorker. Just about everybody else who comes to New York is there because that's the place where you can launch your band or your fashion line or your magazine, and once you've done that, you have to leave because there's a whole line of hungry people behind you.

I remember when I first came to New York, I went to Washington Square Park and was convinced that somehow Bob Dylan would be there because that's what he likes to do—just go play for people because that's what he did once a thousand years ago and that's his natural state, right? And then I realized that, no, people have lives and the reason you play in a park is that nobody else will hear you—you don't have a venue to play in.

Early on, I lived in my head quite a bit.

When I was going to the New School and discovering New York City, *Amadeus* had just come out, and I felt like a young Mozart in Vienna. When I was wearing a hat and learning about the dark art of harmonies from some great beboppers, I felt like a young sorcerer's apprentice learning a form of alchemy. When we'd be playing in Nightingale's to six people, I'd be a young Charlie Parker playing to nobody in Harlem. A little while later, when we were in our first van, it was like we were in a B-17 on a bomber run or—I was big on my history—a band of barbarians like the Huns.

I was also trying to be Batman with my cool harmonica belt. I built my first version in 1989, and then when I came home to Princeton, which shuts down at night, I would walk the streets alone with my belt. I guess in my mind I was looking for jam sessions in case there would be someone out there with a guitar. I don't quite know what I was thinking.

Originally I would carry my harmonicas around in this groovy Partridge Family lunch box. It was the one I had on me when I walked into that building on Myrtle Avenue. I think my sister actually used it in the sixties when she went to elementary school. I put a little skull and crossbones on it, and it would hold my harmonicas and a Shure 58 microphone. I would tie it together with a bandana because the buckles broke, and then I'd put a little strap on it so I could wear it like it was my weapon or my horn or something, and I got known for that. But then I wanted to get something in which I could pull out the harps a little faster, and I was a big believer in building my own things—because the way I was playing the harmonica was so innovative, I wanted to keep building weird devices to accentuate that. And, also, Batman did that.

My first harmonica belt was a 1950s Korean War M1 cartridge belt with two buck-knife holders on the end as sort of epaulets. I discovered that an M1 belt has ten pouches, and I needed twelve harmonicas, so on top of those I added these #110 buck-knife sheaths for the folding lock blades like the Dukes of Hazzard would wear, and I added one on each side so they looked like epaulets.

I filled the belt with harmonicas and memorized which key was where so I could switch harps really easily; it was like fast drawing.

And I would certainly milk that and make the most of it on stage, and then extra gear would accumulate on it to make it that much more special and unique.

When my brother was overseas in Budapest he got me a Soviet telescope with a little case, so I attached that to the side of the harmonica belt. I was reading these mercenary magazines and saw this grappling hook in the back ads, so I bought one. It was a terrible grappling hook, essentially a spring-loaded baton with a grappling hook you wedged on the end—it was a real challenge to compress the spring—but eventually and with a lot of effort I did, and then I hit the little button and it would go *thunk* and shoot three feet. But it had around sixty feet of test line, so I thought *screw the little spring part and the baton part* and just took the line and put it in the telescope case with the grappling hook and figured that if there were ever a real emergency, I could give the grappling hook to someone who was in shape and they could repel to safety and get help. I also carried an actual telescope, but not in that case, that was for the grappling hook. The telescope was much more compact because it was one of those old collapsing pirate telescopes, which I thought was very important because piracy was also in my menu.

I even had some Blues Traveler patches that I glued onto the buckknife sheaths. Around that time we made too many Blues Traveler patches—so many that I still have some. Our idea was to sell them, I guess but they never caught on. So I cut out the cat heads and glued them onto the harp belt so it looked something like Batman's. (The great thing about Batman is that he advertises as he fights crime. That's really important as a crime fighter—to have your logo present at all the important points.) There was a sense of craftsmanship to it because I couldn't use too much glue or else it would soak through and turn the thing sort of gray. I'd then wear it on the subway and people would think, *Who's that crazy dude with all those grenades?*

When we were walking down the street in the wild and wooly eighties, I would do some trick grappling hook stuff like taking out a light bulb here and there, but it was more for show. People always thought there were knives in the thing, so I hid a knife in the back so I could say they never looked there. That was my whole little shtick.

One time I walked into the one gun shop in New York City; it was downtown and had that old-timey revolver over it. It was a hangout for cops, and I walked in to look around. There were all these officers who looked at me with my harmonica belt, so I said, "Don't worry, these are just harmonicas." Then they all they asked the same thing that cops seemed to ask when I wore the belt: "What's in *that* one?" So I showed them the harmonicas one at a time but never the knife. This was back in the Alphabet City days when New York was a different place and it was fashionable to wear a knife.

In the mid-nineties we were in Ireland, and I walked into a store looking for some sort of shawl or a poncho. The guy took one look at the harp belt and said, "I don't know what you're looking for, but they have it across the street." I guess it was sort of fun to intimidate people unintentionally, but it became a problem when people were getting scared of me.

I kept adding to it, with various tool kits and then a big, clunky Swiss Army knife attached to the bottom of one side. The idea was all about weight ratio: if you put a grappling hook on this side, you've got to put jack knife on that side, and I would be endlessly tinkering to make this a perfectly balanced thing. It was really just a hobby before I got to buy weapons. At one point I even had a .22 mini-revolver in one of the pockets until a crew guy found it, thought it was a toy, and shot a chair. Then I figured this belt won't just be in my hands all the time, so maybe I shouldn't have the harp belt armed—somebody's going to get hurt that way.

Eventually we decided to upgrade me to something that was specifically designed to be my harmonica belt, with little Blues Traveler cat heads and black leather. The only place we figured to go was a bondage store to find somebody who designed piss gags and weird cuffing harnesses, and he built a great one. (His collection of piss gags still haunts me to this day.) It was a little bit heavy and a little elaborate and there were a few incarnations of it. The guy who built the last one made a soft leather version with a nice belt to keep it from flapping around—that belt is now attached to an old pirate cutlass that I keep on the bus because you can't go on tour without some kind of a sword—there's just that pirate aspect to it. I must have a cutlass for leading a charge or a cheer, and you never know when you might need to chop something.

When I bought my first gun I wanted to see what would happen if I shot the harp belt with a harmonica in it—maybe it would stop a bullet. So I put a phone book behind it and shot it. Nope. It went right through like butter. And that's an important lesson to know, harp players.

I lost the belt when I lost all my weight in 2000. When you're four hundred pounds, you think, *What's an extra fifty pounds of crap?* But after I shed the weight, my attitude was, *I've got this new body—why do I want to hide behind this elaborate thing?*

When I was doing the TV show *Selfie* in 2014, they wanted me to wear my harmonica vest because there was some line where I was going to threaten the opening band for wearing a vest. They didn't end up using the line, but we got my harp belt sent out, so I figured why not wear it? And wearing it brought back so many memories, in particular how annoying it was to play with a harp belt on.

I'm not sure where all the old ones are, but I remember giving Dan Aykroyd the one I wore at Woodstock '94 for the Boston House of Blues.

These days I keep my harmonicas in a case, and when I set up the case, it's as if I'm laying the harp belt on the ground. So on my left side, as if I'm wearing the harp belt, it would be low G, which is the lowest key, then A-flat, then A, then B-flat, then B, and then C. And on the next side it would be D-flat at the top by my collarbone, then D, E-flat, E, F, and F-sharp. That's the order I keep them in today, lowest to highest. If I were to wear that briefcase, if it were glued to my chest, I could look to my left side and the one closest to my head would be G.

When you start getting crews, they don't know the order, and being all out of order is a nightmare for a harmonica player. I was playing the Blue Note in 2013, and they put my case on a music stand. I got up to do something, and the wire knocked all of my harps onto the table in front of me. So people are picking them up off the floor, and some are covered in beer; one landed on a guy's nuts and I gotta put that in my mouth.

This brings me back to the early days and an incident that happened at the Mondo Cane, which was the next place we wound up after Nightingale's. This was when we worked six or maybe seven nights a week—back in New York in the late eighties we would do that and then take a day off. We did three forty-five-minute sets, but I had the flu that day and was playing when suddenly I started vomiting while I was playing. So the harp sort of clogged, but I was standing over people who were eating and drinking. What I couldn't do was just take the harp out of my mouth like it was a cork and vomit all over everybody; instead, I had to swallow it back down and bite the big chunks. I threw the harp away as soon as I could, and some lucky audience person caught it. I can't say they're a fan—at least they're not a fan now. They probably caught it with glee and then got some emulsified oatmeal—the consistency of this thing—splashed on them and got more and more horrified as they sought to answer the question of what that was.

We started at Nightingale's. You could spot a Blues Traveler gig in the Nightingale's days by this crowd of hippies sitting on the ground and this cloud of smoke. People weren't using chairs so much as using chairs arbitrarily. And it was Monday.

Thanks to Gina, one of the first fans we ever had, a lot of people from the Hippie Hotel on 99th Street started coming down to see us, and it became a thing.

Gina found us, and we noticed her because we would be playing some place like Kenny's Castaways or the Bitter End, where there were chairs and she wanted to dance her hippie dance. The bouncers would come and tell her to stop because they wanted everyone sitting at tables and buying booze at these bridge and tunnel places, and she's about four-foot-nine and 80 pounds and would get into fights with bouncers who were six and a half feet tall and 250 pounds. It was very impressive to see how she could hold her own.

It was about the music for her. She started doting on us, mothering us. Later on she would sleep in the wheel well of our van and do our laundry, working for free just to be a part of it, and it made her feel like family.

One day she wanted a job with us and to be able to define what that job was. So she got help and presented us with a résumé. She wanted to be the assistant to the road manager. So from that point on we created a job that could only be defined as Gina. It was what she wanted

to do to help because she could think of ways that we couldn't to interact with the fans. We were terrible at that, but Gina could get to
know everyone. It was amazing how many people she knew and could
contact. It was like she was our own little Erin Brockovich who would
take care of all the details. We have a great deal of love for Gina.

The song "Gina" was a testament to how bouncers would throw
her out of these clubs because she was dancing—they wanted people
to sit at tables so they could sell them drinks, but she wasn't having it.
So she'd have fights with the giant bouncers and they'd toss her. She'd
be sobbing, "Oh my God, I'll never get back in there." She was always
so upset when she'd made a scene. And that's why the song starts out
"Gina, Gina don't you cry . . . "

A few years ago I went up to this elementary school in South
Bronx—it was a really bad neighborhood—and the teacher used that
song along with a Dave Matthews song to teach kids to read. They all
loved "Gina," and she went up there with me. We were both in tears.
Those little kids knew every word to it—it was something. And I said,
"This is the Gina that I wrote the song about," and they were like,
"Whoa . . . "

She kind of outranked everybody in the crew, and there were times
when she pulled the motherly vibe and outranked all of us. She helped
build that initial audience connection at Nightingale's, and from there
we went to Kenny's Castaways and the whole Bleecker Street scene
with Mondo Cane and Mondo Perso.

We even played CBGB's once in 1989. I was told that Hilly Kristal
saw us and gave us an A rating. I knew nothing about the lore of the
club. The night we had to prove ourselves they put us between two
heavy-metal hair bands where there was a lot of head banging, so it
was easy to be original between two bands that sounded the same.

The sound guy from Kenny's Castaways, Rich Vink, started hanging out with us and became our sound guy, and he knew Dave Swanson, who was the sound engineer working at Greene Street Studios
and became our monitor guy. This was the formation of the guts of the
crew. In 1988 and 1989 those clubs and associations were coming
together.

In my opinion we never left a bad taste in anyone's mouth. We
were generally pleasant to work with—we might have gotten a little

sloppy, but we never really broke anything. We didn't fight over money as a general rule, we usually did as we were told, and we always left everybody pleased. By and large, people wished us well, at least that's my take.

Nightingale's was the first bar that didn't just tolerate us; they encouraged us. But there were others too: Mondo Cane and Mondo Perso and then Wetlands. It's so rare as a band that you get to have your own little club that you get to take for granted. I remember seeing Jono in Nightingale's and saying to myself, *I want that.* We could never quite have that at Nightingale's because of Jono, but we finally would at Wetlands.

First it was Mondo Cane and Mondo Perso and the Bleecker Street scene. Those rooms couldn't have held more than 150 people—I'm probably being generous—but they seemed so important. I remember Downtown Julie Brown from MTV came to Mondo Cane. And one of the bartenders at Mondo Cane, Daniel Kellison, became a talent booker for David Letterman, told them about us, and helped get us on his show.

Adolph, the guy who ran those two clubs, was great. He'd do things like say, "Hey, you dropped that," and that was his way of giving us twenty dollars. Another time we told him how the utility company had shut off our heat, and he came back with this space heater, saying, "I don't need this. I'm throwing it out." He was so aware that some people might be offended by his charity, but we were like, "Cool, a heater." We didn't blink, but we were aware he was trying to spare our feelings in case we were proud. He basically went out and bought us a big-ass heater, and we threw it in our car with the gear, drove it home, and had heat.

He'd also take everyone out for breakfast—the waiters, the waitresses, bartenders, and bands. It wasn't in a pervy or a douchebag way; he just really saw twentysomethings in New York with dreams and without money.

When the lunch box that held my microphones fell apart, I gave half of it to him. I also gave him a tumbleweed. The first time we played a gig in California, we were driving back through Flagstaff, Arizona. It was the first time we had been across the country. The only ones awake were me and Rob Lester, who went to high school with us and was our driver in the early days. He asked, "Is this really Arizona?" and then just as he said it, a tumbleweed blew by. Without a word we looked at each other, jumped out of the van, chased down the tumbleweed, threw it inside, and took it back to New York. We wound up giving it to Adolph, and it lived in the Mondo Cane.

We first heard about Wetlands when some of the people who were working on it came down to Nightingale's in late 1988 and told us about this club that would be opening in February. I don't think we held our breath because at that time lot of people would come up to us and say, "We have this new thing we're going to be doing—come on down and be our band." So we said, "Sure, sounds great," and nothing ever came of it, but Wetlands wound up being a real thing.

We became the house band, and there was that relationship of belief—give me something and I'll give you something; we'll work together. Larry Bloch was among the first to do that, before Bill Graham gave us that feeling. And especially when you're a little band from Princeton, New Jersey, that meant a lot. When we sort of had carte blanche at Wetlands—they made it clear this was our scene and our house—it felt similar to being signed by a label.

When I walked in for the first time, I noticed that bus and all those leaflets and pamphlets and different organizations trying to get stuff done—*Oh God, what is this place?* It had a cool bar and an equally cool paint job. Everybody always complained about the location of the stage, but I always liked the intimacy it created, and I played to more people than I ever did before anyhow.

We had a thousand people in there at times; I know that for a fact, although later on I learned that the capacity was only 389. That's hysterical to me. That's also why I ended up calling it Sweatglands: because with all those bodies in there, the air conditioning wouldn't work, the pipes would drip, and the walls would sweat.

Then we would go downstairs and there were all those pillows, and everyone was smoking weed. You'd grab your girl and start making out, and nobody seemed to be bothering anybody.

I met Bear down there, Owsley Stanley. I was trying to lose weight at many points, and he told me to only eat meat. He gave me this whole spiel about how Eskimos eat seven thousand calories a day. I went to my doctor and told him what Bear told me, and my doctor said, "Yes, because they're in subzero temperatures and burn two thousand calories just trying to stay warm."

Bear was in his mid-fifties and showed me his muscles. He was strong. I think what he was preaching was the Atkins Diet in a sense. I can never eat an entirely meat-only diet because eventually I need ketchup and French fries, but he was a cool guy. We hit it off—we could both tell the other guy was weird.

We were at Wetlands the first month, opening for Sonny Rhodes, and then almost immediately we were headlining. We got signed out of Wetlands. It was the first time the *Village Voice* had to acknowledge our existence. It was also the first time people heard about this scene going on.

I remember looking around and felt like we were in *The Doors* movie for a second. It was cool. We were our own scene. We weren't punk rockers—it was a sort of hippie rejuvenation, this jam band thing, although we didn't call it that. It just felt like we were home.

I remember when Jerry Dugger from the Worms first saw us play. He said, "I really like the psychedelia, but you gotta develop it." That's when I thought, *Oh, so we're psychedelia.* We were definitely into that music, but I never thought, *I'm going to be a hippie and adopt a hippie lifestyle.* That never occurred to me, and in fact it seemed kind of dumb to me. I always wanted to be a friend to a hippie but not a hippie. I wanted to make sure he got home okay. I wanted to make sure he was eating. You always have to make sure a hippie's eating if you care about him.

Shortly after Bobby joined the band, he had all these friends in Princeton who would invite us to play at their parties. They were all Deadhead guys, and I have this tape where someone asks, "Does Popper know the words to 'Fire on the Mountain?'" "Of course Popper knows the words to 'Fire on the Mountain.'" I didn't know the words to "Fire on the Mountain."

Bobby also wanted us to do "New Minglewood Blues," but I'd never heard any Grateful Dead songs, so our version was definitely different. I was really unschooled in singers and bands, so I guess I was sort of trying to do an Iron Butterfly impression, but it really sounded like Bill Murray doing his lounge act. I didn't know how to sing. I had to learn to let my voice go and not try to sing through my head. Drugs helped a bit because then you relax and go with it and can respond to a beautiful moment, and the New School certainly helped me get to my voice.

While Bobby was always trying to steer us in that direction, before he joined the band I felt more kindred with George Thorogood than the Grateful Dead. But improvisation was second nature to everyone at the New School, so it became a little easier to go that way. I also felt a bit like Little Walter reborn, but I didn't want to know any Little Walter songs, just as I didn't want to know any Grateful Dead songs. I thought the key was not to know anything and to go in and be original because it's easier to be original when you don't know what the hell you're doing or who you're referencing.

Eventually I would see the Grateful Dead a few times and come to appreciate their music, but it wasn't easy. The first thing I noticed about the Grateful Dead is that my friends would put on a tape, cue it up to their favorite song, and then proceed to talk during the entire song. I'd want to smack them with a carp so I could hear the song. And when you don't know the Grateful Dead and can't hear them too well, every song seems like they're singing "Ham and eggs . . . "

I can remember the first time Bobby, Dave Precheur, and some other friends took me to a Grateful Dead show. There were two things I noticed as a first-time attendee: everyone wants you to dance, and everyone wants to tell you about the first time they heard a song, so you never get to hear that song. It almost becomes the emperor's new clothes because they're so busy talking about how great it is to be there that you never know what it's like to be there.

I couldn't enjoy the Grateful Dead because everyone was so busy telling me how much I should enjoy the Grateful Dead. I remember being on acid, convinced that people were trying to brainwash me because they really wanted me to enjoy the show, and I just wanted to hear the show before I could enjoy it. That was tough to do. All of my friends were singing in my ear along with the band, and all I could hear was "Ham and eggs . . . "

The one time I was finally able to listen to the Grateful Dead was when I ditched my friends and went off and found a chair somewhere and sat down where I didn't know anybody. The Deadheads around me said, "Aren't you going to dance?" And I said, "No," and just watched the show and got to hear the music, and that was the important thing.

The New School steered me toward the idea that you should know what's out there so you can react to it and rail against it if you must. But it seemed to me that if you don't know what you're doing, you can remain more innocent. The result is that a lot of your songs stay in one or two chords for a little longer, but there was something pure about it that people responded to.

Nightingale's didn't belong to us—it's what we belonged to. If it belonged to anybody, it was Jono's place. Nightingale's was a place where we lived by our wits as a band; it was a proving ground. But the Wetlands took us in, and because they encouraged us to do precisely what we happened to be doing at the time, we got to feel exactly like we did a few years earlier when we were rehearsing or playing somebody's keg party.

They would close the place down sometimes and we'd play an extra hour. It felt like a slumber party—"Hey, let's stay up and tell ghost stories!" We didn't feel like we had to be as professional as much as we got to have fun playing.

I don't think we could even do that today because nobody would let us. But even if we suddenly wanted to go an hour past curfew, now we'd have to think about union costs, we'd have to get to the next gig and unload, the crew's tired, and we'd need to pay everybody. Back then those thoughts weren't really on our mind. It was more like, "This is fun and the crowd's raging—this is what we're here for." Sooner or later, in order to function, you've got to become a business, and Wetlands was the last place we got to be innocent. After that it wasn't worse; it just became efficient.

The first time we played with Bruce Willis was at Wetlands. It was the standard harmonica thing, where we always want to duel, so the first thing I did was rip him a new one. I wanted to punish him because I was angry at all harmonica players, really, but the thing is, he was such a fun guy. Then at set break he was like, "Yeah, you're fast, but can you play slow?" (As if to say, "Do you have soul?") So the next set I took it real easy on him and traded, and it was an instant mutual love affair after that.

He invited me to Idaho to sit in with his band. He plays harp and dresses up his other harmonica player in a Krispy Kreme donuts uniform and says he's the billionaire founder of Krispy Kreme donuts who just goes out on a lark to play with him. So with me, they had three harp players.

I remember he handed me this wooden duck decoy. Apparently he was at some hotel in New Hampshire or Vermont where these ducks were in every room, and he got drunk and collected them all. At first he told me that he had carved it himself, that he was in therapy and his therapist told him he needed to work with his hands. But later he acknowledged that he just said that to people and then handed them ducks.

My other memory of that time is that he was married to Demi Moore, but I kept calling her Diane because this was before *Ghost* and I didn't know who she was. She looked at me dead in the eye as if to punch me and said, "Hey, it's Demi." By the time I visited them in Idaho a decade afterward, it became a funny story, at least to me.

I later invited Bruce to record with us on our 2008 album, *North Hollywood Shootout*. I just wanted him to do some beat poetry. I asked him to write something with a pocket behind it, and he got hold of it, gripped it and ripped it.

As for Wetlands, we would come back and play for Larry long after we were too big to play there anymore. I think I did two solo Wetlands shows where it was just me emptying my stockpile of every song I had written since high school. "Run-Around" was in that batch, unveiled that way. I debuted the original, slower version there, and it was a magical evening for me. Somebody recently sent me the tape, and I just love that it's out there. When you're doing shows like that, you have fantasies in your head that someday someone will remember this, and it feels great to know they really did. Plus, in this case the advantage is that there are so many songs I had forgotten about that I can learn to play again or at least can strip for parts. Thank you, social media.

Wetlands was on Hudson Street in Tribeca on the other side of the Holland tunnel. The area felt very different from how it feels today. It wasn't treacherous, although the rats were big; it was mostly abandoned warehouses.

My mom remembers New York in the fifties when it was exciting to her and jazz was there and the streets seemed so clean. And I tell her, yes, that's because all the homeless people were locked up in giant prisons that were basically snake pits—it's not like they were getting treatment; they were put into holes so no one had to see them.

And in my New York, which I guess was from the late 1970s through 2000, the homeless people were on the streets, so it made for an exciting though really disgusting ongoing saga of the mental health of the entire city. Giuliani did what he could to get them out, but they were still around—you couldn't just sweep them under the rug—and there were lots of crack addicts and junkies. That was our exciting New York time.

And right before us, in the sixties and seventies, it was much more violent. We missed that little party. I remember going into New York then—it was a scary place. And then in the eighties crack was going on, but you knew how to deal with it: you stayed away from certain parts of New York or, if you were some of my friends, you just jumped right in with both feet. It was *our* scary.

I think what happens is that everyone from their generation has *their* New York. And they're always remembering it fondly, even though there's plenty of fucked-up shit about that New York, present New York, and future New York.

For me, when the Virgin Megastore showed up, that was kind of the end of my New York.

I like to think that people from the suburbs are my people, that that's where I come from. I'm Wonder Bread and Miracle Whip and Weaver Chicken Roll and Kraft Singles—that to me is cuisine. Those are my people; that's what I'm made of. I don't stop eating that stuff, because I'm afraid if I don't re-up the Styrofoam that's in my body, I'll start to delaminate and then I'll rot and die.

But that was one thing the suburban people had—the convenience of a mall. And New Yorkers who want everything wanted that. They wanted the comfort and ease of getting their coffee where they also bought their CDs while also doing other shopping. So the Virgin Megastore was the beginning of the end for me. Then there was a Disney store, and anything you could get in a mall you could find in New York City. For me, that was a small victory for the suburban culture.

We finally came up with something that New Yorkers envied, and it wound up being the very poison that transformed it away from the city of adventure that anyone would hope it would be.

That being said, I'm just comparing this to *my* New York because I guarantee there are adventures going on in New York today. I just don't know where they are like I used to. Someone else's New York will be this incredible wild savage time, and then when they get older they'll look back and say, "Man, I remember *that* New York." And that's what New York is supposed to do—it's supposed to be a place where you go face your dreams and try to execute them and either realize them or fail and then get the hell out of the way for the next bunch of kids coming in. That's what I really love about New York. To me, that's the New York we can all share.

New York City's very nature is to be co-opted by everyone else in the world who will say that's *my* city. That is what New York does for everyone, and it still continues to do that—it's just that I won't recognize it and my mom won't recognize her New York in it. And on and on it goes, back to Damon Runyon and P. T. Barnum and all the way back to Amsterdam.

The fuel of New York is that everyone goes through it. I was but a gasoline burp in the engine of New York City, if I was even that loud. It's kind of cool.

As grimy as it is, New York is constantly rewashing itself and endlessly redefining what it means, and a new group of people will discover that. I just love the crap out of that. The key to New York is that you don't fall in love with *your* New York—just be sure to get out of the way and watch what's coming because that's a good way to get hit by a bicycle cab.

9

THE GRAHAM DYNASTY

By the summer of 1989 we'd been in the city for about two years and had created a buzz, first at Nightingale's, then Mondo Cane and Mondo Perso, and finally at Wetlands, which soaked us up and saw us as the perfect house band. We'd also made a demo tape, and people started coming around and approaching us about management, acting like we might be the next big thing.

There was this guy Jose who had lots of cocaine and paid our electric bill one month. He showed up in late 1988 and kept saying that he was going to sign us and that he had connections to Columbia Records. The word Columbia—or maybe it was Colombia—kept coming up, and he had incredible amounts of drugs. We'd go to his house, sit around, smoke cocaine—it wasn't crack, I think it was freebasing, as if there's a meaningful difference—and talk about what we were going to do. The more drugs we did with him, the more we would think, *This guy sure makes a lot of sense.*

I remember on New Year's Eve 1988–89 we were there, and when the band was getting ready to leave, I told them, "I'm just going to stick around." After Chan heard that, he grabbed me and dragged me out of the apartment. It was like the blind leading the blind, and I think that was the last time we saw Jose.

I would say Jose's time with the band lasted four or five weeks. At first he seemed like a white knight who was going to come in and finance us, and then it just seemed like he really needed people to party with.

After Chan pulled me out of there that night he proceeded to lecture me the entire train ride back to Princeton and, in the process, lost his giant white Stratocaster. He left it on the train and never recovered it. If you've ever lost a white Stratocaster, you'll know what that was like for him. It was the one that got away.

The first professional approach was from Josh Warner, a roadie for Anderson Bruford Wakeman and Howe, who told us he was starting his own management company. He began talking to us about how he could get us on tour with Anderson Bruford Wakeman and Howe—"They used to be Yes, you know."

We also started hanging out with Dave Graham, Bill Graham's son, who'd seen us at a Barnard gig. He'd been working with this band Dreamspeak, who were friends of his at Columbia University. Dave heard that we were getting offers and wanted his dad to manage us and he would be the point man because he was graduating.

I remember Dave said that his dad had brought our demo tape to Jerry Garcia, who said, "Nice harp." I dined on that for a long time.

Then we received a letter from Bill Graham himself:

August 16, 1989

Dear John, Bob, Chan, Brendan, and Dave,
Hello,

All this is a bit strange for us and, I feel, all of you, we're sure, because we haven't yet had an opportunity to sit down together. We normally would like to meet and establish a personal relationship before speaking about your business, but your talent has obviously heated up the pace of your career. Both of us listen to and love your music, particularly the Greene Street demo tape, and thus are very much interested in working with you. Your music is simply wailing, and we would like to be responsible for helping to turn the world on to this band.

Because David Graham will not be back in New York until September fifth, there's no way to solidify any exact agreements, but please understand that we wish to manage Blues Traveler and would deliver the appropriate contracts after we collectively decide the most agreeable course of action. Of course we also would like to see you perform live before signing papers, but David's reports and the review we expect from Kevin Burns should speed up the process. I, Bill, will be in New York in September and anticipate seeing you and talking with you. We understand that you don't want to burn any bridges, but we feel we can deliver more than any other offer. We're not asking you to cut your other connections, but we wish to come to you before September fifth if you feel overly pressured by other forces. I would be willing to reschedule my time in order to come and see you earlier. If you have any questions, please feel free to call us. We'll be in touch with you today or tomorrow.

Cheers,

Bill Graham

I was twenty-two and getting a letter from Bill Graham—that was something. So, of course, we waited.

This other guy took us to an Anderson Bruford Wakeman and Howe show, and we saw him getting towels for the band. He was a good guy, but he just didn't have the clout he said he did. It was really a no-brainer for us: anybody else or Bill Graham Presents managing us.

So we waited until September when the Jerry Garcia Band was in town and Bill invited us there. We saw Jerry pass by, and our eyes were popping out of our heads. We were in this dressing room, and Bill came in through this crowd of people and made a beeline for me. It blew me away, just the way he walked up—it was like the seas parted. It was really eerie. Then he said, "I've been looking forward to meeting you for a long time. You are very talented."

And that's surreal. Whenever I start seeing people I've seen in books and TV, my first instinct is to not completely believe it. But I realized I had to impress this guy, so I told him my Indian boil sucker joke. It's set in a medieval Indian village, where, alongside the barrel maker and the tent maker, there's the boil sucker who sucks the pus out of people's boils. A fat lady comes into his tent after a long day of boil sucking, with a rather large boil to suck on the inside of her ass. It's closing time, but he figures, "I might as well—she's in pain." So he has her stand on a stool, hoists up her frock, and there, on the inside of her right butt check, pulsing like a living map of Eurasia, is a giant boil, and he says, "Oh, this is going to be a long one." So he gets under there and gnarls his teeth into the tough hide of this elderly woman. Eventually his teeth break the skin, and the first bursts of hot pus go shooting up his nose and all over his face. There's a lot of flesh in there—it's like a slightly rotted peach—but it just never ends. So he keeps sucking and sucking, and when he's about halfway through, she lets out this giant wet fart, knocking him over and covering him in this brown sauce. He gets up, looks her in the eye, and says, "Lady, you're the kind of person who makes this job disgusting."

So I delivered that punch line, and everyone's horrified, but Bill looked at me and said, "You're going to go very far in this business."

Then Bill needed to see us play officially, so we took him down to Mondo Perso. Everyone there was abuzz—"Bill Graham's coming!"—and he saw us and liked us.

Bill taught us so much during the time he worked with us before he died in that helicopter crash on October 25, 1991. I think most importantly he emphasized that the two things you want to do as a musician are to make a living and to express yourself. Everything still breaks down to that.

The first gig Bill got us was playing the Housing Now March in DC. We'd gone from gigs of a few hundred people to 250,000. It was a homeless rally, and the homeless from New York had walked to DC because someone told them there would be food there, but there wasn't any food there. Eventually the New York homeless started beating up the DC homeless and tried to take their food. It was like, "We've encouraged some transients to come and kick the shit out of some other transients."

Members of the Grateful Dead were there, and I met Joan Baez. Bill was now our manager, and we had been talking to him in a little room, but now he was running this thing and we were very impressed with that. He could see that this rift between the New York homeless and the DC homeless had created angry homeless people everywhere; a number of them were in the front row.

We were about to go on when I looked down at the front row and Bill Graham was tangled in a brawl. His foot was reaching out this way and his arm out another way while he wrestled with homeless people. The king of the world, Bill Graham, was now grappling with eight or nine different deranged homeless men and women and was trying to kick at them.

I saw that, and the first thing I thought was *I love my job*. And then we started playing.

I remember at first it was amazing that this guy who was so legendary would even talk to us. But later, when he yelled at us, we had gotten to this place where we felt familiar enough that we didn't crumble—because you haven't lived until Bill Graham has yelled at you.

Bill was the only one I know who could throw an eloquent tantrum. He taught me a very important lesson that I used until I couldn't scream that loud anymore: if you have a strong argument and you yell it at the top of your lungs, then you're overloading someone because they're hearing your argument and getting screamed at, and they don't know which to respond to first. They want to yell back at you, "Stop yelling like a lunatic!" But you're not yelling like a lunatic; you're yelling sane, salient points, and it's very effective, especially if you're the boss guy. It worked well for years. The problem is that you have to throw a bigger and bigger tantrum every time, and after a while, I'm a musician, I'm not that angry.

There was one night at the Capitol Theatre when Bill just lit into us, and when he was on a tear, he really was the scariest motherfucker you're ever gonna meet. Bill had to get involved because of a power struggle involving Dave Graham and Dave Precheur, our tour manager, who had been with us since Princeton.

I had learned from my Hungarian dad that you just don't want to be the one yelled at—you have to yell something back. Luckily I had something to say to Bill, which was that his underlings kept taking me aside and telling me I needed to fire Chan and Bobby. Maybe Brendan could stay. They told me this was the industry standard. I saved up this information, and when Bill confronted us with the impasse that Dave Precheur and Dave Graham were at, I confronted him with the confusion and lack of cohesion his people created.

Standing up to Bill was a legendary moment for me because I was getting the full force of a Bill Graham tirade. I was able to tirade back a little bit and dilute his argument that "I am of one mind and this is one focused entity." And Bill wasn't prepared to have his underlings undermine his belief in the band.

So I asked him, "So are you through with us? Is this over?" Because we weren't going to get rid of Precheur. And Bill wouldn't answer the question; he wouldn't say yes. He had been trying to scare us with the threat that he was done with us, but he still wouldn't answer. In that moment I felt I had turned what was a complete barrage into a deflection.

A short while later I was over at Bill's apartment in New York with his son Dave, and Bill wanted to sit me down. He said, "We have to do something with Precheur and Dave." He was trying to talk with me and not the band, and he said, "Come on tell me the truth—you know Dave Precheur wants to run the world."

I said, "Look, Dave Precheur wants to run the world, Dave Graham wants to run the world, John Popper wants to run the world, Chan Kinchla wants to run the world . . . "

Bill responded, "Not me."

I answered, "Well, you *do* run the world!" He laughed, and at that point he became conciliatory. Bill was the kind of guy who responded to a funny moment. He was all about the drama of the moment.

And as I walked out, I was in daze—*Did I just do that? Did I win?*

What was really great was that the next time we were San Francisco in his office, he said, "Wait for a second," and then Morty Wiggins and Arnie Pustilnik marched into the office as if directed by God. Each of them individually came in and said in his own way, "I want you to know I really believe in the band, and that includes Chan and Bobby and Brendan. I'm really behind you guys." I got a new taste of what was the industry standard.

I got the greatest ass kissing from these guys who, before then, had referred to us as Dave Graham's pet project, Dave Graham's little toy. I think a lot of people at BGP resented that Dave Graham, just out of college, gets his band, so we met a lot of resistance from them. It was tough-going initially. A little while later they started coming to us for favors, and I was very resentful; it was stupid politics, and I was happy to keep score.

Of course, David Graham was a friend of ours, and he's still a good friend, among my best. One day he invited us to a party at his father's place, Masada. We'd been there before, but this time Dave was throwing a party. It became apparent pretty quickly that everybody was starting to get naked and make out with each other. It was really groovy, and I felt like, *I'm in the hippie capital. I can't really object to this, but I'm sorry—I'm from New York, I'm neurotic. What can I can tell you?*

I think women were running a train on my guitarist.

Masada had several houses, so I was in one of those houses, in somebody's room, and I was talking to this nude woman. I think she was married to this guy who was in there while we were talking. So she and I started making out, and I felt the husband's hand caressing her shoulder. Well, that's alright. But then he reached over to my arm and placed it there, romantically. So I left, and basically I was hanging out while everyone else was fucking.

The thing was, everyone who was there was incredibly good looking. I don't think ugly people show up to orgies, except that ugly guy in the raincoat who doesn't know he's the ugly one. And that was the concern I was having: *Am I that guy?* There were a couple of other people there like me—*Let's just party with the drugs and pretend we took part in the orgy.*

A similar situation took place years later when I was a judge at Nudes-A-Poppin', which is a pageant held at a nudist colony. Both men and women participate, so the key for me was to go to the bathroom when the male strippers came out so I didn't have to do any of that judging. I also learned that when a naked man sits in plastic chair you have to towel it off after he leaves, but when a woman sits in a plastic chair naked it's perfectly fine. I was a judge twice, and the first time I ended up making out with the only person there wearing a shirt who, it turned out, was the date of porn star Ron Jeremy.

A few years after, I returned, met someone else, and we started to fool around in the same room (the couches were exactly the same and had the crunchiest fabric I've ever encountered, which may be why I haven't been back). Well, lo and behold, Ron Jeremy walked in and clearly wasn't going to make the same mistake this time, so he said, "Room for one more?" and started to get undressed. I was trying to be cool, because I was in the presence of porn people, but when I saw the thing he pulled out, I was traumatized. I lost my erection for the next month.

But back in those early days at Masada, we all were relatively innocent. The funny part was watching Bill Graham come back after his son threw a party. Occasionally we'd get some of that rap. We were his son's friends and his house was trashed and Bill was walking around cleaning shit up.

Around this time Bill got us a gig opening for the Jerry Garcia Band at the Warfield. And after our set Dave said, "The B-52s are playing—do you want to go see them?" I said, "Sure," and Bill stared at us like, *What the fuck?* We don't know why he was staring at us— he wouldn't tell us—and when we came back we learned that Carlos Santana had come to meet our band. I missed the whole thing and was so mad. I would have been able to sit in with him if I had just stayed where I was at the Warfield and not gone to see the frigging B-52s.

I did luck out, though. When I came back to the Warfield and heard this, I ran out after him, and there he was. I said, "Oh my God, you're amazing." And he said, "Hey, we're all part of the same thing."

People treated us differently because of Bill. When we recorded our first album, A&M Records wanted the song "Slow Change" to be our single. When we'd do it live, it was eight minutes long and in a 7/4 time signature, but A&M wanted us to cut it down to three and half or four minutes. It was Bill who said, "The single should be 'But Anyway,'" and then they immediately said, "Of course, 'But Anyway.'" He had that impact right away.

The last time I saw Bill alive we finally got Carlos Santana to sit in with our band, and Bill had no small part in it. It was at Golden Gate Park during Ben & Jerry's One World, One Heart Festival, shortly after the media reported that Miles Davis had died. We did a "Mountain Cry" that was twenty minutes long and felt like our high school graduation. I was dueling with him and Chan was dueling with him and he traded with each of us. We were all keeping up with him, and it was a really long, cool thing. We felt like men after that.

Carlos described the way I play—and I think it's the way that Blues Traveler plays—as like a salmon fighting its way up a waterfall. I was very happy when he said that because it meant he was paying attention to us. I remember telling Bill how blown away I was. He told me that was how he felt after he met Muddy Waters.

Bill died less than a month later. It was just so unexpected. He loved that helicopter, and the crash also took the life of Bill's beloved pilot, Steve "Killer" Kahn.

We were at a gig, and I was one who heard about it first, so I called the band members to get on the bus and tell them that he'd been in a helicopter crash. We were all freaking out because we had such plans with Bill. It was a big deal.

My reaction to his death was to punch Bobby in the face.

Whenever we were under stress, a pattern would unfold in which Bobby would be in bad mood and act like a bully. He had this great, infuriating snort, like he couldn't believe what you just said, and he'd give you the middle finger—put it right in your face and violate your personal boundaries.

So the next day we were at the Pancake House. This was the first meeting where we were talking about what we're going to do now that Bill's died—who would be our manger and where we were going.

I think Bobby was getting up to leave to go to the bathroom dismissively when I said, "You can't leave." So he snorted and stuck his finger in my face. I stood up and threw a chair across the room. This was in Winooksi, Vermont, and there were all these old people—it was the senior brunch special. I always forget how large I am, and when I threw the chair, I scared the shit out of the entire place.

I went to leave, but before I did, I just turned around and cranked him one, right on the nose. Then we went out and had a big talk about what was really bothering us.

We were freaking out, but by the time we got to the memorial, it was clear that Dave Graham was really going through a lot: not only his grief over the loss of his father, but, as all things are when a powerful man dies, it was a clusterfuck. He and his aunts were dealing with various issues from the inheritance, and there were all sorts of questions about who would get what and who would run the company.

I remember River Phoenix was there comforting Dave. I'm not sure where they met, but I remember River looking at me and saying, "I'm so glad I get to be useful today." And that really struck me because that was exactly what he was being.

We were comforting him as best we could, and then we'd see someone from Bill Graham Presents and it would take on the aura of a soap opera. There was all this tension because there were a lot of unresolved issues about what was going to happen next. It was a little bit like being in a Mario Puzo book. I think that was how Bill Graham ran his outfit—he was the head and he had a family.

The last time I saw Bill alive was the day I got to play with Carlos Santana at Golden Gate Park. The next time I was at Golden Gate Park, Bill had died and I was playing with the Grateful Dead.

Before the show I was in Jerry Garcia's tent and he was eating a cheeseburger. All he wanted to do was eat his cheeseburger, and there were all these people fussing and not talking to him. I was just staring at the floor. I had my ridiculous harmonica belt with the telescope, and I was playing with telescope. I could see him watching me, and he sort of laughed a little. I could tell he was trying to put me at ease.

Then the room cleared out, and it was just Jerry Garcia and me in this little tent fortification. I heard him sigh, so now I had to say something. This was my moment to talk with Moses, and Moses really just wanted to sit there and eat his cheeseburger. It was a sad day, but I was also very excited to be playing "Wang Dang Doodle" with the Dead. So I meekly offered up, "I'm a flurry of emotions." There was a long pause, then he sighed again and said, "Me too." That was the extent of our conversation.

I remembered Carlos Santana doing a song with the Dead, and it seemed like he was trying to overpower them. They would sort of implode over him, so I was very careful to be humble. I didn't want to impose myself because when you try to establish an ego in a jam with the Grateful Dead, they'll dissolve the ground beneath you and grow over you like vines. So I got my rocks off and put my chops in, but I didn't get greedy and try to outdo them or anything. Afterward I said,

"That was pretty good," and David Graham responded, "Man, you should have gone for it." But there was no way I was going to go up there and try to push Garcia around. It just seemed to me to be the biggest mistake I could make, so I did my humble thing.

Every now and then you see the picture of Garcia and me playing. He's fat but I'm even fatter, so it looks like the lunar eclipse of the sun where you can see me behind him. A Russian doll of fat musicians.

Although that was the only time I played with Jerry Garcia, in the years since I've played with the other members of the Dead, and what I've come to appreciate is how they use music like it's magic. It's not a big thing to them—it's just how they hear it.

When it came time to figure out what would happen next for Blues Traveler, we weren't asking for much; we just wanted to be managed by someone who believed in us. Bill believed in us and Dave believed in us, but the people at Bill Graham Presents never took Dave seriously because he was fresh out of college and hadn't done anything yet.

Greg Perloff was as good to us as he could be, but he was running BGP, so it needed to be somebody from their ranks. That's how Dave Frey became our manager. At first he was working for Dave Graham officially, but it wasn't long before Dave Graham was having problems and couldn't really manage us. We tried to have an intervention of sorts, but the interventions we had weren't by-the-book interventions; it was basically me threatening him with an axe handle, screaming that he had to get his shit together or else I would beat his brains out.

Meanwhile, Dave Frey was able to keep things running by dotting the I's and crossing the T's. Eventually it became clear that he was the one who knew us best. We'd always had someone who cared, but they had to rely on someone else who was delineating the logistics. This was the first time we had a logistics guy who was managing us. From 1992 to 1993 Dave Frey was becoming the guy, although Dave Graham was still in there. By early 1994 Dave Frey had become our manager and would stick with us through 2000.

It was a tough year or two for Dave after Bill passed, but then he started to become the adult he is now. He's still one of my best friends. Bill wanted to make him into another business, guy but Dave's more of a poet. He just didn't have that lethal bastard gene.

10

A&M BLUES

Back when we were just getting looked at by A&M Records, we were scheduled to play a showcase at Wetlands. We had exactly forty-five minutes to play a carefully composed set of all our various strengths and utilities as a band. This was a real challenge for us, but we were told the reason we only had forty-five minutes was because these record people would come to see a whole bunch of bands, and each had the same amount of time.

But before we got on to play our carefully crafted set, meticulously timed down to forty-five minutes, someone came running up to us and said, "Buddy Miles is here! Buddy is here! And he wants to sit in with you guys!"

This is the guy who did Band of Gypsys. How was I going to say no to Buddy Miles? So he proceeded to kick Chan off of guitar and do a fifteen-minute guitar solo, then kicked Bobby off bass to do a fifteen-minute bass solo, then did a twenty-minute drum opera, and finally he grabbed my acoustic guitar, sang a song, and cried out, "Buddy's back!" We were supposed to have forty-five minutes for our entire set, and he took more than that in solos alone.

It was horrifying at first, but it just got so funny at that point. Our entire carefully crafted plan to get signed was ruined. But A&M signed us anyhow because they said they liked the way we handled it.

When it came time to record our first album, however, they made it clear that they wanted it to be a documentation of our song catalog. So for us, the big question was: Who would be the producer?

In January 1990 Bill Graham got us into the Rock and Roll Hall of Fame induction ceremony at the Waldorf Astoria in Manhattan. There I ran into George Drakoulias, who had produced the first Black Crowes record. I knew he would be perfect for Blues Traveler, so we cornered him: "We've got to get you for our record." He said, "Don't you understand? I'm over already." He was about twenty-four years old at the time, so I took that as a blow-off. Maybe he was talking about trends in the music industry, but I still thought it would have been a good album. If Drakoulias had done for us what he'd done for the Black Crowes, that would have been killer. Instead we got Justin Niebank. Poor Justin Niebank. Or maybe that should be poor Blues Traveler.

Justin Niebank had just worked with Jason and the Scorchers as the engineer on their album. That's mostly what he had done at that point for artists like Albert Collins and Johnny Winter.

A&M's approach to this album was, "You have thirty songs, so let's just take the ten best and put them out there." Justin Niebank's attitude was, "You might think you have ideas, but you've never done this before. I've done this before, so listen to me—I'm making sense." We weren't angry at him because this was the most attention we'd ever gotten, and he did make sense about a lot of it. But what came out of that was a milquetoast record.

Justin Niebank was so antipot that he didn't want us smoking before we'd play, which, by the way, is all we'd ever done. Then we went to do "Sweet Talking Hippie" and *had* to be stoned to play that song. It's a big stoned jam in one key. So we snuck a joint and, big idiot that I am, just before the take I taunted him: "Justin, we're all high."

He stopped the take and proceeded to yell at us for a good forty minutes—"You've let your parents down, you've let the label down, you've let yourselves down . . . " Then he gave us this born-again lecture about being stoned before saying, "Roll 'em."

So what you can hear is the most timid "Sweet Talking Hippie" we've ever done because it was four boys having just been lectured by some sort of schoolmarm. No, if you're a producer, you get the take first and *then* you yell at them. The more I look back at that, the more I'm confounded by his behavior.

Basically what we did with our first record was just do as we were told and shut the fuck up. And it shows. We felt lucky to be anywhere and assumed that the way A&M was treating us was normal. Then we saw our friends the Spin Doctors, who fought hard and whose attitude was, "This could be our one and only album." And that's really the way you should look at it. In retrospect I think we should have behaved more like that; we should have made desperate stands.

It was a really bumpy ride getting our album thing going. Our live-show instincts were great, but our recording instincts took a while. We knew how to sell a show, but we didn't know how to make a record. And, truthfully, the Spin Doctors didn't either, but they were convinced they did, and that made all the difference.

They fired their first producer in the middle of their first album. That, to me, takes serious balls. I came in and Eric Schenkman was sitting there with half a bottle of whiskey and asked me, "Is this what it all is, John? Is this what we work for?" They wanted me to sing the harmony on "Two Princes." They were asking for ideas, and this producer was looking at me like, "Help me." You could tell it was not a coast of a session; they were battling forces I wouldn't battle. They fired that producer and got another guy, and then they fought *that* guy.

Pocket Full of Kryptonite is an incredibly concise, brilliantly executed first album. And that's because they fought for it. Our first album is very confused and a little devoid of purpose. Up until *four*, we'd say we were all about the live gig, that you can't capture us on a record. And we had the comfort that people also said that about the Grateful Dead, so we figured it was a thing.

With our second album, *Travelers and Thieves*, we wanted to reach a bit further. Jim Gaines was our choice to produce it, and we were starting to get choices. He'd just finished records with Stevie Ray Vaughan and Santana. He also squeezed us between a half-dozen other projects and was literally falling asleep during our takes. It wasn't entirely his fault—apparently there was a jackhammer at work right outside of his hotel room. So he would come in and say, "I got no sleep last night," and we would laugh about it, but by week two he was showing up and falling asleep. We would record a take and then have to wake him up.

I suppose Jim did the best he could given the circumstances, but there was still this feeling of being neglected and left on our own. This feeling was then reinforced by a situation involving Gregg Allman.

We heard that Gregg wanted to do a song on our album, one Brendan had written called "Mountain Cry." The guys were a bit nervous about telling me, and I can see why, because that's my area but now Gregg was probably going to sing a verse. But instead I thought, *Cool, that's going to be a valuable thing.*

So we were all ready to do this. I was our big hurdle and I was all for it, so there we were, at the session, waiting for Gregg. An hour went by past when he was supposed to be there, and then two hours, and then we get a call from Dave Graham, who had picked him up at the airport and they were at a bar.

Gregg was very carefully babysat when he was on the road with the Allman Brothers and used the fact that he was going to New York to record with us as a way to get away from his handlers and have a drink. Dave said, "Hi, we're almost ready to go down there," and I could hear the concern in his voice. Then Gregg said, "Now give me the phone." He told me, "Hey John, we're almost ready." I could tell he was practiced at assuaging the fears of his handlers, and all I could think was "Oh my god, it's Gregg Allman, and he's talking to me!" So we figured, "Cool, this is what they do. Everybody's late." We didn't care.

He eventually showed up three sheets to the wind. And he was trying to play for me the song on the piano but—this is the sad part— his hands were shaking. I was sitting there, trying to kiss his butt, but I could see in his eyes that he knew he wasn't doing it.

Then after we finished the song, Gregg took me aside into this little vocal booth and said, "I want 10 percent of the record." I couldn't believe it. Gregg Allman, who seemed all powerful, had just laid this surprise on me. We had figured he was getting paid to do this like any other sit-in we've ever had, so I thought we had made some arrangement with him. I didn't know about this. All I could say was, Okay, let me talk to the guys, because we are a democracy and that seemed to be a diplomatic move.

Then he said, "Oh, I'm playing with Rick Danko at the Lone Star Roadhouse on 52nd Street. I want you to come sit in with us." That sounded cool.

So the next night I went to the Lone Star, and the opening band had me sit in with them. Then I went backstage and Rick Danko had taken some kind of drug that made him go, "ack ack ack" like the Aflac duck, and he wouldn't stop doing it.

Rick remained there, while Gregg, the opening band, and I started to play. We were a song or two in before Gregg said, "I'll go see what's keeping Rick," which is code for "I want to do what Rick's doing." So Rick Danko and Friends became me and the opening band for the entire night.

After the show I wandered backstage and Gregg and Rick were sitting up there, arm in arm howling at the moon, when Gregg said, "You know, I changed my mind. I want 20 percent of the album." I couldn't believe this—it was getting worse and worse. I didn't know what to say to him because I was twenty-four and this was Gregg Allman. So I said, "I'll talk to the guys," and he told me, "Don't talk to the guys. Make it happen." I explained, "It doesn't work that way," and he responded, "You know I wrote that song." And now we were at the point when I had to disagree with him.

But then I lucked into the phrase that changed everything. I said, "You're breaking my heart," and Gregg Allman's entire mood changed as if on a dime. He told me, "Oh man, don't worry about it—you don't gotta pay me anything." Then he threw his arms around me and gave me this huge hug. He'd vowed to work for free.

When Gregg was sober, he was the nicest guy you ever met, but when he was drunk, you got the Jekyll and Hyde show that you eventually learned wasn't personal. It was just where his brain was, and he didn't remember a thing the next day. I don't think he remembered asking me for a percentage of the album either time. We paid him the fee that was negotiated in the light of day by managers, and it was as if he had never spoken to me about it.

I think whatever Gregg says he means at the time. He just seems liberated from the responsibility of meaning something for all time, which is what most people expect of the truth. It's a great thing to be that liberated, but I'm not that liberated. Whenever I see Gregg these days I just give him a hug and hold on tight.

We were trying to grow with *Travelers and Thieves*, but we didn't know what we were doing. We wanted to try something in the studio that was impressive like Jimi Hendrix or Led Zeppelin would do, and that became the elephant noises in the beginning of "Ivory Tusk" and all the weird sounds we looped in on "The Tiding" before "Onslaught."

It wasn't like Jim Gaines was falling asleep *all* the time. We were proud of *Travelers and Thieves* because it was further than we'd come. It was a more ambitious record, and I truly believe that the songwriting was improving, but we were still figuring it all out. And A&M was stumbling around just like us, trying to learn how to make records with us. Their dedication was clear when they floated us a bunch of money to keep things going after I had a motorcycle accident because our business was about to fall apart. So these guys were trying to figure out what to do with us.

But then when nothing was wrong, there was almost no budget, and there would be no promotion. We'd sell fifty thousand records, and it felt like they'd say, "That's great. Let's see what happens when we give them even less money."

On the first record they said there would be several singles, but there was only one. This would become a theme, and it's a theme for anyone who's ever put out a record out. The label wants to put all your songs out, but if they don't think it's going to make them money, it's really hard for them to push it beyond a first single. You basically have a month to make it interesting to them.

They let us make a video for "But Anyway" on the first album (there was a second "But Anyway" video four years later when it was rereleased as a single after it appeared in *Kingpin*). MTV rejected it, but it got played at hockey games. It was us using a friend's car and my old high school buddy Tom Brown, who popped out as a newsman, and our girlfriends were in it. So at least we got to have fun. It was wacky and stupid and a very family thing.

With the second record, the label tried to push things a little further. But "All in the Groove" never got very far as a single. The *David*

Letterman band played it better than we did, but at least it got us on the show. It needed horns, and the organ was awesome on it.

This all took place around the time when Herb Alpert and Jerry Moss were leaving A&M. They sold it in 1989 but continued to manage it until 1993. I remember the one time we met Herb Alpert. He said, "There's a buzz about you . . . it's a small buzz, but it's a buzz." And he couldn't have been more right. That was us all along. We seemed like a huge deal—certainly in our own minds—but we were barely hanging on to being a huge deal.

We were always convinced of our absolute invincibility. We just felt that the label didn't sell us right. I would get so upset by those CBS "buy six albums for a penny" ads. I would look where our section was, and we were always next to Elton John. That pissed me off. I feel sorry for my managers because I would call and complain, "How come on the CBS records promotional deal we aren't near Pearl Jam? They're our age—why are we being skewed with Elton John, who's thirty years older than us?" It was more a symptom of what we were going through, in which A&M was treating us like a mainstream band and not getting anywhere with us because we were too alternative for mainstream and too mainstream for alternative.

11

"DIVIDED SKY"
FOR "CHRISTMAS"

Although Phish guitarist Trey Anastasio grew up in Princeton, I never met him until later. He was at the Princeton Day School while I was at Princeton High School and was a couple of years older than me. I believe the first time we crossed paths was when Phish came down to play the Ukranian National Home in New York on December 15, 1989. We'd heard of them and a lot of people were talking about them, so they sort of became the Gimbels to our Macy's.

All of the other venues in New York City seemed to have more personality than the Ukrainian National Home. I was struck by how much it looked like a Cuyahoga event hall. It seemed like a place where you'd have a Welcome to America dance for the new Ukrainians, a getting-to-know-you dance, and the Local 200 Ice Skate Repairman's Union meetings. It was just a big, loud, boomy space, and it was poorly lit. But the most fun part for me was checking out Phish.

We each played two sets, alternating back and forth, with Phish opening the night. I came out during their second set for two covers. My thought was, *Okay, I'm meeting a new band*, so I wanted to show them my stuff. I remember I was very determined to impress them, and that's how it's been ever since. Whenever I play with Phish, I'm always determined to make a good showing. I played on ZZ Top's "Jesus Just Left Chicago," which was blues, and I knew just what to do on that one. I was also on Son Seals' "Funky Bitch," where they got to show something that was more in their wheelhouse. It had that cool Phish thing, in which it seemed like normal funk, but there was a little rhythmic trick to it, and I was really into that.

From the start there was always something else going on beyond the music as well, another level of communication and connection with the audience. That night they decided to prank their former lighting guy, Tim, who would occasionally play harmonica with them, by pretending that I was their new lighting guy, Chris. The band was going to give Tim the tape and say that I was Chris. So before I came on, Trey told the crowd to call out "All right, Chris!" Then after I was done I said, "I'd better get back to those lights."

From there we would do gigs with them whenever we could, and I found them fascinating. We went up to hang with them in Winooksi, and I remember eating with them at the House of Pancakes, the same place where Bobby and I had our altercation after Bill Graham died. I was enjoying this wonderful, intellectual discussion with Phish, while at the next table my band was being all loud and causing trouble, getting their Jersey on. I remember being somewhat embarrassed by them: *Oh the ruffians I hang out with.*

One of my favorite Phish appearances was in February of 1993 when I was in a wheelchair. They had me on stage, and I insisted on being covered with a tarp the entire show so people wouldn't know what I was. Then they unveiled me toward the end and I sat in with them. But just to make the gag work, I sat there the entire show covered in a tarp.

After the show there were some kids who were desperate for a ride back to Long Island. Because I was in a wheelchair, I had a van and a driver. These kids were stranded, so we drove them all the way back; they woke their friend up and we had cocoa.

Trey was the one I clicked with the most and who amazed me the most, although they're all brilliant musicians. Another time we were at a party in Winooski, I think it was at his house, I mentioned fugues. He stopped what he was doing, took me to his room, and pulled open this filing cabinet full of fugues. Some of them were his, some were

Bach's, and some were Haydn's. He showed me all of these fugues and explained the rules of a fugue, how it transports a melody through different variations. The light in his eyes as he was describing this blew me away. I could keep up with what he was saying theoretically, but the execution of it was a really difficult thing for nonclassical musicians.

That's why at times watching Phish is like watching a classical band. They are very intricate in their compositions; it can be difficult to tell what's improvised and what's choreographed. And, as it turns out, they can do both with equal aplomb—they can switch into improvisation or go back to something that's very arranged. They weren't just trying to make stuff move in a jam; they were trying to focus on a single aspect of a jam, and it was really brilliant. Something that Col. Bruce Hampton has always said about Phish is that "the rest of us just play."

Mike Gordon is really cool, always surreal. I remember they had this little tiny box that looked like a beeper, and he said, "Think of a number between one and a hundred." I thought of fifty-seven, they pushed a button, and it said fifty-seven. He would not tell me how they did it and, to this day, still will not tell me. Page McConnell is one of the sweetest, nicest guys. He is always amiable and always trying to make stuff work.

And Jon Fishman is just a madman. I think he didn't always need to put in as much effort to be that madman, but I think he felt that he needed to do so.

The very first time we saw them play at the Ukrainian National Home, Phish opened their second set with Fishman on vacuum. Given my instrument of choice, I've always been intrigued by that. What I found out relatively recently is that I can play the vacuum cleaner in a very different way from Jon Fishman. I find that with the shape of my mouth, I can play notes and really play scales. But he's already popularized the vacuum so much that it would be hackneyed to try to fill his shoes. But someday I hope to get into a vacuum cleaner duet with him. That would be awesome. I'd like to use this book as an opportunity to extend a standing offer.

In 1995 Trey became the first among us to have a child. I was so excited that I sent him every diaper he'd ever need. Literally, a semi pulled up on his driveway and out came every diaper from infancy to toddlerhood. I figured that was something nobody would give him. We calculated how many diapers a kid would need in a year, factoring in that she would have to grow into bigger diapers. It was crates and crates of diapers. He sent me a picture of his little one on top of these boxes with a caption, "Let the shitting begin."

Phish played chess with their audience, they had beach balls going up and down, and each band member played like how his beach ball was being treated—that is beyond music. The reason I rigged a dummy of me to fall through a giant yard trampoline during the 1993 H.O.R.D.E. in Richmond was because Phish did that all the time, and just once I wanted to come up with something like that. It took all of my organizational skills, and I had to own the tour to do that.

Trey wasn't much older than me, and for somebody to be so knowledgeable was one thing, but to see how they could command a stage with one note flying high above an interwoven musical cacophony, that felt to me like he was our Mozart. They were such composers *and* improvisers, and their system guaranteed that their music always was different. They had a much more efficient and effective system of improvising—there was a point when someone had to change something; it was mandatory and it would have to be a little variation. It would give me a headache to play like them—there was a lot to think about, but they did it so effortlessly.

We competed with them for rooms for a few years, but at some point you had to sit back and appreciate what they were doing. They took on musical and theatrical challenges that no other band would want to take on, and that's the thing about Phish. So I went from begrudgingly competing with them to sitting at their feet, and I would always try to take something back to my band. Phish helped me keep my imagination going. They were the pioneers for our generation.

For a while Phish was the only music in my car CD changer, and I would constantly listen to all of their albums in succession. Compared to what we were doing chordally, there was nothing like it. Their song "Divided Sky" was my favorite—the way Trey took this simple melody on his guitar and played it without time for a second, with time for a second, and really milk it—I was obsessed with that song. Then I realized it had the same chords as "Bingo Was His Name-O" and "Hark!

The Herald Angels Sing," which led me to think there was a Christmas melody in there. I wanted to work on something with the same chords that, at the end, would reference "Divided Sky." I tried to get my band to do it, but they weren't Phish fans like I was, so they kept asking, "Why are we doing this?"

But then we were approached to contribute a song to the *Very Special Christmas 3* compilation album benefitting the Special Olympics. I wrote a melody to the "Divided Sky" chords, but it was nothing as elaborate. Then at the end I put the "Divided Sky" reference. Because it was a charity, I called Trey and told him, "I want to use this melody. I want to write this song and give you credit for writing it with me." He said sure and made a few jokes like, "I'll see you in court, buddy," but it was for charity so he didn't mind, and that gave me the license to "Divided Sky" the shit out of it.

There was a part when I put my melody with his, and there were eight harmonies singing each verse. It's one of my favorite songs because you have all these harmonies working at the same time, and it was one of those times when I really hit it out of the park with the lyrics.

It was what I've felt about Christmas, it was what I wanted to say, it was full of all sorts of musical stuff I wanted to do, and it was on a nice vehicle, a Christmas record. And I called it "Christmas" so we could copyright Christmas. I have not as yet received any checks, I have not sued anybody, but if I could somehow sue Santa Claus, it would make one hell of a movie.

"Christmas"

Words by John Popper,
Music by Trey Anastasio and John Popper

Comes the time for Christmas
And I really have to ask
If this is feeling merry
How much longer must it last?
I wish a one-horse open sleigh
Would come carry me away.
But I've been waiting here all day,

And one just hasn't come my way.
Now excuse me if I'm not being reverent,
But I was hoping for a miracle to hold me, wash me,
Save me from my righteous doubt as I watch helpless
And everybody sings.
If it's Chanukah or Kwanza,
Solstice, harvest, or December twenty-fifth,
Peace on earth to everyone
And abundance to everyone you're with.

Comes the time for Christmas,
And as you raise your yuletide flask,
There's like this feeling that you carry
As if from every Christmas past.
It's as if each year it grows.
It's like you feel it in your toes.
And on and on your carol goes,
Harvesting love among your woes.
I want to buy into the benevolent,
And I was hoping for a miracle to hold me, wash me,
Make me know what it's about,
As the longing in me makes me want to sing
Noel or Navidad,
Season celebration, or just the end of the year.
Christmas can mean anything,
And I mean to keep its hope forever near.

As if a cold and frozen soul is warm to love
By love's own hand,
So goes the prayer if for a day, peace on earth
And good will to man.
At twenty, below the winter storm, it billows,
But the fire is so warm inside
And the children, while nestled in their pillows,
Dream of St. Nicholas's ride
And how the next day they'll get up and they will play

In the still-falling Christmas snow,
And together we'll celebrate forever,
In defiance of the winds that blow.
My God in heaven, now I feel like I'm seven,
And the spirit calls to me as well,
As if Christmas had made the winter warmer,
Made a paradise from what was hell,
As if a cold and frozen soul is warm to love
By love's own hand.
So goes the prayer, if for a day, peace on earth
And good will to man.

I wish a one-horse open sleigh would come carry me away,
And I'll keep waiting through next May
Until Christmas comes my way.

12

FELLOW TRAVELERS

When we first signed with Bill Graham in 1989, the first band he put us out there with was the Allman Brothers. We were terrified. We would do our forty-minute set, and then the Allman Brothers would take us to school—that's how we would put it. We would play for forty minutes, and then class was in session.

Dickey Betts was very intimidating. You'd hear all kinds of stories about him, and it's possible that none of them were true: that Johnny Neel, who's blind, was scatting during "Liz Reed" and Dickey punched him out; that Dickey was the kind of guy who would get drunk and use karate, even though most people who were black belts in karate wouldn't use it; that he had some sort of incident involving a crew member and a gun. I gave him a knife that I got in Wyoming—it was an old saw blade polished up real nice—and was told I shouldn't have done that.

He might have a temper, but I never saw it. He's always been very nice to us. By the end of the tour they had me play on "Statesboro Blues" and "One Way Out." And it was probably during the first night when I sat in with them in August 1990 at Jones Beach, that Dickey came right over to me—he had that hat on and he always looks angry when he's playing. I almost shit my pants when he said in this nice, cheerful voice, "We're gonna trade fours, all right?" A bit later he came at me, and I thought he was going to hit me, but it was just to give me a high five. That was when I realized that although they were all very intimidating, they were just dudes.

That being said, they've really lived it and walked that walk. (Plus, there was a time a couple of years later when Dickey had to leave a tour after he shoved a cop.)

Whenever Gregg would get drunk, he'd want to join our band—"Man you guys gotta let me in your band." He once got into a big argument with Chan over whether he could join the band, and Chan was drunk enough to tell him, "No, dude, you totally can't."

So here were these two mental giants just completely sauced, arguing over the silliest thing I could think of. Why would Gregg Allman even want to join Blues Traveler? It never made sense even at the time. I suppose that was his way of liking us. It was very sweet, and I wanted to say, "Gregg, don't be silly." But when he's in that place, what are you going to do? The appropriate answer would have been, "Sure, you can join the band," but what Chan chose to do is say, "No, you can't join the band."

He had no business joining us. We were a very tiny, barely functioning band.

There was also a time many years later when Dickey had Gregg convinced that the band was thinking about kicking out Gregg and replacing him with me. Now that's even more absurd, but apparently Gregg bought into that for a little while. I had to miss my chance at sitting in with them during their Beacon run that year.

The one member of the Allman Brothers I had met before that first tour was Warren Haynes. In the early days I'd always go sit in with people in the New York area, and around 1989 this guitarist showed up and was doing the same thing. Warren was so on fire and so awesome and so understated, but when he started playing, he was amazing and he's kind of been that way ever since. And he really breathed a life into the Allman Brothers.

Another thing I'll say about Gregg Allman is you should never play poker with him when he's drunk. At the end of our first tour, they had a poker night as their end-of-the-tour party—they figured they'd clean up. Well, I was up around two to three hundred bucks, and I was walking out of the room when in came Gregg Allman, ass-out fucking drunk. It was a miracle he was upright, and he was like, "Come on, sit down." I was ready to leave, but he was so drunk that I figured it would be easy—how could I pass it up?

Well, basically, Wild Bill Hickok was asking me to sit down and play cards with him. So I sat down, and he came up with "Jacks are better to open," which is really hard to do when you're playing Texas Hold 'Em and he's pulling jacks and slamming drinks and the drunker he gets, the better hands he gets. I can't figure how he pulled it off. He's either really good or really lucky, and I lost about $250. It was quite a lesson.

They told us that we reminded them of them when they were young. I think we were more like the Allman Brothers than we ever would be like Phish, and we were a volatile bunch of drunken slobs figuring it out as we went along, and we all grew up together. We were like a family going out on the road, being in a band. I think that's a common pattern, and a lot of your great bands are like that.

You drive around in a van. Your best friend is the bottle of Dimetapp you've got for that "cold," and you drive fifteen hundred miles, riding on the floor of a van, eating whatever community Arby's you could scrape together.

The Allman Brothers Band and crew would give us little lessons, and we always tried to pay attention. They'd say, "Don't forget this is the funnest time. You're gonna look back and think that this time was as fun as it gets." It's sort of true because you didn't have any responsibility yet. The IRS wasn't interested in us, we didn't have the commission thing figured out yet. "You wanna go to Vegas?" "Sure!"—you'd put whatever cash you could in your pocket. There's something about a diner the first time you hit it in Muncie, Indiana—you remember those Buffalo wings.

We were living a tribal life on top of each other, and one of the side effects is that we would come to blows. Quite often there were scuffles, and it usually was just half-drunken bullshit. This was compounded by the fact that I really wasn't drinking during this period; my overindulgence was food, so I became something of a slave driver pushing everyone forward.

Bobby and I in particular would have issues, but it was kind of a marriage, and there are few people I'll ever love more than Bob Sheehan. That says something.

I remember one time he made us wait forty-five minutes so he could get a giant nitrous balloon. We were waiting around and waiting around, and we were all late. Then he showed up with the balloon, and I had a samurai sword, so I popped it. He started wailing on me, and I was trying to put this sword down while he was swinging on my back. Then he ran and grabbed my Daisy Red Ryder BB gun and was going to shoot me in the face with it. The gun misfired, then I grabbed his head and began smacking it into the windowsill of the bus. The third component of all this was the stress on Chan because he was clearly the physically strongest of all of us. So he was the great peacekeeper—he would break us up and make Bobby apologize to me. It was a terrible pattern.

I remember another time, when we were driving back from a writing session in Rhode Island, and Bobby couldn't stand the fact that I was playing with this squirt gun I had found in a pile of trash somewhere. So I was twirling it around, being really obnoxious with the squirt gun, and he was very hammered. I wouldn't put it down, so he just cocked me in the face and broke my nose. Dave Precheur was driving, blood was gushing down my face, and I was flailing on Bobby from the back seat like a lunatic.

So Dave stopped the car as best he could, and I got out and ran into the woods. I remember I was still wearing my harmonica belt—because I would wear my harmonica belt everywhere like a crazy person—and threw the harmonicas at him and yelled, "They're yours." Then I marched off into the woods. He came after me and said, "John, you can hit me back," but as I started swinging, he added, "Not in the face!" But it was too late. I split his lip, he had a nice bloody lip, and then I went off to sit in this abandoned school bus until he coaxed me back. At the height of this I'm still quite upset, and I said to him, "So what do we do now?" And he answered, "We're going to go back and get in that car and become rock stars."

It was this weird thing that would happen all the time: Bobby would be a dick, somehow it would devolve into me punching him, and then he would say he was sorry. It was quite the codependent relationship.

He could cut the ace off a cold deck, and I was the only guy who would do that back to him. That was the challenge of him and me.

One time we were sitting in a patch of clover at the Princeton Communiversity (a yearly event at Princeton University), and without looking, Bobby reached down and—*boink!*—pulled a four-leaf clover: "Oh my god, a four leaf clover!" And without looking, to answer him, I reached down and—*boink!*—I pulled a five-leaf clover. I'm not kidding—it was a four-leaf clover with a fifth leaf on the stem. I will remember the look on his face for the rest of my life. He just pulled a four-leaf clover and then got trumped by me. After that, the four of us were digging through that patch of clover and could not find a four-leaf clover of any kind.

That was our relationship: he just pulled off a miracle, and then I said, "Oh yeah? Well, here's a bigger miracle." That was Bobby and me—we pushed each other to heights neither of us would have made without the other. Of all the pressures I could name, like record companies, money, just actual survival, Bob Sheehan was the best and biggest pressures because he wanted action and could not tolerate nothing happening. He was great at that. All action, that guy.

Being in a touring band really is like being in a military empire because you're trying to expand and conquer. You're on a smelly bus with a bunch of dudes and need that espirit de corps. Rich Vink, our sound guy, was in the Coast Guard and was always talking about espirit de corps, so we sort of borrowed from that.

What I can say about the early crew is how much everybody cared about it. There was such a ferocious dedication, and you can't buy that. You can buy professionalism, but you can't buy ferocious dedication. Occasionally we would have bouts of professionalism, but they rarely lasted.

It can be challenging when you have friends in the crew rather than professionals. They're often less inclined to listen to you, but their loyalty was unquestionable.

During this era we had two vans, the crew van and the band van. The band van had Dave Precheur driving, someone would ride shotgun, and then each band member would have a bench they would lie on. The crew outnumbered us, so they had two guys to a seat and all of their gear loaded in between them. I remember the crew van passing us one time, and in the back corner I saw Tim Vega with this horrified look on his face, stuck in corner, saying, "Help me."

Tim was an incredible artist specializing in the tag art that the graffiti guys do. His sister was Suzanne Vega, and their whole family was really passionate, artistic, expressive, and sensitive. I was kind of the sensitive guy back then, but Tim could easily out-sensitive me, depending on what we were talking about.

He did the art for us, the backdrops, but he also went on the road, selling merch. He made the shirts himself and partnered with Darren Greene, who designed the cat head. The two of them rose to any occasion we could throw at them, and eventually another artist, Sandy Garnett, would come in and help out as well. (I remember Sandy would often drive in from Greenwich, Connecticut, to our shows and then head home at five in the morning or later.)

Darren had lived with us in our first band apartment along with Chris Barron. Darren, Chris, and Bobby all had a running tally of the various women they would pick up at the gigs that we'd play. Of course, Chan was far out in front, but for an artist, Darren did pretty damn well.

Tim designed the art on our first album, the spray paint look, and he put it up on the Nightingale's wall, which was red brick. Somebody said he could paint it on there, and apparently we got all excited when we were done and left it there. We thought they might want it there. But apparently the neighborhood block association got really mad, and the police came in and made my friend Bill, who was the bartender, paint the building red again.

Tim Vega did the banner for H.O.R.D.E. He painted the inside of Wetlands—he was just brilliant. I have two of his paintings in my house. You'd forget that when you're touring with the guy because it was all about setting up the sales booth like it was a lemonade stand.

Tim was a real sensitive soul, and I think that led him to drink too much. At some point, after he came off the road with us, he was working at Wetlands as a bouncer and was going through a bad patch, and I think his heart gave out. At the funeral I heard he was heartbroken about Wetlands closing and 9/11. I felt really lucky I got to know him, even though it was fraught with the best kind of agony and

tension—there was very little time he was at peace; he was never satisfied in that way that an artist is never satisfied. He loved his friends
more than anything and was just the guy you would want to go into
business with as well as the guy you would dread to go into business
with if you were at all logical.

As we began touring, I had a map of the United States and would
shade in pencil where we played and fill in ink where we could draw
more than a thousand. That map grew until 1995, when we had all
fifty states shaded in ink, along with Canada and Mexico. That progression was based on the *Penguin Historical Atlas* because I was a
big Attila the Hun fan, being Hungarian. Gradually you could see us
growing. I'd update our conquests in a tour diary that I kept from
1991 to 1999.

Here are a couple of entries to show the flavor (both, oddly, involving Arkansas):

October 18, 1991

We have struck into Canada mercilessly, and in a covert move, we've
pushed deep into her borders. The carnage was complete and exqui-
site. The battle was fought well, the press was with us, and B.C. lay in
ruins at our feet. Success!

As good as our northern conquest is going, news today paints a
dimmer view of the southern expansion of our empire. As we raid
Texas, we are not striking Oklahoma. And Arkansas is lost as well.
The reason for this is simple: our mighty army is expensive and
needs to be fed. These new southern markets are lean on cash and
can't meet our price. We'll just have to wait. It will be all we can do
to expand into Kentucky and Mississippi. They are not definite
either.

Other than them and a tiny annoyance known as Delaware, our
US expansion shall halt and we'll fortify our armies in our established
territories. Reinforcing Texas will make it easier when we do come
for Oklahoma (even so, it's a big state anyway).

But that is November. Tonight is celebration. Tomorrow is rest, as
my wounds are fresh.

October 13, 1994

I am in Detroit. At long last, Kentucky has fallen! This achieved, everything east of the Mississippi River is Traveler homeland! This is a major breakthrough. The southern serpent, once proud, lays reduced to our small territory of Arkansas (a pick-up date in the spring). The fighting was hard but conclusive. The sold-out crowd fell in the end, middle, and beginning. The hardest part was Steve [an audio tech] freezing under fire again. And there was much fire. All three amps at various times were malfunctioning, and he stood there shrugging. He left us on our own to battle on. With such a flank exposed, we spent the entire evening in jeopardy of disaster.

One aspect of this that I realized right away, which wasn't a joke, was the concept of territory. How far have we played? Are we a regional band or a national band? How far down the coast have we been? How far west? So I really looked at the *Historical Atlas* with some sort of occupational seriousness, but most people thought I was just nuts.

I remember Dave Frey laughing. I had my little map I showed him and said, "All right, we've got to get to the Dakotas." He was trying to take me seriously, but at one point he just burst out laughing. I asked, "What's so funny about this?" He told me, "I'm sorry, John. I am used to trying to book gigs where the people are."

Then I gave him the whole "If you build it, they will come" speech. And I was right—they did show up. When you go to places where bands don't usually come, then people show up, no matter who you are because they just want something to come through town to play. Every gig we've done somewhere like the Dakotas is always full. There aren't too many places to play out there, but we consistently do good business. Still, I can't say his conventional thinking is wrong because most people do want to play near a population center.

Our last holdouts in the continental United States were the Dakotas. We got Alaska before we hit them, and then Hawaii was right after that. This was all in 1995. Hawaii was such a party because at that point, everyone in the crew was excited to get all fifty states. I don't think many bands try to tour all over, so there were a lot of firsts for the guys on the crew.

It all seemed not only normal but also logical to me: if there's a spot where we've never played, why wouldn't we want to play there?

Perhaps it was fitting, but in Rapid Cities, South Dakota, there was a stage rush. In one spontaneous moment the entire front half of the house decided to come on stage. I was hanging onto the microphone and getting bashed in the face with it. Chan and Bobby had guitars and were holding them like hockey sticks to hip check the masses. That was both flattering and scary because we were being physically mobbed by a sea of people. That would be the last time we went out without security for fifteen years.

My other story involving audience participation took place in Le Locle, Switzerland. We went to the Montreux Jazz Festival in 1991, and their idea of rock and roll was Toto, who we opened for. They were used to Chuck Berry, and we were much louder—we hadn't quite reined in our sound—so they looked at us like, "What the fuck is this?"

On the way home we booked this little festival in Le Locle on the border of Italy, France, and Switzerland. It was a real local village, where they boarded up everything because it had rained. During that day they fed us—that was part of the gig—and while we were eating we noticed this bagpipe fife and drum corps from Brittany. There were a dozen of them, and they were there for a friend's wedding. They all had sailor suits on and spoke Gaelic French, which none of us—or in fact anybody—understood. I managed to figure out that bagpipes drone in the key of B-flat. So I figured I'd get one of them to come up with us and play in B-flat during our set—how hard could it be? And bagpipes are cool. Through broken sign language and semaphore we came to an understanding that one of them would join us during our performance.

Later that evening we were getting ready to go on, and the band before us was doing classic rock covers in French. The place was rocking, and as soon as they were done, a deluge of rain drove everyone into their houses. When we came out for our set, we were playing to a mostly empty town square. I don't know what happened to Europe in

1972, but the Grateful Dead did not resonate. We were being very psychedelic, real reefer rock that they just didn't get in the Alps.

So I figured it couldn't get any worse, so, what the hell, let's bring out the bagpipe guy in the sailor suit. Except there was a miscommunication, and all twelve of them were there, nervous because they've never been on a stage before. At that point Bobby, Chan, and Brendan were looking at me like, "What did you do to us?" So I called out "Hit it!" They began playing, and I figured we needed some words, so I started singing, "Just sit right back and you'll hear a tale, a tale of a fateful trip . . . " and people started coming out of their houses. The whole place turned into Woodstock. They were doing a soccer chant and there was a conga line around the square. It was absolute pandemonium.

We rocked the town with the theme to *Gilligan's Island.*

What occurred to me was they needed a reference to some recognizable style. After the bagpipes, then every song we did was a hit. I learned an important lesson that day: if you're in a place where you're feeling estranged from your audience, try to bring in some locals to make a connection. If you're in Botswana, bring in a Botswanan band. Even if you bring in a local musician just playing saxophone, his experience somehow translates to the audience. It's a cool trick and one that was born in survival.

Later on I was trying to sleep because we had to catch a plane in the morning, and I could hear all these drunken bagpipers, sounding like they were demonstrating the Doppler effect.

We tried to recreate this at the Jones Beach H.O.R.D.E. the next summer with the help of the New York Ancients Fife & Drum Society. It turned out their name couldn't be more accurate because they sent us a couple of eighty-year-old guys. They were supposed to lead this procession all around Jones Beach, but we had to cut it short because it looked like they were going to pass out.

Then I bought my own bagpipes because we had a band budget for instruments. It seemed pretty easy; after all, it's a diatonic instrument, right in my wheelhouse. First off, assembling the thing was a lot harder than I thought it would be. Second, it is not a rock-and-roll, stage-friendly instrument; it is very fragile, and you have to be careful with how you position the reeds and the drones. It also takes steady pressure when you're working the bag—you have to be constantly filling it with air while you squeeze its bladder.

It all really sounds testicular when you talk about bagpipe technology. While you're working the shaft, you squeeze the bladder with your elbow as you hang onto the bag. And of course, within months, pieces of the bagpipes had gone missing—where did that reed go?—and it's all handmade.

The bagpipes made it to a few rehearsals, but nobody ever said, "Hey John, don't forget the bagpipes." They'd put a pin in it until we got too busy. I love that they bought it for me, though—"We'll buy you the bagpipes as long you don't play them."

13

SAVE MY SOUL

I could never drive a clutch on a car or a motorcycle, so when I learned of Honda's automatic transmission motorcycle, the Hondamatic, I thought, *This was made for me.*

Brendan was always into motorcycles and still is, but he has the right temperament for it, because I stop paying attention at a certain point.

For me it was an eye-opening thing. I remember getting my bike in Nevada before I even had a license. We finished our spring tour 1992 in Vegas with two nights at Bally's, and the next day Brendan and I drove our bikes to the Hoover Dam. We went somewhere we weren't supposed to go and a cop stopped us. Then someone came by and mentioned that he had tickets to our Vegas shows, so the cop asked us who we were and joked that he could *write* tickets. Not only did I not have a license, but the motorcycle was untitled and unregistered. It ended pretty well, though—we took a photo in which he pretended to cuff me on the back of his car. He didn't give me a ticket, though; I just had to put the bike on the back of a semi and send it home.

So I had it hauled out to Princeton, New Jersey. I was living in New York, but I was home in Princeton a lot. I remember riding to and from New York through the Holland Tunnel on that motorcycle. I would occasionally ding a taxicab with my shin, but nothing too bad.

It was definitely too small a bike for me because it would take an extra ten feet for me to stop. What I eventually learned when I got my motorcycle license is that that's why they have those stop tests.

We went off to Louisiana to make our third record, *Save His Soul*, and by that time, I'd had the motorcycle for about six months. It was October 20, 1992, and I was late for work getting from the house to the studio. It was a long drive through these snaky hills and winding roads in gorgeous, rural Louisiana, and I was booking.

I always had been afraid of going fast. I remember a time as a kid when I was on an alpine slide, gripping the break all the way down. People were unhappy with me, and my dad was behind me, shouting, "Don't you listen to those people yelling at you! You go as slow as you want to, Johnny." And that just made it worse. I went back to an alpine slide in my thirties to make up for it and I still went slow. I just couldn't do it.

But on the motorcycle, you get used to going fast. So it wasn't long before I was cruising at seventy or eighty miles per hour, no problem, like I knew what I was doing. So I was late for work on these winding roads where logging trucks were zooming by just as fast as I was going.

I came upon this stretch of road, and there was a blue Chevy Nova just sitting there. I couldn't pass on the right where I would normally pass because there was a ditch and no downshifting on this bike. (Remember, it's automatic only.) That was the problem. I started to realize then that the reason gears are good on bikes is that the gear ratio can slow you down a lot faster than brakes can. So I tried passing the car on the left, but then the car turned left. So I slammed on the brakes and almost sped up into the car. In a moment of herculean stupidity I tried getting between my trusty steed and the Chevy Nova, almost to protect it. They say that probably saved my life because I would have gone head first over the car, but instead I impacted flush with my knee into its back door and bounced backward. I rolled for a while with my broken leg wrapped around my good leg and then landed face down.

A few years earlier I had crashed on a moped and cracked a rib. I remember waking up and getting put in an ambulance, and I was fine.

They call that traumatic amnesia, but in this case my brain said, *John, you're going to feel this.* I tried moving my leg and had the creepy feeling of moving a broken bone and the shudder of nerve endings. If I listen carefully, I can still hear the screaming.

People came running from their houses. I didn't know anybody was there; I thought it was an abandoned road. But they said, "We're not going to move you because you're an accident victim." So I flipped myself over, and that's when I heard the Nestlé Crunch sound when you turn bones into peanut brittle. I started screaming and screaming, and then an ambulance came.

I remember a traffic cop was there, leaned over, and he had the typical traffic cop look—with the sunglasses and Smokey the Bear hat—and he said, "You know this is a no-passing zone, right son?" and he put a ticket on me.

Then they loaded me onto the ambulance and there was a lady there—she was the only angel I saw that day, and that might have been her name, even. She said, "John, we can't give you painkillers for six hours because we don't know if there's internal bleeding." That at least let me pace my screaming.

We made it to this hospital in Bogalusa, Louisiana, and I noticed my bandmates were looking all pale because one foot was at one angle and one foot was coming in sideways. Then the hospital staff tried to put the catheter in, and when they drove that guitar string home, I didn't feel my leg at all.

The thing about a catheter is that they always want to remove it so you can pee. It was this torture test of them yanking out the little guitar string for two minutes for me to pee and then putting back in. It was horrible.

I used to tell my manager, "I got into a car accident—I can't make the gig," just to freak him out. Then I'd say, "No, just kidding." So when I called him from the hospital that day, he didn't believe me at first.

We had a Halloween gig scheduled for a week and a half later, and I thought I'd be ready for it—just a quick trip to the hospital to get some surgery and I'd be right as rain. As wracked with pain as I was, I told myself that I'd never missed a gig. Someone had to explain to me the extent of my injuries, and even then I said, "Yeah, sure." But then reality started to sink in. It was like being in jail because my body wanted to go do something, but I was detained by my own frailty. It was a rough thing.

They had me airlifted to New Orleans, and my feet were sticking out of the helicopter because I was too tall. This is when I built up my tolerance for withstanding surgery, which would help me later with my heart and weight-loss surgeries.

I remember waking up in the hospital bed, and the shin that had crashed into the car was nothing but exposed nerve and welts. Imagine a shin being smashed into a car at eighty miles per hour—that's what it was. The open air hurt. Bits of hair would tickle that spot and there would be shooting pain. When I came to, someone had left the TV on, and there was Jean-Claude Van Damme in some movie where he was chopping down a palm tree with his shin. That was the image I woke up to, and they elaborated the noise. The whole thing freaked me out, made me shudder, and I couldn't reach the remote to change it. There was this whapping noise over and over again, and he was yelling while he repeatedly struck the palm tree with his shin before he took it down.

My initial surgery took place at Tulane Medical Center, where my mom flew down to see me. At some point afterward they needed me to drop a deuce in a bedpan. I'd never gone in a bedpan, so they brought me the bedpan and balanced me, with a broken hip, on it. They put an enema in me, and the nurses were all my mom's age—so there were four sixty-year-old women gathering around while I tried to poop. For some reason they were astonished I couldn't seem to go. They were scratching their heads and trying to figure out what happened. I sensed their frustration and was feeling my own, so they put another enema in me but none of them understood that the fundamental issue was that I couldn't go to the bathroom with my mom and these three other women staring at me.

They meant well, but they were giving me too much attention. Increasingly they got upset with each other and started arguing with one another because they really wanted me to go. Finally I yelled, "Could everyone leave the room?!" Then as soon as they left I not only filled that bedpan, but I overfilled it, destroying the bed and everything in it.

They had to take me out and clean me up. There had been this assumption that because my body wouldn't defecate on its own, my brain had gone with it. And that's what people sometimes forget: no matter what has happened to the patient, there's someone in there.

When you're stuck in the hospital like that, it's like being in prison. Someone has to wipe your butt, and you have to eat the food they want you to eat. Bedpans and catheters are awkward and unpleasant, but the only way out is to fight.

You have to fight to heal and you have to fight for your rehab, but it's also very important that it's for you, not for them. So you have to take any chance you can to be subversive, to break a rule, to sneak a cigarette, to smuggle in some real food—have your friends mail you barbeque ribs as Col. Bruce Hampton did (FedEx did not really make a good barbeque-containing cardboard box, but it came close). You have to fight every time they tell you that you have to do something, and you have to claw your way out because this is the entire process and physiology of what healing is.

Healing is not a natural, calm, soothing experience; healing is a violent, savage, groaning experience that takes tiny little incremental steps and makes you endlessly impatient and frustrated. Each day you feel exhausted, as though *I've only gone the same three feet.* But what you don't notice is that yesterday it took three people to help you go those three feet, and today you're doing it by yourself. But that's imperceptible to you at the time.

There's a feeling I still remember clearly. I felt that I was at the end of my rope and that if one more thing would happen, I would be completely lost and give up and there would be nothing left of me. But I learned that there was far more rope than I realized and that my capacity for suffering was so much more than I imagined. Your brain will never let you know the true end of your limit. The key to healing is to fight and fight and fight. So that's what I did.

From the hospital I moved to a rehab center, and at one point I had a roommate who was this tough dock loader. He fell off a barge on the Mississippi River, broke his back, and finished out his work day. He went to bed that night, tried to get up for work the next day, and couldn't move because it turned out he had broken his back. He finished out his workday with a broken back, and that's the kind of man he was. He was not very articulate, but he was a very sweet man. It became clear to me that no one had listened to him his entire life.

One time I woke up in the middle of the night, and all I wanted was for someone to empty my urine bottle. It was full and I was trying to pinch a little where I could. So I woke up to two things: an incredible stench of human feces and the man next to me, who was never upset about anything, was crying. He had shit himself and what happened was that the nurse would come in and take a whiff and leave it there because there are two kinds of nurses: the professional nurse who cares and the nurse who took the gig because the post office wasn't hiring that week. We had gotten that second kind of nurse.

Part of my instinct is to fight whenever something like that would happen. I would go off because, unlike my roommate, I was very articulate and had learned from Bill Graham how to scream at the top of my lungs and formulate a coherent argument. So I screamed out, "At least open up a fucking window, you heartless fascist!" I made such a stink, if you'll excuse the pun, that they called in the head of nursing. Eventually they cleaned up the poor man, but they came in to talk to me about my attitude.

The head of nursing told me how her grandfather was in a wheelchair, so she understood. I told her how her grandfather would be ashamed, and if he wasn't with us anymore, he would be rolling in his grave with regret and would look down on her with disdain and disgust. And as I'm yelling, I realized that the guy's wife had come in to visit him and that both of them were looking at me with such astonishment because no one had ever spoken up for them before. I wasn't really fighting for them—I just wanted a guaranteed urine bottle that I could pee in—but it really set me off, the indignity that he and I had to suffer because someone had taken the job who couldn't deal with the fact that somebody had pooped themselves. By the time I was done, the head of nursing was in tears and that never happened to us again.

The thing is, you want to be appreciative of somebody wiping your ass because that's no kind of fun for nobody, but when you have to coerce somebody to do it, then you don't know where your next shit is going to land and how long it's going to be with you. It's not a matter of *Please help me*; it's a matter of *If you don't help me, I'm going to walk out of here on my broken leg, find a two-by-four, and pummel you with it*. And that's really how you feel. It's a very dehumanizing experience.

So what you've got to do, just like in prison, is jump in and take some of that raw feces and start throwing it around the room—bring it with you to the head of the hospital ward and slam it on his desk, maybe rub it on his face and rub it on your face, and say, "Let's all dance, let's have a shit party." That's kind of what you've got to do, and then they start to see you as human, and in that process you start to feel human. There's something about demanding your dignity that gives you dignity.

Eventually they let me out, but I was in a wheelchair for two years. I spent the first six months in New Orleans for rehab. I was real messed up because they tried to repair the leg and it wouldn't heal, so eventually they got me in a wheelchair situation back to Bogalusa to finish the record.

After my mom left, Gina came down to Algiers, which is a scary place in Louisiana, and was there every day going over stuff with the doctors and really looking out for me. She rented an apartment and spent a good month or two down there while I was rehabbing. It was pretty hard on her, but without Gina, I don't think I would have made it. For every unpleasant thing I had to go through, at least I had Gina to go through it with. When my mom wasn't there, Gina was there. She drove me around when I could get out and then handled the millions of little details that made it possible for me to function.

They put the leg back together in the fall of 1992 with a pin, but there was necrosis, where the bone dies. So to stave off hip replacement, they put in new pins and eventually, from 1997 to 1998, had to replace the entire hip.

At one point when I was laid up in bed, the doctor noticed I was probably diabetic, and a test confirmed it. This was because I was eating crap and not doing any remedial form of exercise, so I continued to gain weight, pushing north of four hundred pounds. It was very scary—"Isn't that the disease where your foot gets chopped off before you go blind and die?" And then I ran into truckers who said, "I got that shit, man. It's fine. Just don't eat so many Cheetos." That's what it is—you just learn to eat a little bit better. Instead of going to potato chips, have some Wheat Thins. That was just good enough to squeak me through the door. I took medicine, Glucophage, and some other drugs, but when I lost the weight and went below 350 pounds, my sugar stayed under 200.

The other problem with being a big guy—I wasn't super-obese yet, but I was getting there before the bike wreck—was that every wheelchair had to be super-giant-sized, every walker had to be enormous for tall people. But one of many frustrating things about the process is the doctors kept assuring me I would walk in three months . . . and then another three months . . . and another three months . . . and that meant the entire time we were renting things, not getting the good wheelchair, not getting the good walker. And being tall, let alone being close to 400 pounds at the time meant that those were very flimsy.

Eventually we put in the money for the big guy wheelchair. It was a bitch to assemble but at least it could hold me. Our accountant had luckily gotten this incredible insurance deal in which we paid maybe 10 percent of it, which felt like winning the lottery. To their credit, A&M wrote us a check for half a million bucks to keep us going, and that was faith.

Later, when I was in my wheelchair, I would mess with people. We'd be in a tight New York restaurant, and I'd intentionally bump into someone's table and call out, "Everyone's looking at me because I'm in a wheelchair!" I'd say it really loud, like I was crying, and nobody would respond. Some people wouldn't look at me. I really milked that for all it was worth. It was really horrible, but I couldn't stop doing it because it was too fun. The right response would have been, "Yeah, we're looking at you because you're saying stuff." But political correctness was in the air then. I don't think I could get away with that anymore. I'm almost game to try, but I prefer walking.

Meanwhile the band threw the motorcycle into the East River (we call that a band vote), and I never deigned to get on one again. To this day, if a car stops fast, I get a little skittish.

Over the years, being on the road so much, I've wound up being in north of eleven car accidents. And yes, they all suck, but airbag technology is quite superior to motorcycle technology, and I've walked away from every single one. But I tell you, I am not a fan of traffic accidents, and I'd like to point out that I was driving in only about three of them.

I could no longer live in my fourth-floor apartment in Brooklyn, so I had to move to Jersey and back in with my parents. Just being cooped up with your parents as an adult is no kind of fun. But I was in my wheelchair, my dad had a heart condition, we're both Hungarians . . . my poor mom. He and I would get into fights in which I'd try to walk out of the house on my broken leg and he'd scream at me because it was no good for his heart.

I still needed their help, though, so the solution was for me to get a studio apartment above the Laura Ashley in downtown Princeton. For the first six months every song I tried to write started with the word fuck, but eventually being in that little apartment while my friends, the Spin Doctors, were on MTV getting huge put me in a mood to write.

There was a leaky faucet in the bathroom of that apartment, and one day, while I was on the toilet, I hummed "Pachelbel's Canon" to it, using the leaky faucet as a backbeat. I thought, *This could be a cool song.* It became "Hook." I was trying to accomplish a task my brother Bob had set for me when he said I put too many words into a verse. So I wrote the first two verses the way he wanted me to write them, very sparsely, and then the third verse I crammed in as many words as I could, and that would up being the fast part of "Hook."

That's also where I wrote "Run-Around" and pretty much all of our *four* album. I wrote "Run-Around" in a much slower tempo on the guitar. It was for Felicia, and it was supposed to be a love letter of acceptance about some fight we had, and I remember it made her cry when she heard it. It wasn't until much later when we put a backbeat to it that it got to be more of the song that it is now and a much more fun song.

That was my last apartment after Brooklyn. In early 1996 I moved into my first house in Quakertown, Pennsylvania.

At one point, though, I needed to have one more look at my room back in Brooklyn. I hadn't been there for over a year, and it had been cleared out already, but I wanted to ensure there was nothing left. The problem was that I was still in my wheelchair, and our landlord was obsessed with us not marking up the wonderful inlaid wood. We were on the fourth floor, and there was no elevator, so the only way we could think to get up there was having Chan tie a rope around my chair with me in it and another around his neck and, with the help of our landlord, who was freaking out about the metal, we went up one stair at a time—"On, you huskies!" I would yell. Then I got up there, looked around, and shrugged, "Okay, I guess you guys got everything. I can go." But I had to visually inspect it for myself.

When we ended up touring—and we needed to start touring to pay the bills—we put a mattress in a van because I couldn't get on the bus. Then after the show I would get carted up on this mattress in the van, with no windows for some reason (perhaps just to add irony), where I was then driven to the next city by several lunatics looking for work. One of them ran guns for the Hells Angels and one was a former guitarist for 4 Non Blondes, and whenever their song was on the radio she would say, "That's my guitar part, I wrote that." And after hearing the guitar part for the first time, let alone the hundredth, it was hard to believe that somebody would brag about writing that. It was two lines, and I have the guitar part memorized because every time the song was playing, I got to hear about that guitar part. I had to learn it for my own survival.

I was sort of at the mercy of people I didn't really know, flopping around. As soon as the show was over I would get crated up in the van while everyone else got to go have fun.

I couldn't even take a shit unless I had a plastic donut to sit on. I remember one time the plastic donut got sent to the gig rather than the hotel. So everyone was waiting for me at the show while someone ran with the donut back to the hotel. Imagine shitting under that kind of pressure.

Instead of a nurse, we just got a roadie to be a caregiver—poor Grant. He'd been in our crew, and we gave him the nickname Soggy Hoagies. We called him that because tragedy would often befall him, but he'd try to make up for it by bringing us a peace offering of sorts, in case we were hungry. A typical Grant story would involve us telling him to park the cube truck, and he would say, "Sure!" He'd be very chipper about it and drive off, and then you wouldn't see him for five hours, when he'd come back covered in soot with his shirt ripped, maybe a gash in his arm, and mud all over him, holding two soggy hoagies, or maybe four, two under each arm. You'd ask him what happened, and he'd explain, "Okay, I went to park the truck, and I found myself in a mudslide because it stated raining, so I slid down a ravine, and the truck started rolling. So I put it in reverse and tried to back out, but that only made it roll even further down the ravine, and I ended up in a lake. So I tried paddling the truck upside down, and in the process I accidentally dislodged a lighter, and that caught fire on some newspapers that were on the ceiling of the truck because, remember, we're upside down. Then the truck caught fire, and I started rowing really fast because I wanted to get to shore before the truck exploded so I wouldn't have to swim in that lake since there could be sharks in there. I made it just in time, and just as I climbed out, the truck exploded. I couldn't save any of the gear, but I figured you guys might be hungry, so I got some hoagies."

Grant had to empty my urine bottles, deal with all my wheelchair equipment, and ensure that my drivers actually brought me from point A to point B. There was one time Grant couldn't make a hotel key work. I was trapped in the room in my chair, and we were about an hour late for the show. I was feeling all this pressure about being late and making everybody late yet again. So when he finally came in, without even thinking, I threw a bottle of urine, and it hit him square in the face. It exploded all over him. He looked at me for a second and just left. I love this man, we're friends now, but he said he had to leave because he was going to kill me. And looking back, I would have killed me too.

14

H.O.R.D.E TO HANDLE

The idea for H.O.R.D.E. came from my *Penguin Historical Atlas*. In the *Penguin Atlas* you see the people of central Europe being plagued by the Vandals from the south and the Huns from the east and the Visigoths from the west and the Vikings from the north. So I had the idea of Phish fans coming to a particular town from the north and Widespread Panic fans coming from the south and Blues Traveler fans coming from the west. The idea is that the town is being assaulted on all sides by this throng of people, by a hippie gang, if you will.

The thing is that bands never come from different directions; usually everyone's following each other, but I had this great fantasy of everyone converging on the same spot. All of the food in the area gets eaten up by these people. I wanted there to be an air of pillage, so I thought it should sound like some sort of Mongol horde. I figured an anagram is probably the best way to go. Originally it was Horizons of Rock Developing East coast because all these bands we were talking about were from the East Coast, and to me that seemed to be an identification of a scene, because we were definitely not from Haight-Ashbury. But Eric Schenkman wisely said it should be Horizons of Rock Developing Everywhere. And sure enough, the next year we started using bands like Big Head Todd & the Monsters and the Samples from Colorado.

We also saw the success of Lollapalooza. The brilliant idea was that you could get a lot of little club bands out at an amphitheater by combining their draws. So we wanted to see whether we could do that. We'd done a lot of shows with Phish and Widespread Panic, and Spin Doctors grew up with us.

Bill Graham did Lollapalooza that first year, so we got a sneak peek into it. The Graham organization embraced the idea of taking a bunch of small bands and creating a festival that was bigger than any of the individual bands. Then the name Lollapalooza becomes stronger than Jane's Addiction or any of the bands involved. Bill Graham said that to me about the Fillmore—one of the best moments he ever had was when he was in the bathroom and heard two kids come in and one of them said, "Who's playing tonight?" And the other one said, "Who cares? It's the Fillmore." And that kind of identification with a name can be done for a tour when there's not a huge band running it, and that was the idea we wanted to seize on with our scene.

Around this time a few people were floating the idea of possibly joining forces, but because we toured the farthest, we knew everybody. Widespread was still fairly regional to the south and would make occasional forays to the west, the Spin Doctors were a New York band who hadn't toured much, and Phish basically stuck to New England at that time, although they had made some inroads into other regions. But, again, because of my *Penguin Historical Atlas*, we were pushing into every state so I could fill in my map. As a result we had relationships with all of these bands.

So in March 1992 we decided to hold a meeting with just band members, no managers. We had all of Blues Traveler, Eric and Chris from the Spin Doctors, all of Phish (who happened to be in town), members of Widespread Panic, and Colonel Bruce, who was there representing Aquarium Rescue Unit.

We all met in a room in Bill Graham's office in New York. If you've ever been in Bill Graham's anything there's a certain rock-and-roll reverence there—"Oh, look, that's Janis Joplin's tambourine."

Phish drummer Jon Fishman wanted to stage a little skit, so he told us, "Okay, I'm going to run out screaming, and you guys drag me back into the room and everybody will wonder, 'What the hell are they doing in there?'" He got really into it, and while he was yelling, "No, no, don't take me back!" he ripped the door off the hinge. I heard later that people got pissed because of that.

We were trying to figure this all out, and then Trey Anastasio stood up and said, "Why don't we just make it something where the bands get equal billing and equal money everywhere?" So we were fired up—"Yes, let's do this!" Then, and I'm pretty sure this was Mike Gordon's idea, we sealed the deal by shaking hands after we dipped them into a jar of Vaseline that was on the table. I still have that jar of Vaseline.

Working on H.O.R.D.E. that year was kind of like getting stuck between reality and imagination. In your imagination it's world conquest. You're thinking, *We're gonna fill up Shea Stadium!* And then you're disappointed when it's anything less. Then there's the reality that you're amazed you got more than one band to agree to show up anywhere at the same time.

The next day Trey called me and explained, "I talked to my manager, and we just can't do that," meaning the equal billing and money. And that's the reality. I understood why they couldn't. They had to eat, and they had people to pay—Phish had a huge overhead. So my next call was to Widespread Panic's John Bell, and he said, "I understand, but then we have to do the same thing down south." So suddenly everybody was going to their corners. Each band as an entity, including ours, was good at protecting itself, which is what you do as a band, and the hardest thing about a festival, especially a grassroots one, is you have to get all these entities working toward the same goal.

We decided on eight dates, four in the northeast in July and four in the southeast in August. Then Phish said they couldn't do the second half, so we found Bela Fleck and the Flecktones for the August shows. Really, from day one it was quite a mess.

Although Phish was only doing four of the gigs, they wanted us to reconsider the name. They were at some airport where they read these facts about a pilot, and instead of H.O.R.D.E., they wanted us to name it the Clifford Ball and have that be the entire theme of the tour. I have to hand it to them for being abstract. And eventually they did use that four years later for their first major festival at a former Air Force base in Plattsburgh, New York. I guess there's something special about the Clifford Ball that put the hook in them.

As July approached, the Spin Doctors record started happening, and they wanted a different treatment even though they hadn't been touring like the other bands. It all became a feeding frenzy with managers involved and me in the middle.

That's really how I came to run the H.O.R.D.E.; I just knew everybody. They weren't as familiar with each other as they were with us, so I became the go-between. I remember trying to work out an issue with the Docs, who wanted top billing in New York. I was in Princeton with Chris Barron, and he didn't want to talk about H.O.R.D.E at all. He said, "Look man, this is your tour." He made it clear that he had no obligation to deal with this, and I was kind of shaken and wounded when I left there. But eventually I understood.

I became the only one in the band who had the patience to deal with everything, which generally involved lots of phone calls with various entities, each of whom would tell me what they wanted and then I had to go accommodate them while also accommodating the other people. I got Bobby on a phone call in which the Spin Doctors' manager is yelling, and Bobby said, "Uhh, I got to go." He didn't last forty seconds, and I said to him later, whenever he had any complaints about how I came to own H.O.R.D.E. along with Dave Frey, "That's what I do all the time!" After the relative honeymoon of the first year, it became nine months of grisly, ugly work. I'd have to sit there, let people yell, and then pick my opportunity when I got to yell.

Still, it was no picnic in 1992 when we were figuring out how to do this. The Spin Doctors' booking agent pushed really hard, first for the highest billing in New York, which he didn't get, then he made it clear he thought the Aquarium Rescue Unit was overpaid, that they had no national draw—he essentially wanted to push them out. We were not going to stand for that because they represented the spirit of H.O.R.D.E. to us. They did have the smallest draw, but as a group, they probably had the best players. They were sort of our rallying flag.

With H.O.R.D.E. there always would be the money side of things and the artistic side of things, and we tried to make them balance. One of the ways we did that was to make sure we put Aquarium Rescue

Unit on the bill. That felt right to us. H.O.R.D.E. was laden with mitz-vahs, and you got them done back to you. So I guess we were kind of spoiled because we got to do what we wanted and treat that as normal.

Although we had an agreement in place with the Spin Doctors, a week before the first show, their agent wanted an additional $10,000 and the band's split of any profits to double. What eventually happened is that both Blues Traveler and Widespread Panic gave back $2,000 apiece, but we kept their profit percentage as is. Not that it mattered, because although that first year was creatively satisfying, it was not quite profitable. I think the tour lost $7,000 that year and then made $8,000 in 1993 before things started to pick up in 1994.

When we showed up for that very first show at the Cumberland County Civic Center in Maine on July 9, I just marveled, *Wow, this is really happening.* I didn't have too much time to soak it all in, though, because almost immediately people started coming up to me, asking, "What do we do about this?" That's when I realized they thought I was in charge. And that's when I realized that I *was* in charge. I was big and I had the hat on, so you could find me from far away. It was like being a general on the battlefield: "Go to the guy in the hat and ask him what's up."

It got to the point over the years where I'd find a room on site and hide so no one could talk to me. But then when they did, they would be escorted in three at a time like I was Paulie from *Goodfellas.* Some of these things I had never dealt with before and didn't know much about—we needed more insurance at the Garden State Arts Center, for instance, and Jones Beach wouldn't allow tabling by Planned Parenthood, NOW, or NORML—but we did the best we could and figured it out along the way. I discovered that the key to being a musician and promoter was that you wanted everyone to continue not knowing exactly what you knew. It made you an unpredictable quantity, and then you could be useful if there were a real problem.

The first show in Portland was a complete success in terms of the music and camaraderie. We drew over five thousand people, which was a solid start. However, my recollection is that in Syracuse or maybe Oak Mountain Amphitheatre in Pelham, Alabama, on the second leg, our concourse felt a bit more desolate than we had hoped. It reminded me of an emaciated third-world ghetto when the crops went bad, with a beggar trying to shield his face from the dust storms blowing by while a coyote howled. Still, we sold out the Garden State Arts Center and Jones Beach and drew over eleven thousand people to the Carowinds Paladium Amphitheater in Charlotte. The concept had been proven.

Aquarium Rescue Unit had the reverence of all the musicians, and during their sets all the bands would stop what they were doing to watch them. They were an empire within an empire.

Bela Fleck and the Flecktones were a real revelation to me. Their harmonica player, Howard Levy, was just a freak. I think he's the best harmonica player on Earth on the blues harp. I saw him do something that I never saw anyone else do on a harmonica—he can play the way someone does on a piano, where a left hand and a right hand are independent of each other. We did a jam together in which I went rhythmically and he was doing a melodic thing, and we each went places the other guy couldn't go. It was a great little dance back and forth.

I sat in with all of the bands over the course of those shows, which was a goal and a highlight and something I would continue to do over the years. Well, I didn't quite sit in with Phish. At the Garden State Arts Center show they brought out trampolines for their routine during "You Enjoy Myself"—Mike and Trey would play while they were jumping. They also brought out one for me, but mine was rigged to break. So on my first jump, I broke right through it and walked off stage all dejected. We planned that as a gag. But everyone thought I had really broken it and tried to cheer me up—"Don't worry, John, not everybody can do a trampoline." I kept trying to tell them it was rigged to break, but nobody believed me. And that would lead to something the following year, when we one-upped it, because now I had something to prove.

Given my original inspiration from the Mongol hordes, it also seemed to me that we needed to have ceremonial swords. So I found a sword maker who had the time and wherewithal to follow through on the concept.

We made a H.O.R.D.E. sword for every band. Each band only received one because we weren't made of money, and we didn't want to arm all the musicians because that only lends itself to sword fights, which would not be a good recipe with that much booze lying around.

I received them just before the end of the first leg of the tour. These were fully functioning broad swords with 36-inch blades. They were really heavy, the same weight that knights used with a fairly strong hilt. Each had a claw holding a green orb, which I think was a nod to the movie *Heavy Metal*. On each blade it said *mota et volute*, which means rock and roll in Latin, and on the other end it said *modulare et vincere*, which means jam and conquer. Then the other side of blade had each band's logo (Phish, Widespread Panic, Aquarium Rescue Unit, Spin Doctors, Bela Fleck and the Flecktones, and Blues Traveler).

They were wicked sharp and really heavy, and we wanted to see how they would work. So we put a peach on top of a bucket on top of a road case, thinking this would be a safe way to see how much damage one of these swords could do to a peach pit when we cut through a peach. Trey took a big swing straight down, a good cut, and it went through the peach, through the pit, through the bucket, and through the road case. With no damage to the sword. We were very impressed.

Still, my favorite moment from that first year is a weird one. After the show at Lakewood Amphitheater in Georgia, the end of the whole tour, we were leaving and I was hungry—I hadn't eaten yet. So we hit a Burger King on the way out of town and they were out of food. That to me was one of the best moments of H.O.R.D.E. We came into a town and emptied their fast food joints. That was as close as reality and imagination came together in my bizarre Attila the Hun fantasy: the Burger King in Georgia.

By the end of the tour people were talking about next year, and in 1993 the same problem existed: we wanted to get out of clubs and into sheds. The Spin Doctors were off doing their own thing, so we couldn't count on them, and Phish had made the decision not to commit to a multiband festival. But we found other bands: Big Head Todd & the Monsters, the Samples, and the Dave Matthews Band on a few dates. Rather than eight shows, we did twenty-six, opening with two nights at Red Rocks on July 2 and 3. All in all it was a solid showing, with the exception of two dates we had to cancel due to low ticket sales in Darien Center, New York, and Syracuse (no doubt the coyotes would have been howling again had we returned).

By the second year Dave Frey said, "We're doing the all the work. This is our tour—we should incorporate." There was an extraction on Dave's end from Bill Graham Presents because they had funded the first year, at least on paper. So BGP would get a disappearing annual percentage, and eventually Dave and I would own it, fifty-fifty.

Dave did the vast majority of the logistical work, and I was the figurehead. I would call people and find out what our party position was, what we needed to talk them into, and try to sell it. Then I would try to find out what *they* needed. I saw my job as attempting to accommodate everybody. Eventually, though, there was this point when everybody wanted to be accommodated in ways that were impossible, and by 1998 we were fed up.

That first year, in order to appease the guys in my band, I had given them each 5 percent of our promoter's funds. Of course on top of that, they also were paid to be on the tour. Rich Vink, our sound guy, had been spouting off this idea, had spiritually been talking about this, so it seemed wrong not to cut him in for something. So he got 2.5 percent. And Dave Precheur, our trusty road manager who was with us since high school, got 2.5 percent as well. That left 40 percent each for Dave and me.

There certainly was some amount of resentment from the band over the years, but they had to begrudgingly acknowledge that I was earning it. If need be, I reminded Bobby of the Spin Doctors' call from 1992. A few years later it was reinforced via this band Red Thunder. They were a Native American group but were sort of manufactured: one guy was Apache, another was Shawnee, and one claimed to be Aztec (which is almost indiscernible from being Mexican), but they had formed a native supergroup, and they'd do new age music with a tribal influence. They tried, and I thought they were okay, but none of us thought they were a great band. The reason they were on the tour is that they were opening for one of the other acts, who had said that they would only appear on H.O.R.D.E. if we could find a slot for Red Thunder on the bill (which also demonstrates how things had changed since year one and also how the live touring business often works). The day before the tour started Chan went on a drunken tirade in front of everyone in the commissary—the room had to clear out—screaming at me because Red Thunder was on right before us. I had to sit there and listen to him yell for what seemed like hours, and he was like Frank Sinatra on a bender. I was the one who was sober back then, and I just filed it away thinking, *Someday you're really going to regret that you did this.* Well, here's that day Chan—enjoy the book.

H.O.R.D.E. was like a real job. It wasn't songwriting or playing; it was more about planning and negotiating. I was willing to do it, but I'm a musician; we cater a little more to imagination than reality, and that's really a better job for me. That's when I think I gained a lot of weight. I had to be the guy who explained to James Brown's manager why he wasn't worth fifty grand in New York City in 1993. Try living with that karmically. Go on, I dare you.

Who decided that James Brown wasn't worth fifty grand? It wasn't me; it was the local promoter, who during that time in New York would have been Delsener/Slater. They have numbers that are facts, and you cannot escape these facts. They saw what James Brown pulled in the last few times he appeared in the area and then deduced mathematically how much he's worth as a draw. Then they have some sort of algorithm to decide what James Brown would be worth on a festival, and that number becomes what it is. There's no getting around that number, no matter how creative or artistic you are—you're stuck in that number. So really I was just relaying to the musicians the bad news the promoters gave to me, and it just felt like I was on the wrong side of that.

Phish met the tour for two shows, and I was able to follow up on the previous year's trampoline gag. (I feel you out there reading this, not believing it was a gag, but dammit I am going to prove to you retroactively along with everyone who was there, that this time it was a gag.) I was still in my wheelchair that summer, and we got another wheelchair and a dummy dressed exactly like me, playing the harmonica, and dangled it above the stage. Then at the end of the show there was a big jam session, and in the middle of that jam, with no explanation to the crowd, the crew brought out a giant yard trampoline, as Phish jumped on their regular tiny trampolines. Then the audience could see what they thought was me dangling from the top of the stage in my wheelchair over this giant yard trampoline. Surely the giant yard trampoline could hold me, right?

I was offstage on a wireless mic, playing, and at the very end they dropped me right through a giant yard lawn trampoline, which was also rigged to break (I swear to God) while I was offstage, saying, "I'm okay, oww . . . I'm all right" The cool part was we ran so long that as soon as I fell through, the lights had to come up due to the union guys, so some people thought I was really hurt, and it looked as though something really wrong had happened. For the following several years I had people say to me, "I was at the Richmond show—are you okay? What happened?" It was the only time I ever made milk come out of Trey's nose from laughing, and that to me was my proudest moment (it might have been beer, but I'm still proud).

The next year we had the Allman Brothers Band as the headliner. I always enjoyed playing with them, and they had appeared on a couple of 1993 H.O.R.D.E. dates as well. The most memorable of those in 1993 was in Stowe, Vermont. Apparently Dickey had a physical alter-cation with a police officer the previous evening and got arrested. He couldn't make it to the show, so Jimmy Herring from Aquarium Res-cue Unit played guitar with them. He would do it again during the summer of 2000 after Dickey left for good, but that night in Vermont was huge for him. I was still in my wheelchair, and I sat in for about half the set. Jimmy and I were on cloud nine, and I remember looking over at him, and we both couldn't believe where we found ourselves. "In Memory of Elizabeth Reed" was really the moment for both of us, and I kind of owe it to Dickey for punching out a cop.

The main stage opener for most of the 1994 H.O.R.D.E. tour was Sheryl Crow. We also ended up touring with her that fall, which was a lot of fun. She was opening up for us, but we all knew she and her band were a big deal because her song "All I Wanna Do" was all over the radio. I got to play on it with them every other night, and I re-member one time our tour manager said, "That's the number-one song in the country you just played on."

There was one night at the end of the tour with Sheryl when we harassed James Taylor. We had a big dinner with both bands and ev-erybody's crew at this sushi restaurant in Atlanta. We were all on A&M, so Al Marks, our A&R guy was throwing us a dinner. While we were waiting for our table, Tad, Sheryl's bass player spotted James

Taylor. He was in this private little booth. We wanted him to come out, so Tad and I started singing:

> You just call out my name
> and you know wherever I am

And nothing happened.

> I'll come running
> to see you again.

Still nothing.

> Winter, spring, summer, or fall
> all you have to do is call

And finally he came out—"Would you stop that?" It was hysterical. I think he recognized Sheryl because at the end of the dinner he came over to say hi, which blew us all away.

Sheryl and her band were always up for that kind of thing. Brendan's rule (which continues to this day) is that when someone had been touring with us, it was our job to prank them. It was usually silly string, and I always prided myself on being the godfather about it and not ever being there when it went down. But in this case we went all out and silly stringed the shit out of them one night when they were onstage. We just nuked them with silly string. So they decided to prank us back. They ran out while we were playing and started mopping up. Then Sheryl came out with a little waitress apron, brought us drinks, and danced off. I thought that was really cool of them.

Back to H.O.R.D.E. By 1994 we had expanded to two stages, the Gonzo and Mondo stages. In fact, Sheryl was originally scheduled for the second stage, the Gonzo stage, but after her album took off, she moved to the opening slot on the main stage for most of the shows.

Eventually we would have three performance spots. I was particularly proud of the workshop stage. Someone had carved a life-sized blue whale out of one piece of a redwood tree, and we brought that around with us as the workshop stage. This was where someone from one band could perform with someone from another band. We had a lot of good jams over the years with Taj Mahal, Dave Matthews, and Sheryl. I was involved with quite a few of them, including one with Warren Haynes, Allen Woody, Jaimoe, and LeRoi Moore. Of course, Warren was in with plenty himself, including a spontaneous performance by Warren and the other members of Gov't Mule joined by Ben Harper and Chris Barron. Another one that people still talk about was a bass jam with Les Claypool and Marc Sandman from Morphine.

The year 1995 was big for H.O.R.D.E. because that was the first time we outdrew Lollapalooza. The combination of us, the Black Crowes, and Ziggy Marley made for a really nice package.

The Crowes were very determined to have something that was not corporate. They thought we were too corporate and didn't want to play with a beer banner behind them. To our minds, H.O.R.D.E. had grown organically to the point at which we *could* sell beer.

This was a time when it seemed everyone was turning against sponsorship. But the fact is we were being paid a million dollars, and most of it we were paying to the Black Crowes. We figured out another sponsorship that made everybody happy, but ever since the Andrews Sisters in the 1940s, beer companies have been paying bands to play, and I never saw a problem with it. It would be one thing if a beer company was promoting death to puppies as a political practice, but they just wanted people to drink a beer that a lot of people tended to drink anyway. If that's not your brand of beer, I guess that really matters to you, but if it essentially comes down to brand loyalty, I think that's silly. I would go with the beer company that pays the most money, although admittedly I'm not much of a beer drinker. So am I betraying my art for trying to make a living? I don't think so. There was no other way we'd get the Black Crowes on the bill. So I'm glad we had sponsors pony up the cash—it allowed people to have a lot of fun.

We really tried to make the Crowes as happy as we could. They liked the medicine show idea, so we took that angle of a weird carnival and just ran with it.

Ziggy Marley had the best pot ever, and they gave everybody a jar of the finest ganja we could remember—if we could remember. Their drummer, Squidly, was on our bus every day, and we took pride in the fact that we were the only band on the tour besides his own whose weed he respected.

Here's a related Marley story Dave Frey tells from that tour: "We were playing the Waterloo Village, in Stanhope, New Jersey, and there were a lot of traffic problems because it's a field out in the forest, with a two-lane road coming in and out. They were stuck out there, but their tour manager had one of the first cell phones. So we called him and explained that we'd send a state trooper to lead them in. And there was this profound silence on the other side because we realized what we'd asked them to do—because usually the state trooper would be leading them somewhere else."

That was also the year the Rembrandts were on the tour. I said that was okay so long as they didn't play the theme from *Friends*. I suspected they would but I wondered how they would respond to that kind of challenge because did the Rembrandts have any other songs? As you can imagine, they wound up playing it anyway. They came with Sheryl Crow, who had jumped on for a few dates—again, there was always an accommodation we had to make for somebody.

Then 1996 was the year when it *really* got huge. It was the second year in a row that we outdrew Lollapalooza, and that meant something to us. We had Lenny Kravitz, the Dave Matthews Band, Natalie Merchant, and King Crimson.

Dave Matthews was on fire but was just an easygoing guy and really easy to work with. One of my favorite moments playing with Dave was a version of "All Along the Watchtower" that we performed acoustically on the Blue Whale Stage. It was so odd to us how somebody we met at the Van Riper's fest and perhaps Wetlands as an opener become so massively huge, but they were really such an effortless band to play with. Boyd was nothing but optimistic, and LeRoi was the exact opposite, and that combination was in their playing styles—it was so wonderful. Stefan on bass was just so nice and completely conducive to making whatever jam work. Then you have Carter who, in my opinion, is one of the best drummers in the world (I would later nab him for my solo album *Zygote*, where he would save the day—stay tuned).

In June 1994 I had joined them in the studio up in Woodstock, New York, to play harmonica on "What Would You Say" (a song that would later be up for a Grammy against Blues Traveler's "Run-Around"). They sent a crew guy, a runner, to drive me up there in a rented Gremlin, and you should just never drive a rented Gremlin. The car broke down on the highway en route to the studio, and I really needed to head back to catch the only flight remaining that day to England for a tour. So I only had time to lay it down twice. I think Dave went to the bathroom, and when he came out I was done. That became the track they used on the song, so I felt like a badass, but really I just had to go to England.

Back in those days women were throwing themselves at Dave. My friend Felicia was a huge fan of his, and she and I would get into this argument where I'd say, "Oh, you just think he's got a great butt." She was dying to meet him, so of course I introduced her with "This is my friend Felicia—she thinks you've got a great butt," which made her mad at me for the whole following year. Then we went to see Dave Matthews at Madison Square Garden, where I sat in with him, and she reminded me, "I can't believe that's how you introduced me to Dave Matthews." So we were at the after-party, and I said to Dave, "Could you maybe say something nice to my friend Felicia? She feels bad about the way I introduced you." And a few minutes later Felicia came up to me and reported, "Dave Matthews just made out with me in the bathroom." And that's what Dave heard: "Can you make out with my friend Felicia? She feels a little neglected."

As for the 1996 H.O.R.D.E., the weather really affected the performances that summer. The heat was brutal in July, and Lenny fainted during the Dallas show, where it was 105 degrees. He simply refused to take off those leather pants. Lenny had a leather outfit and eventually went shirtless but then fainted. Had he worn jeans, he probably would have been okay. Then a couple of weeks later, in Salt Lake City, a dust storm drove him from the stage. I believe lightning struck the stage as well during his set. Another interesting thing about Lenny is he always wanted to make it seem as though he had driven his motorcycles into a given town, but what really happened was his truck would park outside, they would offload the bikes, and then he would ride into town. That poor bastard worked his ass off that summer. It is not easy being as cool as Lenny Kravitz.

Meanwhile we were getting used to the headlining slot. We closed over forty shows, all except for one in Austin, where we left that to the Dave Matthews Band. We took nothing for granted, though. In St. Louis I wrote a set list with a record-breaking sixteen-song segue. Audiences really responded to what we were doing and to the bill as a whole—we drew thirty thousand to the Saratoga Performing Arts Center and twenty-eight thousand to Chula Vista, with plenty of other crowds topping twenty thousand. I sat in with Lenny, Natalie, and Dave a number of times, while at Randall's Island in New York City, Bruce Willis and Chris Barron sat in with us.

We were having a lot of sound trouble on that tour because I wasn't connecting with my sound guy on what my harp sound was supposed to be. And during this era sometimes I would play with my glasses off. That night at Randall's Island I knew Bruce Willis was going to sit in at some point, but I wasn't sure which song it would be, and the sound of the harmonica was terrible. So someone who I thought was my crew guy Greg Hester walked out with a baseball cap on and a big dumb smile and said, "Isn't this great?" And I couldn't believe that he came out like he didn't have a care in the world, asking me, "Isn't this great?" when the amps sounded terrible. So I looked at him with absolute murder in my eyes and bellowed, "What?" as if "I want to eat your head." But then as I stared at him I started to realize it wasn't my sound guy at all; it was Bruce Willis who was so excited, that he ran out a little early. My response had just drained all of the color out of the cheeks of this person who I now realized was Bruce Willis, who suddenly got very scared. He asked me, "Am I supposed to be here?" And I quickly said, "No, no, you're okay—I thought you were someone else," and I wrote him a letter about it later.

We were doing so well that we decided to pay seventy grand for a hot air balloon that we used twice. My fantasy was you'd be in Chicago, let's say, and open your window, and there's a giant Blues Traveler cat on a big purple balloon that says H.O.R.D.E. But it turned out you can't fly them anywhere near cities or telephone lines or if there's wind that exceeds twelve miles per hour, which is generally all the time. This might explain the decline in the past century of ballooning as a popular sport. So we basically hired a "balloon captain" (yes, there is such an occupation) to lick his finger, stick his finger in the air, say, "Nope," and then get drunk all day. On top of that, the balloon had to be hauled around on a flatbed truck all tour. That balloon remained in my garage for nearly a decade.

Many years later, in 2013, we're playing a balloon festival in New Jersey, and looking up, I was reminded of my folly in trying to create a H.O.R.D.E air force and that $70,000 balloon that sat in my garage for about ten years before I could sell it for six grand. Or, as I like to call it, my $64,000 loss. And sure enough, as I'm thinking about it, I look around, and what do I see but that very same balloon that some-one in the know probably bought from me and sold to someone else for sixty grand. There it was, looking brand-spanking new, and in-stantly I stopped the show and told this story. So if you've been to the balloon fest in Readington, New Jersey, you'll know what I'm talking about. Curse you, balloons.

By 1997, even though H.O.R.D.E. continued, Blues Traveler de-cided not to do it. All our compatriots were getting huge and doing their own summer things—Dave Matthews, Phish, Widespread Panic. But what we ended up doing was going to Europe and trying to break into that market, which wasn't exactly the same.

So our headliners were Neil Young and Primus. The only problem was that although each of them loved the other band, they were also worried about the other band's fans messing with their fans—"Could you keep Primus on the bill but not have their fans come?" Well, I guess we could, but that would defeat the purpose of having Primus on the bill. To us the answer was telling them, "Let's try to build a solution, but until then, let's go along as though you want to work together, which is what you're saying, right?"

We had to get Neil a bus covered with inlaid wood so he could carve it. His house is exactly like that as well; it's like a Hobbit hole, only a little more above ground. Every hallway is ornately carved. It's just beautiful. His son needs sunlight because of his cerebral palsy, so Neil created a room that was all colored glass in a bubble—wherever you are in the room, there's sunlight.

I saw Neil's place in 1997 when we went out to do the Bridge School Benefit. I hung out in a teepee in his backyard with Marilyn Manson. That's what gave me the idea to get a teepee and put it in my own yard, but this was right when the *Blair Witch Project* came out so then I was suddenly too scared to go out and sleep in it. I've got more guns than Fort Knox and I was literally twenty feet away from my house, but I heard those Blair Witch noises in the woods and said,

"Fuck this, I'm going inside. Why am I out here? I've got a perfectly nice house right over there."

Before I walked onstage the first time at the Bridge School show, Nigel James, who was doing the production and had worked with us on H.O.R.D.E., whispered in my ear, "Go sing to the kids." They sat behind the musicians, facing the audience, and they all had cerebral palsy in one form or another. So I tried it, thinking it was a pretty good idea, and it was overwhelming, people started to cry, and then after us, everybody started doing it. To turn your back on fifteen thousand people to sing to these fifteen kids was more powerful than I thought it would be. In fact, I got choked up. I really have to credit Nigel—it was such a coup. It affected everyone and elevated our show. It worked so well, I felt a little guilty about it.

I also remember Chelsea Clinton being there, and all her Secret Service men were dressed like hippies with tie-dyed shirts.

Back to Neil and his tour bus. He was an incessant carver. Neil was working throughout the tour, and by the end, the van looked like something out of Tolkien. It was a work of art.

In August we joined H.O.R.D.E. for a few dates, but we clearly had miscalculated. The tour ended up being perfectly fine, although people really missed us. We didn't quite catch on that we were a necessary part of it.

We also had a problem when we played a show in New Jersey on August 11. This was our first performance in the Northeast since New Year's Eve, and A&M had released *Straight on till Morning* a month earlier. We were contracted to play five songs with the Paramus Symphony Orchestra. Medeski Martin & Wood and Me'Shell Ndegéocello also appeared, both H.O.R.D.E. alumni. But the way it was sold to people in New Jersey was as a regular Blues Traveler show with an orchestra. We didn't know about that, and there was no time on our schedule to put anything else together and rehearse a full two-hour show with the orchestra. Classical orchestras are not known for their improvisation.

So we did our five songs, and it was clear that people were unhappy, so we did another and then we came out for an unplanned encore. There was some gap we didn't catch with our audience in which they wanted a big, long show out of us, and we weren't giving that to them. We thought we were done, but people were chanting "Attica!" in the parking lot and a riot started. What this actually had to do with Attica, I have no idea, but I'll admit I thought it was pretty funny, so I have to get part of the credit for the riot to Al Pacino.

By 1998 it became much more difficult to plan H.O.R.D.E. With the Lilith Fair and Smokin' Grooves tours, it seemed bands increasingly were being divided into whatever category they seemed to occupy. Then radio stations became involved and started putting on multiband concerts, telling groups, "If you play our summer jam, then we'll put you in heavy rotation." We had nothing comparable to offer them that was remotely on that level, so it was kind of doomed.

That year we put together a package with Ben Harper & the Innocent Criminals, Barenaked Ladies, and Alana Davis on all of the shows, with plenty of other acts rotating in and out like Gov't Mule, Galactic, and Mighty Mighty Bosstones.

There were some good nights, but I was getting a little weary of the politics, and Blues Traveler had been on the road nearly nonstop for a decade. The guys kept reminding me that so many of the bands who had been a major part of H.O.R.D.E.'s success had moved on to their own careers and their own summer tours. So, going into it, we had a strong sense this would be our last H.O.R.D.E. Our scene was in full flower, but what happens to a flower after it blooms? It *was* blooming, so we felt like we wanted to get out.

At one point during the tour I approached Steven Page from the Barenaked Ladies and asked him whether they would be interested in taking it over. He seemed almost horrified and said "No! I guess they wanted to do their own thing. So I decided, *Okay, that's enough for me. I'm not going to offer that to anyone else. I'm going to keep it and just retire with a balloon in my garage.*

I went out in style, though. Every year I sat in with every band on every stage. That was a big thing for me. I looked at H.O.R.D.E. as a way for me to play with so many different artists who I never played with before. And the entire last day I would be on a golf cart to see whether I could do it. It was a full-day affair, making the rounds every hour, pulling up to each of the three stages. I really loved doing it, and that was where I felt the most useful.

Over the years, through luck or timing, we ran into an immense amount of really talented bands. From 311 to David Garza, each of them had something different to offer. The Smashing Pumpkins were not a band we'd normally play with, but we got them on the bill—it was such a great an opportunity for us to play with so many different people. Again, I liken it to our desire to play more states than anyone else and get around and see more: you get an incredible view when you experience all sorts of different bands and play in their musical fields. It makes you a stronger band, and we keep coming back to that conclusion, as evidenced by our most recent record. The thing I feel grateful for is that people attribute such a heritage to H.O.R.D.E. We're honored that we could do that, but basically it was trying to solve a survival problem with playing in sheds. All the rest of it was paths of least resistance. I think if we had tried to make H.O.R.D.E. as cool as it became, we never would have succeeded.

When we started, the term neo-hippie was thrown around, and a few years in, people talked about the jam band scene. H.O.R.D.E was probably a reflection of that. Chris Barron once told me that he thought we all had shaped a generation, but I'm not sure I agree. There's always that debate—"Are you doing the shaping or are you being shaped by your generation?" And it's really hard to tell.

15

THE RACE TO 430

I was always a fat kid as far back as I can remember. I think that makes a person seek to be funny as a solution. To me, that was the identity I had even in my own family. I wasn't the only fat one, but I was fat and that was my thing. That was also the perception in school as well as my identity there—as a kid, you get tagged with an identity.

As I got older and went out into the world, I still saw myself that way, even if people saw me as talented and weren't really looking at that.

When I got really obese, it had to do with the motorcycle wreck. I spent a year in a wheelchair and gained a lot of weight. I wasn't moving around. You're kind of like a frog on a hot plate when you get that obese. I was past four hundred pounds and didn't notice it, especially when everybody was helping me out of chairs. Then I had four guys helping me out of a chair, and I just got used to that. Then I got used to not walking very well, and this gradually became how I saw myself.

I won't go so far as to call it a mixed blessing because it's bad to be that unhealthy. I think everyone in the band had some sort of addiction, whether it was drugs or alcohol. For me it was food. That was the thing I was used to, a continuation from when I was a kid. After I got fatter, it became something for my friends to focus on, telling me I needed help. Well, of course I needed help, because there was this hopeless feeling. I think I perpetuated it and got used to being alone that way.

I used to torture the flight attendants who would discreetly hand me the belt extender when I got on a plane. Their "discretion" would piss me off, so I would always say very loudly, "Stewardess, I'm sorry I'm so big and fat, but I need the super-fatty-fat belt extender for extra-fat, fat people. I'm sure you weren't counting on me being so big and fat. I'm sorry I'm so big and fat." I've never seen a woman run so fast to get a belt extender just to shut me the hell up.

There was always this feeling that being fat or famous was something to hide behind, so it wasn't my fault if I wasn't connecting with people or being rejected by them. That was always a weird thing for me because I went from fat to famous, so there was always a reason to be isolated on one level or another.

It's weird being famous when you're 436 pounds. I think perception-wise, the crowd was rooting for me because I was that fat guy they knew, but I was also talented. And in some ways it sort of helped us because we were that band you rooted for. But I also said that if I had Dave Matthews's ass back then, I would have gotten laid a lot more.

I recently looked at some pictures of the band from 1992. Brendan had shaved his sideburns completely off, as was his custom at that time—he had kind of a Euro look with a Clash T-Shirt. Chan was the lady killer—he had the long metal hair and was wearing a vest like he was Richie Sambora (he also knew how to smell good—at first it was patchouli, but he was quickly learning his fragrances). Bobby knew how to wear a baseball hat and could always go to the Deadhead thing, so he pretty much looked like someone who was on his way to a party, which was accurate more often than not.

And then there was me. I'd be wearing overalls, and it wasn't that I was making a statement about overalls; it was, "Hey, these things fit me. I'll put them on so I won't be naked." Which is about as much thought as I put into it.

Or instead of a belt I'd tie my belt loops together with a piece of rope—"Hey, my belt's broken. I guess I'll use this rope." I wasn't thinking that was fashionable; I was literally in my room, and there happened to be some rope there.

In all the pictures, the shirts I'm wearing, you can see the buttons hanging on for dear life, and it's because I didn't know when a shirt was too tight or too small, and the shirt was invariably some form of horizontal stripe or vertical stripe to make me look like Charlie Brown.

Unless I was wearing purple. In 1995 we hosted the season premiere of *Saturday Night Live*. We got the show because Prince canceled, so I wore a purple shirt in his honor (along with his symbol on my harp belt). I wore the same damn shirt at Woodstock '94, and what I later came to realize is that if you're a really obese man, you should never wear purple. People just instinctively think of Barney the Dinosaur when you're giant and purple. So unless you're really terrifying, little kids want to run up and hug you and sing the "I love you, you love me" song. It was just very bad on so many levels.

I recently saw the *Roseanne* episode I was on, and it is amazing what they would allow me to wear on a TV show. Or in *Blues Brothers 2000*, where I brought my clothes, but what other clothes did they have in 6X? So I pretty much wore whatever smock or muumuu I could squeeze into, and everyone just figured, "Yeah, that's what he wears." But maybe they should have suggested something that was a different color or with buttons on it instead of just a tent cover. And my hair. . . . The things I would appear in when I was really overweight—they would let me do whatever I wanted: "Have it stuck to the side of your head. It doesn't matter—you're gigantic." It was a weird double standard.

After I lost the weight people told me, "You know, maybe you should try some mousse or something." I'll never wear mousse because the fun part of being a dude is that you roll out of bed and you're ready to go. I don't need to fuss and preen my hair, but it's nice to have that as something to worry about, to look at your face and ask yourself, *Should I shave?* When you're obese, who cares if you shave? You're 436 pounds—is it going to help? You're so strange-looking anyway, just go with it. I could have literally painted my head bright blue, and people would have said, "Yeah, he's probably doing a thing."

In those days my clothes just screamed, "Help me! I'm clueless!" And I was the lead singer in the band. I've told Brendan and Chan,

"You guys should have dressed me better. I needed help, and I was your lead singer." But to them, I think, it was part of the charm— "Come see the weird crazy man play the harmonica." I think that was sort of the attraction, and I really did live it.

I had an old girlfriend who said, "Back in those days you didn't care about anything." And she said it with such admiration.

I'm kind of a lunatic. I'm a much more sociable lunatic now, but back then my lunacy made me sociable. There was a point when that sociable lunacy became more of a mania, in which I literally couldn't drive past a fast-food place without ordering something.

If I have a drug of choice, it's probably McDonald's. You have to bear in mind that this is one of the addictions your parents and grandparents teach you to enjoy, so you associate it with very fun times in your life. In my family every Sunday we would all go to McDonald's, and it was a big treat we'd all look forward to. McDonald's has this culinary expertise of infusing meat and sugar at every point. It's the sauce on the McRib or the sweet-and-sour sauce with the McNuggets or, the most famous example, the special sauce on the Big Mac. It's just a lot of sugar on everything, and they slather it very close to or on some meat. It's an artistic achievement really. They talk about the bliss factor in Doritos, but McDonald's discovered this years ago.

I would say that by the mid-nineties I turned this into a thing. Everyone else said, "It's just fast food. I don't eat fast food anymore." So I became a champion of fast food. Back then I might smoke pot occasionally, but I was not drinking at all. Really the only thing I would do to mindlessly destroy myself and feel this euphoric rush was go to McDonald's or Burger King or Taco Bell and eat a big meal. Wendy's would suffice, I guess, but it had those baked potatoes, which countered the whole point of fast food. They had actual pieces of broccoli, and that's just wrong.

One time I went to a McDonald's drive-thru and then right to a Burger King drive-thru to combine the two, and that made me really ill. Somehow the grease in each restaurant counteracts the other and creates a deadly poison, much like the Japanese blowfish. So do not cross your fast foods. Just a tip there, kids.

I would see a McDonald's and would get scared—"Can I drive past this thing? Maybe I'll just have a cheeseburger"—and the concept that

I couldn't drive past one was really crazy. I'd drive by one, and to reward myself later I'd go to McDonald's.

So I'd eat the food, and for about ten to twenty minutes I would feel this euphoric rush of flavor, which is the meat and sugar and the association of all the other times I had this feeling. Then about a half hour later I would feel sick, and maybe three hours later I would want more McDonald's.

It was part of a daily staple—twice a day some days. It wasn't that way all the time because there was room service, but many, many times it was.

Back then I could eat a dozen donuts by myself, which is horrifying. Who does that? Although a lot of people do that who shouldn't, at the time I was proud of that, like it was an accomplishment, which is even kind of scarier still.

I remember we were sitting in a van somewhere, and I was eating a donut. Brendan said, "John, that's just a fat pill." But I knew how to expertly use the guilt he felt in saying that to me—I could turn it around and get to eat the donut. That's what I was great at. I knew about people, and really, all I wanted was the donut.

During this time I moved to the fast-food capital per square mile in the entire country, which was Quakertown, Pennsylvania. I like to say that was an accident, but I also like to say magic is just being super-observant. I think on some guttural, subliminal level, my nose just knew I should live there.

You can start to feel it in the wind—"Wait a minute, there's an Arby's coming." I developed a skill, and when I'm eating a lot of fast food, I can still do it; I can tell by the grease in the air what kind of fast food it is, and I'm uncanny. It's like I feel it on my skin. I can tell you when there's a Burger King within half mile of me.

Even today, if I'm not careful, I can eat at McDonald's every day. I have to tell myself there will be another McDonald's up the road. To this day I look at any time I pass up McDonald's as one in my column because I'll always wind up eating at McDonald's.

Always look for the McRib if you can. I know it's made out of yoga mats, but it's the best damn yoga mat you ever had. What it's taught me is that you can literally put the right kind of barbeque sauce and onions and pickles on a yoga mat, and I will eat it.

Here's what I won't do. I'll eat good things, but I won't pretend that the green drink I have to take in order to live is somehow better than McDonald's, because it's not. It's healthier than McDonald's, it's better for me than McDonald's, but to say some leafy thing is going to replace meat and sugar is insane.

I've always said that the purpose of life is ice cream. You should try and consume as much ice cream as you physically can. Now, if you go to an ice cream factory and eat a metric ton of ice cream in a month, you won't live very long. But if you eat as much ice cream as you can while staying healthy enough to support the digestive system needed to eat that ice cream, then you're gonna get a metric ton in. My rule is you gotta drink the green drink to eat the fun stuff.

But back then, there were no green drinks unless they were Shamrock Shakes.

16

ODE TO
THE LATE-NIGHT SPONGE

The advantage we had with *Letterman* and, later, Stern is that we were fans first. When people were getting on Letterman, particularly during those first few years at NBC, they might have thought of it as just another booking—"I'm used to being on Carson and now I'm learning this new show." But to us Letterman and Stern were our Carson. I think there was this evolution in which I got Letterman's humor more than most people who were getting on that show, and I think most people in my generation did.

He once sent me a note congratulating us on our first gold record, and I have it framed on my wall. I really felt he was rooting for us. I think he felt we were something new, and we felt he was something new, and I wanted to be a comedian, so his show was really important to me.

The first time we were on, in early 1991, they made it very clear that only Chan and I could play. I remember Brendan and Bobby really objected to it—"We're a band and we only go on as a band." But Chan and I were like, "We see your point, but we really should just take any offer they give. But it really does suck." Chan and I weren't overplaying our hand, but we thought, "Let's do what they've asked us to do and then try to get the whole band on the show that way." Our manager agreed, and I'll never forget, Chan and I quietly left the room and then started dancing around and high fiving.

All of my *Letterman* prep work really paid off, though. It was really my kind of humor, and being on that show felt natural to me. I knew how sometimes they would cut to Biff Henderson to watch his reaction for comedic effect. In fact, everyone on Letterman's staff knew they might be on the show if they were on the set and had a stupid expression on their face. When I first went on, I sat in with the band as well, and while I was listening to Paul, I was trying to pay attention to the conversation, trying to have a stupid face ready to go. And because I was a weird-looking guy with crazy hair and knew how to mug for the camera, they cut to me a few times. And getting a laugh from just having a silly look on my face was my favorite moment on that show, more so than doing the song.

I nearly ended up in a Miloš Forman movie because of that first appearance. Miloš saw me on that show and shortly afterward called our management to say, "We want to hire John to star in a move. It's about an American sumo wrestler who wants to become a full-blooded sumo wrestler and compete in the sacred Japanese competition." I agonized for weeks: *Do I want to be in a movie in a giant diaper? Is that who am I? Have I worked that hard at music to be in a movie wearing a diaper?* And there's something about being performer and you say, "Of course, that's what music is for, to dress up in a diaper and parade around in a diaper and wrestle other guys in diapers. That's a great honor." And then I began to think about the money; anything at that time would have seemed like a lot.

Miloš wanted me to come in to audition. So I went into the place and there was some other fat guy coming out, looking all nervous. I don't think anybody was very excited about this movie—"Oh my God, I'm trying out for a movie to be in a diaper." I walked in there, and Miloš was very nice to me and asked me to read some lines. They hadn't sent me any sides to read in advance, and I'm terrible reader—to read something naturally off the page was the worst thing for me. So I had the shittiest audition ever, and he said, "Thank you." I left. That was the last I ever heard of the movie. I found out later it was never made because the Japanese Sumo Association didn't approve of the script.

I was on *Letterman* twenty times. Each time I watched the show afterward, and it became a torture test of, *Will they cut to me?* One time I had a conversation with Dave, and they bleeped out the word tracheotomy. He said to me, "How do you play the harmonica so fast—do you play two at a time?" I said, 'No, you need a tracheotomy for that," and when it aired, they bleeped out "tracheotomy." I couldn't figure out why. My best theories are that they wanted it to sound dirty or thought I was saying something worse.

I always had a special relationship with the show, at least in my mind, because of my initial connection from high school. In 1983 or 1984 my friend Tom Brown took me to Rockefeller Center and we got tickets to see *Letterman*. Then we waited outside afterward to meet Dave, and he gave us an autographed picture and sent us a *Late Night with David Letterman* sponge. I couldn't believe that a person on TV actually existed. And the sponge was something I saw on TV every night; the sponge was famous to me. It would be thin when he gave it you, but after you added water, it would swell into a proper sponge. Eventually, I think ten years later, I finally did wet it to make a full-size sponge, and that was the beginning of its end—it started pilling and falling apart.

I also got an autograph from Steve Jordan, who was in the *Late Night with David Letterman* band because he played with the Blues Brothers. Then I saw Paul, and my first question for him was, "How come you weren't in the *Blues Brothers* move?" Paul was in the Blues Brothers band, and once you've done that, you could do no wrong in my eyes, but I never understood why he wasn't in the movie. So Paul explained to me that he was committed to *Gilda Live!* on Broadway, which is why Murphy Dunne is in the film. It's too bad he wasn't able to be in the film, because over the years I've heard Dan Aykroyd talk about that blues bar he had with John Belushi, and Paul was very much part of that scene.

If I had a real book or fake book, it was the Blues Brothers movie that led me to all this other music. I made cassette tapes of those songs and learned them religiously. Through his work with the Blues

Brothers on *Saturday Night Live* and on tour, Paul was part of reawakening the old blues music, and for me that was a great way to get into the Stax sound. I was an ignorant kid in the suburbs and had no desire to learn the Stax history. I just thought, *Wow, that really sounds good—it's that* Saturday Night Live *sound.* I was proudly ignorant. It was terrible and wonderful. If I had homework to learn about Stax, I wouldn't have done it, but because it was on TV, that was my world. It allowed me to treat it with the reverence needed for me to get good at it. I really think it would have fucked me if I knew about things. That's why Arnie Lawrence called us the Dummies because our ignorance was bliss.

And when I made my final appearance on the *Letterman* show during its last weeks, after I played some riff, Paul leaned over and said, "Arnie Lawrence would be proud." I thought that was pretty cool.

Actually the second time I met Paul after the time I got an autograph outside Rockefeller Center was through the New School. We had a field trip to a studio where we got to watch a session and meet Paul. He introduced himself and said, "Hi, I'm . . . Paul."

Then the third time was a few years later when I was on the show. He had heard that Bill Graham was managing us and was very deferential. For me it was mark of coming up in the word, how Paul Shaffer reacted to us.

Over the years, when I was on *Letterman*, Paul would usually give me a call earlier in the week. Then on the night of the show I'd have about forty minutes before the show, if that, to work out the songs we were going to do, and the band had already done their homework (the real homework was that they were so generally prepared and such solid musicians that it was pretty easy for them; they would decide songs on the fly quite often). The way Paul worked with me as an improvising musician was to say, "I'll cue you, you blow for a while, and we'll throw it back to a melody, the head. Then just keep your eye on me, and we'll stop when the commercial comes in." Bernie Worrell was in his band for a while, but he had to leave because he wouldn't stop for the commercial breaks; he would keep on playing.

The whole time I was on *Letterman* Paul would be telling me stuff in my ear—"We're going to do 'Low Rider' next in the key of G—be ready." Or, 'We're doing to do this Animals tune," and he'd name it.

I'd say, "I don't know how that goes," and he'd sing me the melody because I am not an encyclopedia and he knew how to handle that.

When Blues Traveler got bumped the first time, I was sitting in with Paul's band, so I didn't know about it. He was the one who told me, "We ran out of time; you're getting bumped. You can't play because we're mean, horrible people." But I felt like it was all part of a rich tradition; it felt like a great show-business moment—"I'm being bumped, how professional."

What's ironic about being bumped is that we were bumped for Bill Murray—that was the first time we ever met Bill Murray—and the cool part is we were all in first class, flying out to play *Letterman*, and he got bumped out of first class because we took all of the first-class seats. So it was kind of a mutual bumping.

In 1993 Paul hired me for his *World's Most Dangerous Party* record. He later played on *four*, he did something on "Stand" and he's in our "Hook" video. On the *Party* record I did a session with Dana Carvey and Mike Myers. The two of them were trying to talk to me, and I kept forgetting to respond to them because I was used to just looking at them on TV—"Oh, you're talking to *me*." You forget that. It's not like you're an imbecile; it's more like you're hypnotized.

Another important thing I have to say about *Letterman*, though, is that one of the first times I did it Julia Roberts walked out and kissed me square on the lips. It was like she had a thing she wanted to do, and then she sat down to talk to Dave. It was so surreal, I couldn't believe it. I knew I was on TV, so I was respectful, but the whole time my lips were tingling. I remember thinking, *Wow, the sexiest woman alive just kissed me full on the lips.* And that woman's got some lips.

In January 2015 I was playing in a brewery in Taos, New Mexico, with Scott Rednor's band, Brothers Keeper, and I'm not much of a beer drinker, so I mentioned that I'd like someone to get me something other than a beer. And this woman wearing glasses kept coming up throughout the night to bring me vodka. When I thanked her I realized it was Julia Roberts. She had her glasses on and was dolled up, but she was regular dolled up—she didn't have her TV hair on. She had her regular going-out–to-have-fun hair. At one point I told her, "I loved it when you kissed me on *David Letterman* in front of America." She said "I can't believe you remember that!" At first Jordan, my then girlfriend, now wife, was a little jealous, but then she realized who it was, and her friend said, "If she makes $20 million per film and her husband's there, I don't think you can get jealous."

Speaking of January, Letterman always liked the studio really cold. Your average air conditioner gets to 55 degrees if you really crank it but he put in a special air conditioner to get it to 45 degrees because he figured that, with the lights, that kept it below 60. It's true, and I always found his stage quite refreshing. It's eccentric, but I could see the methods.

Another rule was that when Dave walked through the halls coming to or from the show, nobody was to be in the hallway: "Everyone must be out of the hallway—band, cast, crew, leave the hallway to Dave." He probably didn't want to talk to anybody while he was getting pumped for the show, and that's part of it, but I think he was also something of a nervous wreck.

One time I left a CD in the dressing room and Gina went back to get it. Everything was locked down, and she was trapped in the hall when he was coming back from the show. She tried to make herself really tiny, but apparently she didn't make herself tiny enough because Dave muttered, "Who the hell are you?" as he walked by. Gina was destroyed. She felt like she'd done something horrible. I think Dave just never wanted anyone to see him in this state because he was afraid of what he would say to people. It made me identify with him in a weird way because we're all a little crazy, and as long as you know you're crazy and set up precautions, I say be as crazy as you want.

On my final show I had one mission: to thank him for thirty years of comedy and for starting our career and then to get the hell out of his way. It felt like senior year of high school when you know graduation is coming. Everybody on the show was walking around saying, "We're going to miss you," and "Thanks." I think they had been doing that for the last three months. I looked out the window at the remains of Roseland across the street, which really drove home the point that an era was ending for me. It also reminded me of J. R. R. Tolkien—the elves were leaving these shores. It's no longer the era when late-night TV holds the same kind of sway.

It was a little bittersweet, but I came in with a mission to observe. I just wanted to see it one more time and wear that terrible earpiece while Paul and the band are talking and deciding which song to play while I'm trying to watch the show.

One of the songs we played was "But Anyway," the first song we did on *Letterman*. Paul went back to a harmony that was a little wrong, and I told him. So he asked, "Oh, I fucked it up the first time?" And I said, "Yeah, you did." He got a kick out of that and said, "So I'll fuck it up again?" And I said, "Yeah, for old time's sake."

Whenever I'd do *Letterman*, after the show I'd go out the stage door, and there would be fans there who wanted me to sign stuff. One time I was out there and holding up Tony Danza's limo because I was signing so much stuff. And he was probably trying to get to another show to promote his thing—his book or his TV show or whatever—and to him that's not where he normally met his audience, but for me that's always where they were, wherever the hell they are.

So he came up to me and asked, "What are you, lonely?" And that has been ringing in my ears ever since.

We really busted our asses to get to *Letterman* that final time. It was his last month, so we had to take whatever he gave us, which was right after we booked a gig in Kentucky two days before and a gig in Vegas the very next day at three in the afternoon. So doing the taping meant I would have to fly on no sleep to Vegas. It was a really annoying day the next day, but what spurred me on and made me feel better about doing it was the excitement I heard from people and the messages I received on Facebook and Twitter. The people who supported us were so excited about us being on *Letterman*, and that made it a more worthwhile enterprise. Because historically we'd never get a bump in sales when we'd go on Lettermen, and sometimes we'd grouse a bit because with TV, you always want more than they're willing to give you, and they always want to give you less than you want. But it always excited our fan base, and that just reminded me that the reason we were there was the right reason to be there—we're lucky to have somebody to do it for, to have people boostering us on.

So to answer Tony Danza's question: "It's good to have an audience to write autographs for. So yeah, I guess I am a little lonely." And the question, Tony, is: "Why aren't you?"

17

WE WILL BREAK YOU

People say, "You were smart to wait until your fourth record to get huge." Yeah, that was our plan. Actually we were happy to be able to make a fourth record. All along the way we weren't sure whether we were going to get a chance to make another. Our attitude was, "Thank God A&M wants to keep doing this." After each record we had ideas about what we could do with the next one.

If it didn't happen, though, we still had this fully flourishing business. We always looked at it as two businesses: the record business and the touring business, and you use one to feed the other. Hopefully they feed each other. That's really what happened, and that's been our biggest success. The reason people buy the records is that they saw us and we reminded them that we're still out there, and the reason they hire us is that they like the records.

The albums certainly helped us tour, but when the albums weren't out, we could still tour. And that's kind of the way we've found it the whole time, with a slight interruption by a successful album in 1995.

Before we got there, though, our third record saw these two worlds come a bit closer together. Our sound guys began pressuring us for a chance to produce—"We think we can do better." Dave Swanson, our monitor guy, was a hot engineer at Greene Street Studios, and our front-of-house guy, Rich Vink, had theories on mixing everything. So we told A&M, "Okay, we tried it your way two times. We want to go with our guys." They responded, "Okay, we'll give you enough rope. We hope you don't hang yourselves." And that's when I had the motorcycle accident. As it turned out, I think Dave and Rich did a pretty good job, because the albums before and after *four* are my two favorites (although I will acknowledge that because *four* became so successful, it's hard to see it; it's hard to have perspective).

But what A&M also said was "We'll let your guys produce if we can find you guys to mix." They found Steve Thompson and Michael Barbiero, who wound up producing *four*. That's how we met them. I think the record company knew what they were doing—"Let's introduce them to the guys we want to produce their next album." Thompson and Barbiero certainly understood that as professionals: "Our job is to get you comfortable so we can do the next album."

I love the songs we wrote for *Save His Soul*, but some of them were too long. In mixing the album, Thompson and Barbiero instantly showed us some of what we were missing, and we were finally ready to utilize their experience for *four*.

Our relationship with A&M did progress a bit with the third album. They had given us money to keep us going after my bike wreck, and we appreciated the faith in what we were doing. They even let us make a video for "Conquer Me," although I defy anyone to remember that video—I can't remember that video.

I can remember the video we made for "Defense and Desire." It was shot at Nightingale's, directed by Dave Dobkin, who has gone on to direct such films as *Shanghai Knights*, *Wedding Crashers*, and *The Judge*. He's the one who put us in touch with Lorene Scafaria, who wrote and directed *The Meddler*, in which we appear as ourselves, performing on a boat at a lesbian wedding—the cast includes Susan Sarandon, Michael McKean, and J. K. Simmons, who won the Oscar for *Whiplash*.

I think they believed in us and were trying to find a way to promote us, but part of it was that they just didn't quite understand us. We had to win over their departments.

Just like with the previous records, they set out a singles strategy with us, explaining how they would release a second and maybe even a third. Then they gave maybe a month to see what the first single could do before the whole thing was kiboshed. We had our live following, though, and when they sent us into the alternative department, the people there said, "You guys are doing it. We have no advice to give you." So we couldn't even catch a break at alternative.

But things changed with *four*.

Michael Barbiero and Steve Thompson were amazing producers, and their enthusiasm was on a whole different level from anyone we'd met. They were the first outside producers who really seemed to get us. Rather than, "I need to save this weird, backward band," they were like, "Wow, these guys have a sound—let's go after it. There is something here." *four* was the first album where the producers related to us like we were the artists. By getting Thompson and Barbiero, we were getting actual producers who were not resting on their laurels; they were doing things now. They had worked with Metallica, Tesla, and Guns N' Roses, so it was a much more aggressive posture.

On *four* Thompson and Barbiero confronted me about songwriting, and that to me became the first time we made a professional album. If you get lucky, that's a moment you might have on your first record, but you have to prove yourself before people will even say you're good enough that they want to fuck with you on this. I was getting somewhere, but I needed help. That was the biggest songwriting education I had yet received because they wouldn't settle for pretty good, and they pushed me on that. And from that point on, once you learn that discipline, you can't ignore it. You notice that you can say the same thing in a simpler way, and the simplicity of it makes a more impactful statement. "Whoop, I think it's right there" is nowhere near as good as "Whoop, there it is." I love that as my example. But what really motivated me was that I would see the results almost immediately.

We were at the point where we loved playing music but wondered why our albums didn't sound like what we heard on the radio. They introduced us to the things that are true about songs, like repetitive choruses that people can sing over and over again—don't go the Bob Dylan road, where it's long and drawn out. And songs should be about three and half minutes on a record because a record is to show people the idea of the song, and then you go play it live however you want.

"Price to Pay" originally had a few more verses, and Thompson and Barbiero knew how to say, "Look, if you pull this away, you're still getting to your story. You have nice images that you're painting here, but remember, you're trying to paint a story." So I looked at my images, and what I found was that the ones I trimmed away really weren't that important—and that has happened almost every time since. I find that I can take the good stuff from verse two and the good stuff from verse three and make one verse. I really wasn't doing that before Thompson and Barbiero.

I wrote "Run-Around" as a slow, sad dirge. When I sang it for Felicia, she cried, and that was the desired effect. It was sort of a sad song, and they heard us rehearsing it and told Brendan to put in a backbeat to it make it faster. Suddenly it was a peppy song almost instantly, and we all knew, "Wow, that's different." It was like in *That Thing You Do!*, where suddenly you put a backbeat to something and the song takes on a new life. If we tried to sell "Run-Around" the way I originally wanted it, which was this sort of sad, touching song, it wouldn't have gone very far. Thompson and Barbeiro caught that.

Everybody at A&M was freaking about "Run-Around," so we decided this was our moment to take a stand. After three previous albums, where they had broken their promise to go two singles deep, we figured we could finally make them commit to it this time. When we went into our meeting about *four* they wanted "Run-Around," and our mission was to force them to wait and do another single before they could get to the single they wanted.

I walked into the meeting dressed in a bathrobe and Buffalo Bill–fringe gloves and carrying a saber. I plopped my saber on the table, pulled a Diet Coke from my pocket, and said, "Let's talk." I was trying to take a note from Vinnie "The Chin" Gigante. After the meeting, I told this to the label president, Al Cafaro, who referred to the mob boss as if they were good friends. He told everyone, "Hey, he was doing Vinnie."

That was during my performance-piece era. I remember in my first interview with MTV I was holding a teddy bear at knifepoint like he was a hostage throughout the entire interview. I never explained why I was holding a teddy bear at knifepoint, and I was always proud of that. I wanted people to make up their own minds. You have to let art speak for itself.

We sat at the table, and everyone else was on the side of J. B. Brenner, the radio guy. He wanted "Run-Around." But we argued the case: "Why can't we have the single you want released after Christmas, and we do this other single, 'Hook'? Let's work 'Hook' first, and then if you really believe in our record, then you can go two deep." Slowly but surely we won our argument.

But along with that, we had to do all this ass kissing. One thing we had to do was play for all the A&M people at some private party at a bar. I remember Al Cafaro, came up to me, grabbed me by both sides of my head, and said, "John, I promise you, we will break you." I remember wondering, *Does he mean break us or break us?*

But there seemed to be something different in his tone. That was when we saw how you could really make things happen back then if you were a record company. It was weird. Doors were opening that we never thought possible.

We were told to go to Z100 in New York and play for the DJs. They brought us into a little room, all the DJs came in, they put out this little plate of ziti that they ate, not us, and we played only for them. At the time we didn't know why we were doing this, but it was because they knew that the next day, after they put us into heavy rotation, everything was going to be different—"We are about to put you on this vast apparatus in which you will be exalted and never take our calls, but before we do that, kiss the ring." Bear in mind, *we* didn't know this. I had just put my Labrador retriever to sleep and went into a meeting. But we kissed it because that's what the label told us to do, and that had never happened before. But we really had no grasp until the machine was turned on and we saw the results. Needless to say, we still don't call those radio people.

From the nineties perspective, when they decided to push you, it was just a matter of them deciding to do it. They could tell an audience which songs they should like by saturating them. Now, the song would have to be good enough not to annoy people, but basically I think there was something to the infrastructure they created: we're going to put enough standees in windows so there's a percentage we can guarantee will buy this. We know how to capitalize on that percentage, we know how to keep your disc in a store, should we decide to do that, and we know how to go to radio stations and say, "You like bands on A&M? Well, if you want Soundgarden, you gotta play Blues Traveler."

"Run-Around" was put into heavy rotation in early 1995. We didn't play any live dates until February 15, when we went down to open for Hootie and the Blowfish in Atlanta, and that was when we realized that the buzz had started to catch. We were playing our set, and people liked us, but then when we played "Run-Around," it was like a Beatles concert. Something was definitely different. It was as if somebody had gone around and paid everybody a hundred bucks to scream at that song. Were they aware of the excitement difference? They liked our music, but when we played the radio-backed one, the one that Mike and Steve had said would be a hit, the applied science of making a single, of making a song catchy, was suddenly not theoretical anymore. It was direct proof. It took us about a year from conceiving the album, writing it, and then finding out the results.

Suddenly we were told to do a tour of radio shows for little or no money, but we'd be glad we did it. By that summer we were making so much stupid money and we were working so hard that we didn't even get to appreciate it, really.

I do recall one moment, very early on, when the album was just starting to go but we hadn't quite felt it yet. Brendan and I were walking through Times Square and saw that this new restaurant was opening, the Official All-Star Café. There was a red carpet there, and Brendan said, "We have a song on the radio—we should try walking on the red carpet and see if that works." Everyone else was dressed up, and we were wearing our street clothes, but I loved that it was Brendan's idea, so I said, "I'm game if you are."

So we tried, and sure enough, everyone let us through, with no credentials or anything. We did a circuit, we were on E! Entertainment Television—"And here's Blues Traveler!"—and it totally worked. Shaquille O'Neal was there and all sorts of people along with free food at a time when free food was a big deal. So immediately Brendan and I got on the phone to Bobby and Chan: "Get your asses down here right now!"

John McEnroe was there, and he had a band. The finest moment was when, in between his sets, John McEnroe was sitting in a chair, grumbling to himself—"Man, I screwed that up"—just like he was in a tennis match. I had always wanted to sit next to John McEnroe in that situation and say, "Look, you did okay, you did fine. There was nothing wrong with it. You'll bounce back." And I got to do that, as I happened to be somebody that he kind of had to listen to because I knew what I was talking about—it was music. Eventually Blues Traveler backed up John McEnroe, so we basically infiltrated and then took over that party.

That was a strange time. I had people try to climb into my car when I was driving. When I would order in a pizza, the delivery guys didn't want cash tips—I had to give them harmonicas. One time I ran out and someone said, "Can I just have some stuff?" So I gave him some stuff. When I would go the supermarket, kids would talk to me, and I would have them help me put my groceries in the car.

Things became a little confusing for our fans as well. Some of them who had been around since the beginning were really put off by these new kids who treated us any like any other pop band, waiting for the two songs they knew, bored by everything else. These new fans would create such manic energy for those two songs that it would almost balance out their apathy for the other stuff. We had hoped older fans would help educate the younger fans—I had seen that happen with Phish—but it was more like two factions who could never reach détente.

One really satisfying thing happened during this time, though. That very first Blues Traveler record went gold around the same time that *four* did. It took the time for all those other records to steadily, incrementally sell, and then when *four* went gold because A&M decided it would and the system green-lit it, *Blues Traveler* went gold at the same time. We had two gold records, and that was a really fun moment because we did one the official way and one the real way.

Something else took place years later, after Bobby had passed away. He had contributed "The Mountains Win Again" to *four*. It's his lone solo songwriting credit on any of our albums.

"Mountains Win" was about a girl he loved dearly, and he had gone through this thing with her, and her first love was snowboarding. He came back and said, "I've got this song." He would rarely write all the music to everything—he would usually write great sections—but this one had all the words and all the music. I was ready to critique him because that was my job, but it was all great.

Actually the thing that sticks out in my head was the line, "It looks like rain again." I told him he didn't need the word again because he already had rain, which rhymed with pain. But he said, "No, it's rain again," and that was important to him. So we compromised, and on the first verse I would let the rhyme fall on rain and the rest of the time I'd do it the way he wanted.

I think "Mountains Win" really should have been a single. We made a case for it, but we were starting to wane after milking "Hook" and "Run-Around." Years later it got used in a Busch commercial. I thought that was awesome, although it had taken some time before the rest of the band was willing to allow our music to be used in ads, much less beer ads for some reason. I don't know why, but apparently beer ads are the devil. It never made sense to me that some ads are okay but *beer ads are the worst.*

I was a whore from day one, but everyone else was much more dubious. Shortly after Bobby died, Chan, Brendan and I were talking with our manager, who said, "Mitsubishi has an offer for you. If you let them play the fast part of 'Hook,' they'll give you a hundred grand." I was all for it, but my trusty partners said, "You know, Led Zeppelin never made a car commercial," and they stuck with it. I was so frustrated because I wrote the song, but my partners did not want to take the money. So for the next five years I got to see the fast part of the Barenaked Ladies' "One Week" in that exact commercial in which people were sitting in a car having fun. We went back to them with a no, and they realized, "Oh, 'Hook' lifts right out, and you can put 'Chickity China the Chinese chicken' right in there." Nothing bad was happening, it wasn't cheesy—the radio was playing. There was zero harm to the Barenaked Ladies.

I've never let them hear the end of it, and I want this in print that I was right and they were wrong. Wrong, Brendan, wrong. When that happened, I vowed that for the rest of his days, I would haunt Brendan and get my hundred grand's worth of torment. Finally, last year he did admit he was wrong but added, "To be fair, it would have been twenty-five grand." And that's true, but goddamn it.

Oh, and the capper? Right after we made the decision, Led Zeppelin came out with a Cadillac commercial.

18

DROPPING SOME MSG

As New York musicians who grew up in New Jersey, we always lived in the shadow of Madison Square Garden. We never imagined that we'd have the opportunity to play there. No, we imagined it, but that goal seemed very distant from reality. But as my conquest maps and road fantasies seemed to remind me, we were never too tethered to reality anyhow.

Our first opportunity to play MSG came through the Spin Doctors. They were at the peak of their popularity with *Pocket Full of Kryptonite* when they asked us to join forces on a show at the illustrious venue. More specifically, they asked us to open a show for them at the illustrious venue. It wasn't that bad an offer, and they couldn't understand why we wouldn't do it.

As I mentioned, it was weird watching them get huge because they were our little brothers. We had it set in our minds that they would always open for us. They had different ideas, though. I can remember, before their record hit, when I came to see them at a gig, they each pulled out an article they had saved that described them as "Blues Traveler's favorite opening band." They had saved it with a purpose, and if I were them, I would have also saved it with a purpose.

But MSG was a hill we wanted to assault on our own.

On New Year's Eve 1995 Phish had *their* first shot at it. Our show that night was at Roseland Ballroom, which was about twenty blocks away, so before we went on I decided to go down there and check it out. I can remember they were in the middle of some jam and Page was looking up into the endless ceiling that is Madison Square Garden. I desperately wanted to get into the damn room, but in just watching them play, any sense of competition kind of left me.

We finally had our chance one year later, on December 31, 1996.

There was some added stress, though, because they kept telling us right up until the show that we'd only sold six thousand tickets. We were having some shitty gigs around then too, so we thought we were heading into doom. But it turned out that when they were doing their calculations, they had somehow forgotten about all these other tickets, and we walked into a sell-out.

Our heads didn't get too big, though. There was this kindly looking old elevator operator in the uniform of a doorman with the epaulets and the bright orange hat. I could tell he'd been there since the thirties or forties, maybe even the twenties, because he looked like he was ninety years old. He'd clearly shrunken with age, and it looked like this had been his entire life's work. I could picture him as a teenager helping Louis Armstrong onto an elevator. *Man*, I thought, *he must have seen it all.* So I said to him, "You look like you've been here forever. I bet you've seen Sinatra, the Ali-Frazier fight, the Rolling Stones how many times. What's your favorite act you've seen?" And he looked up at me with those cute little eyes and said, "Get the fuck on the elevator." And that was Madison Square Garden.

A day earlier, while we were rehearsing for our big masterpiece, ten-years-in-the-making Madison Square Garden show, we met a guy at the rehearsal studio who had this human fly musical suit made of synthesizer parts. If you touched one part, it would say, "Blues, blues, blues" and another would say, "Traveler, traveler." None of us really thought much of this guy, but Bobby was such a sweetheart and so enamored of the technology that he had this guy open for us at Madison Square Garden. He asked him on all of our behalf, and then Bobby looked at us with such childlike eyes, we couldn't say no. The guy promised it would be a five-minute introduction, but on the night of the show he wound up doing a forty-five-minute set. We could hear the roar we'd been waiting ten years for, and then everyone slowly became bored and started mumbling amongst themselves. So I turned to Bobby: "You gave away our ten-years-in-the-making standing ovation in Madison Square Garden."

I want to say it was one of those days, but you only have *one* of those days.

My other memory of that night was the death of the black cat.

This was our New Year's Eve ritual, which began in 1990. It largely had to do with Dave Graham and was sort of a tribute to his father, Bill Graham, who would dress as Father Time for the Grateful Dead every year. One night while Dave and I were inebriated and I realized there were nine years left before the next century, we hit upon the idea that one of the black cat's lives would be sacrificed each year, with Dave on stage in costume dressed as the black cat.

The first year at Roseland Ballroom he came out as a black cat, and all we could afford to do was throw him off stage. The next year, in New York City at the Paramount, we had a little more budget, and I mean a *little* more, so curiosity killed the cat. There was a question mark on a garbage can, and he when he opened it up, it exploded and he died. Then in 1992 I'd just had my accident, so we put the cat on a motorcycle and he crashed into some barrels.

By 1996 we had finally made it to Madison Square Garden, so our lighting guy, Paul Morrill, convinced us to let him do something special. Back when we had a band van and a crew van, he constantly asked whether he could ride with us because he thought he was an artist. He would also try to hit us up for a lighting fee *and* a designer fee during an era when we barely had any money to pay the crew, so of course we put him in the crew van—it was great.

What Paul pitched us was that because we finally were in Madison Square Garden, what better thing than King Kong? The cat would be dressed in a gorilla suit and would climb the Empire State Building far over the skyline of Manhattan, where cartoon planes (as promised by Paul) would fly out of the sky through some holographic projection, swoop around, and buzz him like flies, causing him to fall off at precisely the stroke of midnight.

By the way, none of our strokes of midnight were ever on time. There was never an exact counter, although, to her credit, Gina really tried her best without access to a Navy clock. So in the era before iPhones, if you came to one of our New Year's Eve shows, you were at the mercy of the house. That was keeping in the tradition of "Leave the time to us when you enter these hallowed halls." The New Year's countdown could take place at 11:58 or, far more likely, at 12:03, but what was really important was that you came in on December 31 of one year and you left on January 1 of the next year. Who really cares when it's midnight? We're focusing on a point together, drinking champagne, and hugging.

Really, that's how a New Year's party goes, unless you're lucky enough to have the TV on where they show the ball dropping. A timely ball dropping is always good, but sooner or later all balls will drop, and remember, where the ball lands is where you want to keep your hands.

Another problem we had with the New Year's Eves was keeping track of the black cat's lives. The first few years we started counting down, but somewhere in the middle Gina started counting up. We knew that the whole thing would end at 1999 but there was some confusion about what to put on the shirts. What does number six mean? The sixth time we're doing it or that there are six lives left? I don't think anybody else noticed, but one year I lost it: "Oh my god, the whole thing's ruined! Now nobody knows how many we've done and how many are left." That was as annoying as it gets.

But back to Paul Morrill's New Year's Eve spectacular. The day of the show arrived, and instead of a backdrop of Manhattan, all he could get was a backdrop of Pittsburgh, which was troubling. Also, his Empire State Building looked exactly like the Williamsburgh Bank Tower in Brooklyn. Then, instead of an actual gorilla suit, he had a gorilla chest and six pack, which he would duct tape to Dave's belly. The airplanes, which he touted as cartoon projections independently flying through the air, were just light gels that would spin around where the lights were hung, so in no way would they be bothering the cat. You would just hear airplane noises.

When the moment arrived and the black cat climbed up to fight these imaginary airplanes, his gorilla chest and six-pack fell off, so it looked like he'd been vivisected. And then when he fell, no one lowered him. He just hung there like in a bad school play. So being the improviser he is, Dave Graham just died right there, hanging.

So the grand effect at midnight on New Year's Eve with Blues Traveler at Madison Square Garden 1996 was that the King Kong cat climbed up the Williamsburgh Tower in downtown Pittsburgh, had a hallucination, vivisected himself, and died a mysterious midair lynching.

It cost us forty grand, and, oddly enough, I believe that was the last year Paul Morrill worked for us.

Another thing we learned was that all the production costs were part of an exquisitely perfected art form in how to bleed you. The unions, for instance, were required to be there for anything that had to do with shipping and transportation, and they earned three times their normal rate if you went into overtime on New Year's. So we ended up doing four times the work and earned a little less than what we'd normally make.

But in spite of all that, we wanted back in.

However, you needed to reserve Madison Square Garden more than a year ahead of time. In the summer of 1997 it turned out that Phish was already sitting on MSG for December 31, 1998. They had what's known as "first hold," and we had decided to challenge them for it, in which case we put up half the money—it was over a half-million bucks—and they had forty-eight hours to respond, when they had to put all their money down. Finding a time when they were without resources or the ability to respond in that forty-eight hours would require chicanery.

We picked a time when we strategically found out they were in Scotland. This was in the nineties, so there weren't really good phones in Scotland, especially at 2 a.m., which we decided was the perfect time to start the clock ticking. The only person representing Phish in America was their accountant, and he was the guy we had to stop, so I sent a stripper every fifteen minutes for eight hours to his office to read from Sammy Davis Jr.'s *Yes I Can*. His office was destroyed because every fifteen minutes someone would show up, take her clothes off, and start reading this bizarre book, and he wanted to know who was sending these strippers. It never occurred to him that it would be us; every stripper took a stripper's oath (I wasn't aware of one, but I was grateful) not to divulge who had sent her on this errand of evil.

But to his credit, Phish's manager, John Paluska, using a borrowed telephone and wire transfers, made it in the last two hours. We held him off for forty-six hours, but with two hours to go, he transferred nearly $600,000 to Madison Square Garden, and I had to just give him a salute. I gave him everything I had, and he survived it. I don't even know if he knows this, but I'm ready to share that info now.

19

INTIMACY WITH STRANGERS
IN THE DARK

I think it's important for songs to be autobiographical—you need to write about what you know. Charlie Parker said if you don't live it, it won't come out of your horn, and I've taken that to heart. And if you don't mean what you're saying, then there's no way for your song to connect with other people.

When a comedian tells a joke, there has to be truth in it so someone else says, "I know exactly what you're talking about." There's no shortcut to that, and the only way I can see to solve that is by writing autobiographical songs. I stopped telling people what songs are about a long time ago because if they loved the song, it would be about something in their mind, so that would ruin it.

The best example is the song "Just Wait," which I wrote about my friend Felicia going off to Yale. She wasn't making friends there yet, and I wanted to cheer her up. Over the years I've had a number of people tell me that the song helped prevent them from killing themselves. One guy, this big guy, came on our bus in Philly, sat down, and started crying. He told us he had been planning to kill himself; he'd gotten a big brick of heroin and was going to do heroin until he died. Then "Just Wait" came on, and he saw a picture of his family and decided to give his life over to Jesus. He became a born-again Christian and never touched heroin again.

He told us this, and as soon as he said, "give my life over to Jesus," all of us on the bus were like, "Uh-oh, this isn't going to go down well." But it really did. You don't know what to do about something that big, and you don't want to tell him, "It's about my friend going to college and worrying about making friends." You learn to shut the hell up because what you originally wrote the song about is not the important thing. Just like tone, truth harmonizes. If you write something that's true to you, it doesn't matter what the song's about; the important aspects of it resonate in somebody else's experience, and then the song is more about what they want it to be about. "Just Wait," if you look at the lyrics, is much heavier when you apply it to that guy's story than mine.

Whenever someone says, "You saved my life," I respond, "I'm really appreciative that you're alive, and I'm really honored that you used our song as a totem. But *you* saved your life. I don't want to take the credit for all the work you did, and I want to remind you that *you* did that." We were a part of it, but *they* did the work.

Plus, that really is something I need to deflect, because where do I go from there? "You're welcome. I *did* save your life, and now your life belongs to *me*! Give me the contents of your wallet, and prepare yourself to follow my little plan . . . "

Where does that lead, and where does that end? The next thing you knew you've got ATF outside the gate to your compound, and all of your wives are twelve years old. The fact is that that guy did save his own life. He heard my song, and I'm very honored and grateful that there was something in that song that connected to him, and that's all I was trying to do. He did all the rest, and that's what I try to remind people. And if I do that, then maybe I won't go to hell. I look at it as my karma credit card. I get away with a lot of shit, and if I do good things, it kind of equals out. At least that's what I'm hoping.

I've always likened what I do to being a stripper because it's intimacy with strangers in the dark. The only thing you've got to remember is to not replace that with actual love. As long as you know that, it's a very acceptable and healthy form of expression, but you just can't look at it as true intimacy.

You make a trade. When you say to the entire world, "Look at me, look at me, look at me" and then you wonder why the whole world is looking at you, you don't quite have the same rights because you kind of started it. I sort of invited myself into a dialogue with people who don't know me.

So I try to be supportive, listen to what people have to say, and 99.99 percent of the time it's something really nice and positive. Although there was one night at a mafia bar in Rhode Island when I invited a drunken fan into our dressing room, and within a few minutes he started insulting the women and spilling drinks on people, so I asked him to leave. Then, as I was escorting him out the door, he took a swing at me and knocked my hat askew. Before I knew what happened, my left hand went up and I broke his nose. I was torn, thinking I had failed because handling drunks is part of my job, but another part of me said, "Wow, it's nice to know I can do that if I have to."

But as long as people aren't belligerent, I don't mind having a conversation with them. Provided they don't slap me on the back. I hate back slappers.

Picture, if you will, this hearty, jovial man, and I always picture him having eaten a large barbeque or drinking a lot of beer, more of a soccer dad, who walks up behind you, filled with love and admiration—they only want to say something nice. But the way they express themselves is by taking their flat open hand and whapping you like you're the biggest smash return in a tennis match, and saying, "Hey man, I love you!" or "How's it going, brother?" with a familiarity that's just so inappropriate to being slapped hard on the back.

You haven't even seen this person; you're just minding your own business and get a big loud slap on your back and a stinging red mark. So your first instinct is you want to turn around and take a swing at whoever just did that to you. But as you turn, you realize that this person meant well, that they're not being a dick. They feel like they know you, and they're genuinely happy to meet you.

The thing you've got to remember when you're dealing with a fan is that they might say something you hear over and over again, but for them it might be the only time they'll get to say it. I try to be there in the moment because it's really about the person who's having the moment with you. They want to tell you something amazing about you that you don't want to believe, and what you're really aware of is that this person believes it, so fuck what you believe. And you let the person tell it because it's really important to them that they had the courage to tell you, and this is their moment. They don't do this every day; they don't go around looking for musicians to tell this to.

So I try to be supportive and listen to what they have to say. It's almost always something really nice and positive.

But what happens is that you don't feel any different—what makes it matter is that they've imbued it with power: *you* haven't, but *they* have. So what you're really getting is their reaction to what you do, and that gives you the actual wisdom they claim you have. So it's a really weird symbiosis, and I think that really is the key. You just stand there and let that moment happen and try to pay attention, if you can, to what they're saying. That gets harder when it's a bunch of people, but you've got to remember the objective. You've got to remember the point, which is that what you did really affected somebody.

And people have affected me as well. There have been a couple of people I've been too scared to talk to, like Michael Jordan. I've been the worst kind of fan, a back tapper who wouldn't leave him alone. He was meeting kids in wheelchairs and was surrounded by cameras, and I was behind him—*tap tap tap* . . . "Mr. Jordan?" . . . *tap tap tap.* Then finally he turned around and barked, "What?" I said meekly, "I'm a big fan," handed him a harmonica, and just slinked away. I still don't know if he knew who I was.

Another one is Jack Nicholson. There was a Bulls connection there too, because I became friends with Dennis Rodman. One time Dennis was sitting at a table after a game with Jack, and I just couldn't bring myself to join them. I sat somewhere else, and instead, my road manager, Dave Precheur, went up to him and said, "I just wanted to say hello" and Jack responded, "Well, hello." And I don't even have that. That's my Jack Nicholson story—talking about how Jack Nicholson said two words to my friend because I was too chicken-shit to approach him myself.

A better Michael Jordan interaction came when I was a fan in the crowd at the United Center in Chicago. It was game six of the 1997 finals against the Utah Jazz. The Bulls were down in the fourth quarter, and it looked like they might lose. Jordan walked onto the court after a timeout, and I sort of fearfully cheered and lifted my beer. Then he looked at me and gave me this wink, like, "We got this." It was a priceless moment that any fan could have.

The Bulls really blew me away, especially during the second three-peat era. Michael Jordan had gotten me into basketball. It was like watching Babe Ruth play baseball—you didn't have to be a baseball fan; you'd just get it. Jordan had some moves like that fadeaway, where it was almost like slow motion, the whole place slowed down, and even the other team said, "Wow." I was hooked immediately.

I began buying box seats and going to games whenever I could. My accountant couldn't understand why I'd want to buy a gun or a cool sword, but Bulls tickets made sense to him, even though it was about a thousand bucks a throw. Dennis Rodman eventually invited me to sit in his box, which made it a lot cheaper.

Then I started hanging out with him. There was always a late-night party, especially with Dennis and the team winning a lot. There were a lot of celebrations. I wouldn't hang out with Jordan, but I'd see Steve Kerr, Scottie Pippin, and, eventually, Phil Jackson toward the end, but he was not a big hanger-outer.

I can remember one of the first times when we went looking for Dennis, he was at some place called the Crobar in Chicago. I walked in with Bobby, and the first thing we saw was a man dancing naked in a cage. It turned out that Dennis and the Bulls were hanging out around the corner, but Bobby and I saw the naked cage dancer, looked at each other, and started to leave when this hot blond girl said, "Hey, you're that guy from Blues Traveler. Come dance." And we started making out while we were dancing to electronica music. I remember thinking it would be cool if I made out with her for the entire length of the song, but I didn't realize this was a techno tune, so it really lasted a good long while. Bobby was blown away because he was the guy who was used to taking over the room. Some days I do have my moments.

I never assume that anybody knows who I am. Whenever I think everybody knows me, that's when nobody does. And whenever I think they aren't paying attention to what I'm doing, that's when they know precisely what I do. So I've got to be ready for both.

I can never tell which way it's going to be. As soon as I try to get out of a ticket, I get a ticket hard, and as soon as an older cop who does not look like my demographic pulls me over, he's like, "Hey, I saw you on VH1" and he lets me speed. It's nothing I can ever count on.

When I meet someone I'll usually say. "Hi, I'm John." And if they say, "Of course, I know who you are," I'll respond, "Well, I still reserve the right to introduce myself."

And if there's one lesson in the racket of being famous or being pseudo-famous, it's this: never ask the question, "Do you know who I am?" Because if you have to ask, the odds are they don't.

Sometimes the whole thing gets kind of murky when someone maybe, sort of, kinda recognizes me.

I remember we did a NORML benefit at the Playboy Mansion. Bill Maher was there hosting. I think I've been there three times, and every time I get into that grotto, the same experience happens: there are no women in there and a bunch of dudes are asking, "Are they any women in here?" It's like Christmas when you walk in, and then your heart sinks when you see a bunch of dudes who look just like you: schlubby, horny, and overeager. And then right behind you comes another guy who looks like a kid on Christmas morning until he gets the same look on his face when he sees you, and that makes you realize, "Wow, I'm a pervy slob too." Then he feels like a pervy slob when the next guy comes in behind him. It's like this endless machinery of agony.

Then I walked into one of the little houses. It had a pool table, and I was pretty sure Thora Birch was playing pool. I thought she recognized me, but we both weren't sure. I was like, "I think that's Thora Birch," and she was like, "I think that's that Blues Traveler dude," which is what most people call me. But we were both too nervous to talk to each other. I love awkward moments like that.

My favorite one is when Lukas Haas came to say hi to me and I got it into my head that he was Henry Thomas. I was like, "No way, man! I loved you in *ET*! My friend was obsessed with that movie when it came out. We hid in the bathroom and saw it like fifteen times." And he was so sweet about it (but crushed too) that he pretended to be Henry Thomas the entire night. He wrote me a note later explaining, "My name is Lukas Haas. I was in the movie *Witness*, among other things." Of course, I loved *Witness* too, and I loved Lukas Haas in it (and when I read that I recognized him in retrospect instantly). He just didn't want to let me down, so he pretended to be Henry Thomas for me. And I asked him questions about working with Spielberg and what Drew Barrymore was like, and he would give me polite, positive answers. But the sweet little note he wrote me was just awesome. I got to see him later and make it up to him. It was one of the nicest things anyone's ever done for me.

The question, of course, is would Henry Thomas pretend to be Lukas Haas for me?

Hollywood is strange. I'm glad I don't live there because I would be such a whore about it, like, "Oh my god, Christopher Walken said 'Hi' to me again!"

I met Christopher Walken after Alicia Silverstone invited me to her *Excess Baggage* premiere. I was newly famous and didn't quite understand how that worked, so I figured I'd just try it out. I'd read some article that said Alicia Silverstone was starting her own production company and thought that was cool, considering how young she was, so I wrote her a fan letter and she invited me to the premiere.

I was smitten with her, but she had a boyfriend—now her husband, Chris. She called me Johnny and I loved it. When Chris called me Johnny, I loved it considerably less. She'd always try to go motherly on me and feed me vegan food options—which were pretty good—and then she'd show me movies of animals being slaughtered and I'd say, "Yes, but they're delicious." Even so, she ended up being a really cool friend.

But at her premiere I met Christopher Walken and went up to him and said, "I'm your biggest fan." He said, "Of course you are."

Ken Ober, who was a friend and appeared in our best-known videos, was once doing something for the LA Lakers and walked by Magic Johnson's locker. He saw Magic Johnson's Mennen Speed Stick and stole it. I asked him why he did it, and he showed me that there was a single armpit hair on the Mennen Speed Stick. He built a little shrine around it.

Ken was a good guy, one of the sweetest people. He was exactly like me because even though he got into this line of work, he still cared about things much as fans do. We're all fans at some point, and he proved it by building a shrine to Magic Johnson's armpit hair. It was the high point of his apartment, and I kind of loved that about him.

But what I still need to come to grips with is that the people I see on TV or the movies are people who are weird, just like me, and sometimes they get to do special things just like me.

Bill Murray wants to be funny; it's what he does. It's not all he does—he's not the Terminator—he just has the instinct to be that guy I look up to. And there's an instinct in me that has no social acknowledgment, where I could put my hand in Bill Murray's food and yell, "I touched Bill Murray's food!" (No, Bill, I haven't ever touched your food.)

Whenever I meet famous people, I tend to become this bumbling fan. I treat them the way Chris Farley did in that *Saturday Night Live* skit in which he hosted the "Chris Farley Show" and mostly just said to his guests stuff like, "Remember when you were in *Ghostbusters* and you said, 'Let's show this prehistoric bitch how we do things downtown . . .'"

I think it really helps when people come up to me and treat me the way I fear I treat Bill Murray. People come up to me, and I can't tell a joke without them going way too nuts over it or they won't let me tell a joke because everything I'm saying is super-profound. I run into people like that, and it really kind of helps because what I realize is that whenever you're doing something that's seen by a lot of people, it takes on an impact, especially if they saw me when they were young. That's what I'm running into now, and that's something Bill goes through on a much larger scale.

Michael J. Fox was hosting this benefit a couple of years ago, and he had me attend to be part of the band. Elvis Costello was there, for God sakes, and I could barely talk to him, but I held my own, I think. But it was still that kind of thing in which I went home and giggled to myself that I was normal around Elvis Costello—so you can't quite count that as normal. I was close but I wasn't quite there.

Roger Daltrey came all the way from England to this benefit, and Michael J. Fox forgot to call him up on stage. I was talking to Roger, and he suddenly said, "Wait, that's the song I'm on." So Roger Daltrey showed up to get blown off by Michael J. Fox.

Michael J. Fox had all these musicians around him because he likes to play his guitar, and as the first song was being counted off, right there in the first note he cried out, "Wait! I'm not plugged in!" And then the song started.

Those two moments made it really awesome because I was watching someone I'd seen on television since I was teenager, and television is super-important to me. It's the parent that never has a job. Yet here he was, so intimidated by the musicians around him, myself included, that the guy I'm intimidated by was not even plugged in.

The older I get, the more I've gotten used to people putting me in that position where I can be Fonzie for a second and hit the jukebox and make it go on. That's a fun opportunity, and I don't want to waste that. It also helps me see the position that someone like Bill Murray is in.

Ultimately it's about empathy, and that goes two ways. There's empathy for someone who looks up to you for stuff that isn't quite true, and there's empathy for someone you're looking up to that isn't quite true, and everyone wants to come through for whomever's looking up to them. But they also want a chance to interact as a normal human, so there's a schism of your empathy. There's an empathic schism, and it's weird and takes time getting used to.

One of my favorite comedians is Larry Miller, and in getting to do *Politically Incorrect with Bill Maher*, one of the fun things was that I got to be on with Larry Miller. I couldn't stop freaking out about Larry Miller; it was almost unnatural. Why is this rock-and-roll-band guy freaking out about this balding comedian? He's wasn't cool or trendy, but when you get into stuff, you care about people who are good at it. I always wanted to be a comedian, and he's just funny.

Adam Carolla is a really cool guy, and the great thing about him is that he makes you feel normal. He remembers very well that he's a carpenter. He feels like a carpenter, and the fact that he's famous is very weird to him. He's one of the few people I can really identify with in that way because he can express it. I think everybody's who's famous feels weird that they're famous, but you get used to it because it's what you've got to do; you learn how to handle it. But I think Adam feels first and foremost like a carpenter—and he loves cars, so maybe he feels like a gearhead too.

Me, I'm a musician. And in the discipline I come from, musicians aren't necessarily known. They do the backup stuff; they're the backup band. That's the musician I prepared myself to be when I was growing up. I was trying to be famous, don't me wrong, and to the extent that I've succeeded, I'm happy with it. But the discipline I came from requires that you're there first and foremost to play music.

That's why things sometimes get weird when people want to debate me about whether I'm me or not.

I was once getting my driver's license, and there was this girl with her mom. She whispered in her mom's ear, and I could tell what was going on. The mother said, "I'm sorry you just look so much like him." I responded, "No, I am him." But they didn't believe me, so then I wanted to prove I am who I said I am. Except I was in line at the registry of motor vehicles and had just turned in my license, so this was the one place I had no ID. Finally I got my license and held it up: "See! I am me!" And the mother said, "Oh I don't care." That was quite a zigzag of my ego.

Something I noticed after I moved to Quakertown, Pennsylvania, in 1996 was that people would ask, "Why would *he* live here?" speaking in the third person about me. And I wanted to answer, *Why? Was there a chemical spill?*

There also were people who would demand proof: "No, you're not John Popper. Prove you are." That took me a while to work out in my head. You want to show them a license, but then you realize they're making you do stuff. So where I came down was, "No, I don't need to prove to you that I'm me." I agree with the mom—I really don't care either.

I like working the job and saying, "Look at me! Look at me!" But I also don't want to get upset to the point where I'm obnoxious.

A few years ago a girl was convinced I was in Sister Hazel, and there was no talking her out of it. I actually got my Wiki page out on my phone with a picture of me to show her, and she said, "No, it's okay. I just like your band." And I said, "I know, but I'm in another band."

I'll admit, though, in a moment of weakness I was trying to impress a girl I was with.

Originally I had said, "Thanks," but the girl I was with asked me, "Why don't you tell her who you are?" I said, "Because it doesn't matter. Why don't I be in Sister Hazel for her?" When in doubt, be Hootie. I've been called Hootie plenty of times. Let them call you Hootie. If it makes them happy that you're Hootie, just be Hootie.

Then this other girl started to feel slightly annoyed that I wouldn't admit I was in Sister Hazel. So I said to the girl I was with, "See, this is why I don't do this." And then I said to the first girl, "I *am* in Sister Hazel. I'm sorry—it's just this girl I'm with thinks I'm in Blues Traveler."

That's something Lukas Haas taught me. If it's really important to you that I'm Hootie or that I'm in Sister Hazel, then I am. I'm in Marcy Playground too. As long as you're happy about it.

20

JOHNNY APPLEHARP

My fate is to walk the Earth, distributing harmonicas.

They call me Johnny Appleharp.

During the band's first trip to Europe in 1991 I was hell-bent on placing one at the place where Attila the Hun was toppled at the Battle of Chalons in France. I'm a big history buff, and I was reaching back through history to kiss Attila the Hun's ass. So I had to go to a museum to try to locate it. I was trying to speak French, and it was a spinach field and our van got stuck in the mud.

I've left a harmonica at the Acropolis, Napoleon's tomb, Louis Armstrong Park, Buddy Holly's grave, Graceland, and the Pyramids of Giza. I also placed one where I thought Julius Caesar was stabbed on the Senate steps. It turned out it was configured differently back then, so I may have buried it where Caesar walked by or went to the bathroom. But, hey, it's the spirit that counts.

I placed one in Heroes' Square in Budapest because that was my homeland and I had returned. I vowed never to return until I had a gig in Budapest. It was a very tiny gig, and the band who was supposed to go on before us conveniently got amnesia and forgot to show up until after we played so they could headline, which is a pretty cool trick, actually. But I was able to place a harmonica where Arpad, the Magyar chieftain, led his little tribe to Budapest and founded Hungary.

I've given them to plenty of actual living, breathing people as well. When I lived in Quakertown, Pennsylvania, I kept a basket of harmonicas by the front door to give out as tips or when people would come by and ask for them, which was a bit strange.

I gave one to Bill Clinton. I gave one to George W. Bush, but his people took it away. You're not allowed to assault the president with a harmonica—apparently I could have stabbed him with it or something.

I gave one to Mitt Romney at one of the Republican conventions. He was the governor of Massachusetts at the time, and none of us knew who he was. He said, "Here's a band who feels the way I do about the Second Amendment," and then he looked back and winked at us.

I gave one to Quentin Tarantino, who used it in his acceptance speech at the MTV Movie Awards for *Pulp Fiction*.

I handed a few to Dave Letterman throughout our career, and he'd play them during commercial breaks. I gave one to Jay Leno. I gave one to Jon Stewart on the *Daily Show*, and he said I was made of harmonicas.

The only man who ever refused to take one from me was Hugh Hefner. I went to the Playboy Mansion, and there was Hef in his robe. I said, "I'm a big fan, so I'd like to give you something," and he told me, "Oh no, I don't take those." I was kind of stunned because no one ever denied a harp from me before—admittedly, that is a little conceited of me—who the hell am I? But the question I had was, who else has offered him a harmonica so that he made this a policy? Did they used to hand them out like candy in the sixties, but he had bad trip with one? Was he going cold turkey after snorting them or ingesting them in some way? And then being Hugh Hefner, you assume he was thinking about doing something dirty with one. Maybe what he was thinking was that it could give him hepatitis or a communicable disease?

Speaking of *Playboy*, I once had Anna Nicole Smith come up to me after a show. This was the first time I had met her, and I noticed her right away because she was six feet tall and gorgeous in this enormous leopard-print-leotard thing. As she walked up to me, I was trying to intellectualize, *I don't succumb to the charms of women like that. I'm above that.* This is what you tell yourself when you're a fat guy. *There's more to me than just looks.* I guess somebody had given her a harmonica I'd signed, and she came up to me, pulled it out of her cleavage, and asked, "Could you sign this for me again—I put it in my boobs and it sweated off." And I looked at her with everything rational I could muster and said, "Okay!" and greedily signed it like a little boy. We got to hang out a few times afterward, but Anna Nicole completely floored me, and that was a good use of a harmonica.

I gave one to Steve Lemme from the Broken Lizard comedy troupe, who was really excited about it until he found out that I also gave one to Kevin Heffernan from Broken Lizard. Then he was crushed. Apparently he thought he was the only person who ever received a harmonica from me.

I was in LA doing Broken Lizard's podcast when they were telling this story, and then this drunk guy came up. He didn't know us; he just started bothering us because we were doing *something.* So to get rid of him I said, "How would you like a shiny new harmonica?" So I gave him one, and that just destroyed Steve again.

When you throw a harp out in the crowd, that's its own little adventure. It all started because when harmonicas break, you can't fix them. Howard Levy, who, in my opinion, is the best player out there on the blues harp, treats the reeds on his Golden Melodies and tries to repair them, but I find that once you bend a reed, you fatigue it to the point at which it will never be the same again.

So we came up with this ritual where we'd throw old ones into the crowd. It's like when baseball players have got a bum ball and toss it into the stands. So by and large we throw them out there and then I sign them.

Here's the bitch. Harmonicas started out at $10, and I signed a 50 percent endorsement deal, which is the best Hohner offers. You could be Moses and they would not let you have any more than a 50 percent deal. Eventually it crept up in price to $40, and I was Hohner's biggest customer by far. I would buy more harmonicas than any six music stores in the country. They had my picture all over the thing, so I was paying twice as much money for the privilege of a package with my face on it. The picture should have just had me giving myself the finger.

The band pays for them collectively. So there have been nights when the sound is bad and I'll throw a whole set into the crowd to punish us—there's 250 bucks we'll never see again.

This seems like a fine moment for some brief harmonica theory, with the core idea being that, as a diatonic player, I require twelve harps for a complete set. Diatonics are built around chords. When you exhale on a C diatonic harp, you get a C major chord; when you inhale, you get a G dominant chord (which is major except the seventh is flattened). What we blues-style players tend to do is use that G dominant as the root chord and the C as the "four" chord in relation to the tonic (G), so we'll use a C harp to play songs in the key of G. This simple transposition makes a lot of traditional blues riffing possible and is commonly referred to as crossharp. The diatonic approach requires twelve different harps, one for each key. Every bluesy harp player and folk player from Little Walter to Dan Aykroyd to Bob Dylan or Neil Young uses them.

Chromatic harmonicas are almost an entirely different instrument. They are not built around chords but rather to have all notes available as would any other instrument. They achieve this with a button that shifts air access to equivalently arranged scales a semitone higher to cover all the notes in the Western twelve-tone scale. Concert greats like Toots Thielemans and Stevie Wonder favor this instrument, as do most symphonic harmonica players (it's probably best not to incorporate the slang term "harp" when discussing symphonies, as they have actual harps in their arsenals). Robert Bonfiglio comes to mind, or Blackie Schackner, who made every harmonica sound you've heard in the *Brady Bunch* or late-sixties television.

Anyhow, after decades of buying harmonicas only to literally throw them away, things finally changed in 2015 when Fender debuted my signature model. They got together with the Seydel company from Germany, which is an even older harmonica company than Hohner. They're laminated brass, and I've been able to give my input all along the way because I'm the one who's going to be using them. It's pretty cool. Rather than paying 50 percent, I actually get a small percentage of sales. These harmonicas aren't disposable; they have replaceable reeds, which come with a low price, but it feels free compared to what I was used to.

Now we may have to get cheaper ones to throw to the crowd, and I'll feel like an asshole doing that because what was fun was the purity of taking the harmonica I just played and then tossing them out there.

There are perils to throwing harmonicas from the stage. You have to gently lob them because they can be like throwing knives. They have weight in the center, so if you really whip them, there's a spinning aspect.

In the old days we used to really try to get distance. And I don't have good arm, so I'd give them to Chan. He could hit the end of a really large room any day of the week. But that changed one night in Boston when someone threw it back at him and hit him in the mouth. He left the stage bleeding, and I really milked it: "Maybe we can get him back out to play," and eventually he did.

After that we tried to throw them lightly, but invariably we'll hit somebody in the head. That happens from time to time when they take a weird hop. Lawyers get involved.

One night at a H.O.R.D.E. concert this guy ran up to me with this bloody impression of a harmonica on his forehead and said, "Dude, I totally caught one of your harmonicas!" He clearly hadn't seen a mirror, so I signed that thing right away before he could sue us.

The hot girl in the crowd wants one—I don't know what she's saying, but she seems really smart—but invariably that girl is terrible at fielding the harmonica. Everyone around her snatches it, so it takes four or five to get to her. And if you finally get it to the hot girl, she immediately gives it to her boyfriend—"Look at what I got you, honey!"

What I hate is when one lands right in the hands of the little hippie chick and then two frat guys' elbows pincer her on each side of her head. Then she gets that blank look in her eyes and goes down into the crowd. The scary part is that you never see her again. There isn't a bloody stain; you don't see a body—she's just gone. Where does she go? I never know where they go. I'm worried they'll be waiting for me on the other side.

These days people are bringing their kids to shows, and you'll get one to that little kid and then you'll see his sister, all horrified: "He got one!" So then you throw her one. Then you realize this is a Mormon family and they've got fifteen kids, so the parents give you a look like,

I'm sorry. We know we have too many children, but you have to equip us. I actually feel sorry for them because I'm giving them harmonicas in different keys, so the ride home sounds like traffic in Hong Kong. Have fun with that, Mom and Dad.

As I've said for nearly thirty years now, the harmonica is like life: sometimes you suck and sometimes you blow.

1 That's me at an early age, jockeying for what provisions were left in a family of seven.

2 I'm much more charming after I've had a meal. Just look at that face! I must have been three or four.

3 Here's my family when I was age six. I know this because my brother Tom was practicing juggling me on his feet, and I went flying into the piano and busted my arm.

   I don't know what to say about what everyone was wearing. It was the 70s. We were a noisy, dysfunctional, and happy family. Dad's taking the picture. That's mom in the middle.

4 Here we all are at my parents' 32nd anniversary during my senior year of high school. Note my Hungarian grandmother Nagymama not long before her passing, and this time my dad is in the picture. Also my little brother Ted (in the straw hat and 1920s garb) held the exact pose throughout the roll of photos and convinced his friends at school that this was a life-size cardboard cutout of him because he couldn't attend. In my family, everyone's a character.

5 Here's I am at age eight. That's the piano that busted my wing behind me. Being distantly related to a famous cellist, the family thought I should start with that instrument once I showed any musical aptitude. It did not go well.

6 Here I am at good ol' Stamford Catholic High School before we moved. It was talent night, and I believe I was doing my Chuck Mangione impression, which was a very horrible trumpet noise. My partner in crime is Tom Brown, who is now a director out in San Francisco.

7

8

9

10

7 That's me at Princeton High School on my trusty moped. I would later wreck it but not nearly as bad as the motorcycle wreck that would follow. The lunchbox in the front is where I would keep my harmonicas. Yes, it came to New York with me, and so did that vest. Wasn't I a character? Do you like that gas mask on the front of the moped? That was just for style.

8 Brendan Hill and myself at Princeton High School circa 1983–84. We were just starting what was then known as Blues Band. Oh, what dreams we had!

9 I am with Chan Kinchla in 1987 at the PHS spring fling on the steps of our beloved high school. At this point I was just out of high school and coming back on weekends to continue this garage band that was about to become Blues Traveler.

10 Here we were playing later that summer. At that point we were called Blues Traveler. You can even see our fellow PHS alumnus and road manager Dave Precheur skulking by the amps. There's my mom's minivan in the background.

11

12   13

11 Blues Traveler back in Princeton for the weekend playing Princeton University's Communiversity. Chan's dad was a professor at Princeton, and he always got us in for gigs there. That patch of clover in the background is where we sat at break time; Bobby found a four-leaf clover, and then I found a five-leaf clover. According to the popular 80s movie *Manhattan Project*, the odds of finding one of those is near impossible. Maybe they're treating their clover with uranium.

12 Blues Traveler in New York City. Here we are with Dave Precheur on the stage of Mondo Perso. We would start at Nightingale's and wind up at Wetlands before leaving NYC, but Mondo Perso and Mondo Cane represented the bridge and tunnel places that constituted the bulk of our livelihood. It was at Mondo Perso where Bill Graham came to see and officially sign us. Again, look at what we're all wearing. A band needs to dress its lead singer, that's all I'm saying.

13 One of the very first musicians I met in New York was Joan Osborne. She would introduce me to Jono Manson and the entire Nightingale's scene.

14

15

16

14 Spin Doctors and Blues Traveler backstage at Wetlands when it was new, before all the stickers and graffiti. Anyone in this picture or who knew us back then need only look at who is sitting with whom and can guess at the intrigues afoot. That's the kind of scene it was and why I love this picture so much.

15 Chris Gross (or sometimes Chris Barron) was a best friend from high school long before he was ever lead singer of the Spin Doctors. He came with us to New York and did great things. Here we are on one of those nights in the thick of things while Bobby has our back. Wetlands and lower Manhattan were Bobby's kingdom as much as anyone's.

16 Here we are having just signed with Bill Graham and his son David, playing for Dave's twenty-first birthday party, which Bill had booked for him on a chartered boat around Manhattan. At this point we were beginning to feel like we ran this town. This was Blues Traveler at the height of its nexus of power and innocence. We felt like we could do anything and often did. It's hard to describe the feeling of only being twenty-two and feeling like you've conquered New York. By the way, I wore that harp belt everywhere. It scared the shit out of people on subways.

17

18

19

20

17 Here we are backstage in the dressing room at Wetlands. The woman with Brendan is his present wife, Sophie, and there's our trusty manager Dave Graham, who along with his father Bill would kick some doors open for us.

18 Bill Graham and me, on what would be the last day I saw him alive, which was also the day we all learned that Miles Davis had passed away. I received a lifetime's education from Bill in the short time we worked together, and many of those lessons still apply today.

19 Here I am about a month later playing with the Grateful Dead at Bill's memorial in Golden Gate Park. It was at approximately the same spot where I had last seen Bill. It was a very emotional day for everybody.

20 Here are the freshly cast H.O.R.D.E. swords I had made for each of the bands the first year. They arrived just in time to give to Phish, who were leaving after the first leg. It took a lot of work, and sword forgers are not slaves to your schedule, trust me.

21

22

21 The very first H.O.R.D.E. tour in '92. This was the first time the like-minded bands on the Eastern Seaboard galvanized into one scene and became aware of each other.

22 Blues Traveler's first trip to Europe. I was so obsessed with seeing where Attila the Hun had taken his horde, which was somewhere in Orleans, France. Today it's some sort of spinach field with very few markings to reveal this. I think Attila would be proud to know that we got our Riot van stuck in the same mud that his ox carts must have been stuck in. Here the illustrious Blues Traveler crew tries to free said van. It was quite a day.

23

23 Bill Graham had us touring the with the Allman Brothers, starting in 1989. Here we are in '92 playing with them at Red Rocks, which at this point we'd only played once before with Widespread Panic. This was our first two-day run at Red Rocks. It was the Allman Brothers' idea that instead of competing we would flip-flop opener and closer status each day. This is perhaps the only time we had the Allmans open for us. They were incredible teachers to us and still are.

24 What happens when you try to drive a motorcycle through a blue Chevy Nova? The answer might amaze you. Here I am recuperating in Louisiana after the crash. You'll notice the harmonicas are not very far away, but it not was not a very musical time. Gina came down to take care of me, as did my mom at some points. It was the beginning of some pains that are still with me to this day.

25 Life in a wheelchair . . . the doctors kept promising that in three months the bone in my leg would heal, and I'd be walking again. The problem was the way I had broken my leg put all the weight on it, and it would not heal for almost two years and eventually required an entire hip replacement. We needed the money, and the only way for us to go on the road was to put me in a tiny van and ship me from place to place like so much cargo. Don't even get me started on what going to the bathroom was like, let alone the other creature comforts.

26 I still got to sit in with lots of cool people while in my wheelchair. Among them was a gig opening for Neil Young where I got to play with Pearl Jam. I love the look on Eddie's face. He was so cool, he walked up to me, gave me a shot of the wine he was drinking out of the bottle and said, "What's up dude, I'm Ed." We'd have had many strange experiences together. He's awesome.

27 Here's the band with producers Mike Barbiero and Steve Thompson along with Paul Shaffer presumably putting his tracks on what would be our *four* album. This was the album we made after I was out of the wheelchair. Even though I'm sitting, I had the full capability of standing at this point, although I'm not sure how. Look at how huge I'd become. And I mean physically.

24

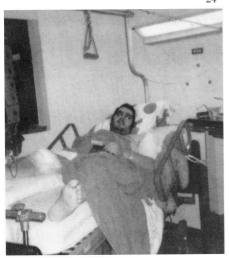

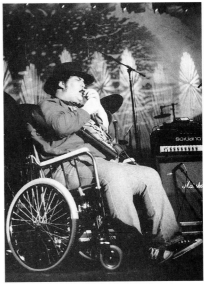

25

26

EDDIE VEDDER LEAD SINGER OF PEARL JAM STUNNED!!!! POPPER HITS A BULLSEYE ON VEDDER'S FOREHEAD!! During "Baba O'Riley" encore Popper sharpened his aim with PEARL JAM members. The stunned & confused PEARL JAM crew wrestled the psychotic harmonica player to the ground. The 2 bands shared the stage together this summer in Toronto, Canada with SOUNDGARDEN & NEIL YOUNG. Luckily razor sharp harmonicas are in vogue due to the new alternative body piercing.

27

28

29

28 Our record broke huge in late '94 and throughout '95. We were gigging nonstop and getting more attention. Bruce Willis had actually been playing with us since Wetlands, but it became a big thing for the crowd when he would show up on the road when he was doing a movie. He would ultimately wind up improvising, riffing some poetry and blowing harp on our 2008 release *North Hollywood Shootout*. But that would come way after this picture. Love that guy.

29 The years from 1995 to 2000 were quite a blur. Who knew what my next aspirations would be. . . . It was crazy time, and from what I remember quite a bit of fun.

30

31

32

30 This was the very first gig without Bobby. We were trying out Tad, and we would try out two other bass players. Of course it was weird, but we had an idea of what we were doing, and we knew this new chapter had to happen. I was just starting to get ready for the gastric bypass, so you don't see much of a difference yet, but you will in the next picture. This is one of the three rare gigs before we had our keyboard player Ben in the new lineup. Despite the nepotism, Tad clearly did the best of the three in sounding original and not like some ghost. And so began our next chapter.

31 Now you see the difference with the gastric bypass. Here we are in Bosnia. The war on terror had broken out, and we wanted to do our part. No, they wouldn't let me load the damn thing, but they did allow us to play and begin what was to be a longstanding tradition of meeting gallant military personnel and their families. That tradition continues today, and we've been able to see parts of the world most civilians don't get to see. We're very honored. Damn, I wish that M240 was loaded.

32 I've been doing radio with Adam Carolla since 1994, back when he was hosting Loveline with Dr. Drew. To this day he'll have me on and remind me of some song I've forgotten about like "Look Around." Gotta love the man for that.

33 The great thing about getting older is the company you keep, the friends you make, and sometimes the reputations you incur. I have always loved this shot. It's at a Dead gig that DJ Logic brought me to. Unbeknownst to me and on Logic's advice, we ended up stealing Bob Weir's wine, which we were required to return. Still, it was a gorgeous sunset that day at the Gorge. Logic and I had just finished making our record together, and we were just having fun.

34 I love this picture with Conan taken at Bonnaroo just after he left his show on NBC and right before embarking on his new show. He was very seriously considering just doing a live show on the road and bringing bands out with him. It was fun to see the guy open to so many possibilities.

35 Here I am in 2009 at Michael J. Fox's benefit for Parkinson's. It was an honor to be thrown into such an odd collection of musical talent. I, of course, was mugging for the camera. As was Tyler.

38

39

36, 37
   Politics makes the strangest bedfellows, and anyone who's ever been to bed with anyone knows it's the strange ones who are often the best.

38 The Duskray Troubadours was a motley band, seen here in their outlaw hideout in Chupadero, New Mexico. This band was comprised of awesome players from the old days along with some new guys from recent years, all headed up by myself and Jono Manson. Jono's the one holding the whip.

39 This was taken at SXSW right after making the Duskray Troubadours album. I don't even want to say what we got into that night, but it cost a few of C3 Management's top employees their good standing and possibly their jobs. Don't blame me, Matt, Woody, or Logic. Blame it on the bossa nova. If that's what the kids are calling it these days.

40

41

42

40 Stevie and me in rehearsals before the big show. That was an awesome night all by itself.

41 Renee Zellweger's Christmas party afterward was an awesome night all by itself, as well, even though the two events happened on the same night. Sometimes you can't have a bad day in Hollywood.

42 Blues Traveler, as it stands today, though this picture is from 2012, taken as promo for our *Suzie Cracks the Whip* album. It's been quite a journey with this lineup, and as with the other lineup, we've grown so much together.

43

45

44

43 Here I am with my then-girlfriend, now-wife Jordan, Scott Rednor, and John Michel from Brothers Keeper, doing our New Year's tour where we ran into my old friend Julia Roberts. What an awesome way to kick off 2015.

44, 45

By summer I got to congratulate Trey for playing at the Dead's fiftieth, and then finally sit in with Dave Grohl. These events were long overdue. P.S. Trey owes me some diapers.

46

47

46, 47

Jordan and I at the wedding and the day after delivering our new daughter, Eloise. It was quite a year. And then I wrote a book.

21

BANNER YEARS
(OR TOOTIE GOES SHOOTIE)

I've played the "Star-Spangled Banner" quite a few times in my career, but my two most memorable "Banners" are the one that was postponed and the one that I missed.

It all goes back to high school. I'd go to gym assemblies and play my harmonica to advertise an upcoming Blues Band gig. The first time I did it, I just walked up to the mic, played a solo and then said "Come see our band!" From that point on everyone knew who I was and I started to begin feeling famous. People would pass me in the halls and call out, "Hey, Harmonica Guy!"

Pretty soon every time there was an assembly, people would start chanting for it. It became a thing. I always had a harmonica on me—that's the great the thing about the instrument—it's so portable. I'd play, and the whole place would go crazy. The vice principal would put up with it because everybody liked it.

There was this big kid who was upset because I would play the same thing over and over again because I was a crowd pleaser. One time he yelled out, right before I started, "Do something different this time!" He was that one asshole.

So I was determined to have something up my sleeve at the next school assembly. This was when I was worshipping Jimi Hendrix. I had watched his "Star-Spangled Banner" at Woodstock so many times that I decided to work on my own "Star-Spangled Banner."

So when my moment arrived at the next assembly, I stepped up and played it. That first time it was closer to the normal kind of blues shuffle. Later on I'd learn how to feedback my amp, so I did that, and everybody was looking at me weird, like, *What the hell was that?* Then there was a murmur and I heard booing, which confused me. It turned out the vice principal was behind me, kicking me off because he recognized it was the "Star-Spangled Banner," and apparently that was disrespectful.

Over the years I would drop it in here and there, mostly in tribute to Jimi, and then finally, in August of 1992, I played it at my first Major League Baseball game. This was during the southern leg of the initial H.O.R.D.E. tour. I played it before a Baltimore Orioles day game, during the first season at their new park. What you have to keep in mind at a baseball game is that it's not rock and roll; it's baseball— what they want is more melody with no feedback in it, so you need more rudiments.

My next big "Banner" was at Woodstock '94. I had mono, but there was no way I was going to miss that gig. (I would miss Woodstock '99 because I was recovering from heart surgery.) So I came out there wearing my regrettable purple shirt (Barney again!), and I knew I was going to do my version. When I started I could hear the roar of two hundred thousand people, and that's when I got a little scared, like the ghost of Jimi Hendrix was going to get me. But the *New York Times* commented on it, and I felt fancy. When I read the critique that Hendrix's "Banner" was about the war and now it was about chops, I thought, *Yeah, that's fair.* I just knew that someone was going to play it, and because we appeared on Friday, I was the first guy able to do so.

I think Game Four of the 1996 World Series in Atlanta was the biggest one. By then I had done the Orioles and the Colorado Rockies along with some hockey games and some basketball, but when you go to the stadium for the World Series, it's crazy because it's an international event. That was probably the largest coverage of me doing it because of the television broadcast.

I was supposed to do Game One at Yankee Stadium, but George Steinbrenner bagged me for Robert Merrill and the Yankees took a twelve-to-one pasting. At the game I did do, the Yankees came from six runs behind to win—the biggest comeback in World Series history since 1929—and then they won ten straight Series games. I like to take credit for that, although I'm not sure I can.

When I hit the high note and the crowd went nuts, I left my body for a second. Later, when I heard what the TV announcer said, I knew I had hit a good one. To me it always felt like hitting a ball—do you hit it far or do you hit a grounder? And that one was out of the park.

After they bumped me I made a big enough stink with MLB that they offered me Game Four, and the Braves said it was fine with them. I was allowed to bring a friend, so I brought Col. Bruce Hampton, a big Braves fan who was putting as much mojo on the Braves as I was putting on the Yanks. That was quite a game.

Asides from the Yankees comeback, the other surprise came when I was on the pitcher's mound about to do the anthem and realized I was carrying a Glock in my fanny pack. I was used to doing gigs out on the road where the places we played could be dicey, so it was a thing I'd tuck away and never think about. This was pre-9/11, and I was licensed to carry in Georgia. They had waved me through security, and I had forgotten all about it until I was on the mound. Then I had nowhere else to put it, so I just kept it there.

After I finished the "Banner," I went to my seat and was next to Tootie from *Facts of Life* (Kim Fields) and right behind the president of Panama. I was thinking I could have assassinated the president of Panama and thrown the gun into Tootie's hands. I was imagining the stories that would run the next day—"Tootie runs amok at World Series, blames it on Blues Traveler guy, nobody believes her—Tootie Goes Shootie." How fun would that be? I mean it would be really horrible, but just for the headline.

There are places you shouldn't have guns, and I think airplanes and sporting events are two good ones, especially when you're behind a world leader. Try not to be armed when you're behind a world leader unless your job is to protect the guy. And I would like to state for the record, to all mental health officials, that I do indeed recognize my job was not to protect the president of Panama. It's very important when you're dealing with real bullets to know real things.

The next time I was really excited about performing a "Banner" was before Michael Jordan's final home game with the Chicago Bulls at Game Five of the NBA finals. I was a big Bulls fan and a friend of Dennis Rodman, who by then was allowing me to use his box seats.

Eddie Vedder was another major Bulls fan. I first met Eddie while playing with Neil Young in Ontario during the summer of 1993 back while I was still in the wheelchair. Five years later, at one of the Bulls' parties, I remember Eddie was trying to explain to me his views about the world while I was going to take a leak. There was only one toilet in the bathroom of this little club, there were no stalls or urinals, and I was standing there for a while as he wouldn't stop talking because he was so excited. I finally said to him, "I can't go while you're standing here." And he apologized, but instead of leaving, he turned his back to me and turned on the faucet. So then I felt like the guy who couldn't pee because he turned the faucet on and became the guy who couldn't pee in front of Eddie Vedder.

I was really looking forward to this "Banner" at Jordan's last home game in Chicago. The only complication was that I was in DC getting ready for the Tibetan Freedom Concert at RFK Stadium, which took place the next day. As it turned out, there was a problem with my flight. We had to land in Peoria and then I had to catch another flight to the game. Meanwhile Eddie, who was also playing at the concert, was able to get on an earlier flight. When the Bulls found out I wasn't going to make it and that Eddie was already there, they made him sing the "Star-Spangled Banner."

I finally arrived toward the end of the second quarter and was so bummed I had missed my chance. So I walked in, and Eddie Vedder came up to me, gave me the finger, and walked away. He thought I was doing some sort of diva thing. I guess because of the night we bonded in the bathroom, he felt comfortable enough to give me the finger when he thought I was pulling some prima donna shit.

Later on he apologized after he found out about my plane. We flew back to DC on the same flight, and he was trying to be incognito, with his hat pulled down over his face, while I was signing every autograph that came my way. He was probably nervous that I was going to point him out to people.

That whole incident highlighted the distinctions between him and me. I was dying to do the "Star-Spangled Banner"; he was pissed he had to do it. He was hiding from people, and I was high fiving everybody. That'll tell you who sold more records. Clearly, him.

So we made it back to DC, and a few hours after Blues Traveler performed at RFK Stadium the Bulls won the championship in Utah. But it still haunts me. What a "Banner" I would have done for Michael Jordan.

22

FOUR PLAY

The response to *four* really felt like the culmination of a decade's work.

In early January 1996 we learned that we had been nominated for a Grammy. "Run-Around" was up for Best Rock Performance by a Duo or Group with Vocal at the ceremony, which would take place on February 28, 1996, at the Shrine Auditorium in Los Angeles. A&M Records, which was also based in LA, invited us to come over the morning of the Grammys, where they laid out a new contract in which each band member received a million bucks. It was quite a start to the day.

From there we all got into our limos to head over. Brendan and I took our dates to the Grammys in one limo, and Chan and Bob took their dates in another limo. When they called our category, which was pretty early, Brendan and I had made it inside, but we didn't know where Chan and Bob were.

To my mind it didn't matter so much because we were up against Dave Matthews Band's "What Would You Say"—you'll remember, I had played on that song—which I thought was going to win. Still, as they announced the nominees, I was trying to calculate the fortitude and the logistical planning needed to run up on stage when they won to accept the Grammy with them. This was years before the soy bomb bullshit and Kanye. They were nice guys, so I figured they wouldn't punch me; all I had to do was stay away from LeRoi. They were about to announce the winner, and I was jumping up, expecting to hear, "'What Would You Say,' Dave Matthews Band," when they called out "'Run-Around,' Blues Traveler." I was in midjump and so stunned that I popped my knee. I couldn't walk on it, so I had to hop on one leg to the stage.

Meanwhile Chan and Bob were in the other limo "parking," which I took as some thinly veined metaphor for drugs. I don't know whether they were smoking it or snorting it, but they were late. They missed their entire Grammys speech. Brendan and I went up there, and I was hopping on one leg in blinding knee pain; Brendan was the only one with any reasonable composure. I was supposed to thank Howard Stern because I vowed I would, along with my teachers and all these other people. But I didn't really prepare a speech because I didn't think I was going to win. So I asked Brendan, "Who should we thank?" He answered, "I don't know—our parents?" So we thanked our parents, half the band, and then we sat down. This was when Chan and Bobby showed up—"You guys missed it! We won! We totally won!" Bobby immediately wanted to leave—"Oh fuck this!"—and he did. I think eventually Chan did too, but Brendan and I watched the rest of the show with our dates.

So it was win a million in the morning, win a Grammy at night. You work for ten years to get a day like that.

The punch line came when we were walking outside afterward, being all hot shits, and this little girl who was playing in the parking lot looked up at me and asked, "Weren't you in that movie *Tommy Boy*?" And that was awesome because it deflated me in the best way. My ego had been so puffed up. Then I tried to sing "Run-Around" for her and she said, "Nope, never heard it." And there's the reality of it.

Although *she* didn't recognize us, our profile was on the rise, which led to some really cool new opportunities.

Dolly Parton wanted me to come and record with her. Dolly didn't ask me to play harmonica either; she just wanted me to share vocals with her on a Merle Haggard tune. This was for her comeback album at the beginning of the new country music. I think she asked me because I was this rock-and-roll guy and it would represent a connection to something new. I was grateful because she still had the voice I had heard for so long, and it still melted raw steel.

I had my puppy with me, Cice, a blue heeler who was a terror back then. (I named her after a Magyar she-warrior who saved her master from the Mongol hordes.) Cice promptly trotted into Dolly's vocal booth and took a watery diarrhea shit all over the carpeting. Dolly's response was "Bless her heart." Now, how sweet was that? You can't top it. Poor Dolly, though; it wasn't the scented candle that I later learned Chris Robinson preferred.

Paul Simon was someone else from this period who only wanted me for my voice. When he made a demo of *The Capeman*, the musical he was working on for Broadway, he had me come in and play the role of the redneck. He was one of the hardest taskmasters I've ever worked for. He wasn't a dick; he just knew exactly what he wanted and would not be persuaded otherwise.

A couple of years later he had me back in again, this time to record harmonica for his album *You're the One*. That was hard too because he was the one guy who would not fall for my trick of "Let me blow all over and you can trim and use what you want." When I did that for Paul, he said, "Yeah, the problem with that is it makes more work for me later, so I'd prefer you do exactly what I'm thinking."

In defense of my approach, I really do think it can be the best way to get the most out of me. There was a time when I'd say that every harmonica solo I did was the best harmonica solo ever. Now I'm quite willing to allow someone to let me blow through something a few times, and then they can cut it and link it to another take—they always fit like Lego blocks on beat one. I can understand Paul's reaction, though. I can't say I blame him.

Still, he was asking quite a bit of me. It was some melody he heard in which I had to arpeggiate like I was a guitar; I worked for hours. Eventually I got it done, but he ended up not using it and instead he went with Howard Levy. I got Levied. If anybody was going to trump me, it would be Howard Levy. Not only can he sight read but he can also play chromatic scales, which I can't do. Eventually I figured out I would need a few harps, but it wouldn't sound smooth. Howard Levy was the right musical choice—he was the one guy who could do it. To expect that out of a harmonica is pretty insane anyway. When you've got a harmonica part that only one man in America can play, that's an ambitious harmonica part—"We need Albert Einstein to figure out this little math problem." Howard Levy's the mad scientist, so between the two of us, I'd give it to him.

Around this same time I played on a Hanson album (fifteen years later they would reciprocate on Blues Traveler's *Blow Up the Moon*). I had no problem with my solo, but trying to play this one melody for that Hanson song was like working for Paul Simon. I just couldn't play it for some reason, but Taylor could. So, oddly, I got Taylored. And you pay extra for that.

Although I no longer believed that my every harmonica solo was the best solo ever, I will say that one of my best harmonica flurries ever is on the opening credits of the *Roseanne* show. It appeared during the last season—Chan did a little guitar thing and then I did a lovely little flurry like Charlie Parker. It's just fun every now and then to turn on one of the cable channels and hear an example of a really nice burning harp solo that I did. Once you've done that and it's on national television, I think it eases the constant need to go into sessions and demand that your work can't be touched because you've just laid down the *perfect* solo.

We were obsessive *Roseanne* fans, and at the time she invited us on to her show in 1995, that was our favorite prime-time sitcom. So to get to go on the set and be in that kitchen with Roseanne and Dan Conner in Lanford, Illinois, was surreal. We played Dan's former band—my name was Stingray Wilson—and he came on stage with us for "Sweet Home Chicago." We watched that show religiously at a time when we were living hand to mouth. That show really spoke to us, and then we were in the TV.

Standing in their kitchen, which I'd seen on television so many times, was almost dreamlike. I knew consciously and rationally that I was talking to Roseanne Barr and John Goodman, but they were in costume. I had to open their refrigerator to see what was in that fridge, and sure enough, they had fake bologna. It was made of rubber and looked like real bologna. It was stunt bologna.

I started to look around after I closed the fridge, and I remember John Goodman's expression was like *He's going to blow!* I nearly had one of those sensory overloads that I hear people have when they're in a foreign land and don't quite understand what's real anymore. For a second my brain told me that maybe I actually was in Lanford, Illinois. But, of course, I wasn't. It was the stunt bologna that got me because, *If the bologna isn't real, then maybe none of this is real.* But then a voice in my head said, *Of course none of this is real. You're in Los Angeles.* The overload almost led to a conniption, but I held it together.

Roseanne was a sweetheart to me. We hit it off like lemurs and pie, and she later played an important role in helping me lose my weight, but she had a fight with John Goodman in between the scenes and yelled at somebody else on the set. She would be ashamed afterward, though. It reminded me of my actress sister, who's known to have a temper.

Before the last season she came to me and said, "I'd like you to put words to my theme song." I was so honored that during the very last scene of her entire series, when she was reminiscing like all of those episodes were part of a book, Phoebe Snow was singing my words a cappella.

A few years later I would work with John Goodman again on the set of *Blues Brothers 2000*, which came about through my friendship with Dan Aykroyd. The first time I met Dan Aykroyd was in Los Angeles in early 1995. He was there when I sat in with Steve Vai. That was quite a night because Steve Vai was in *Crossroads*, a film that also had its hold on me growing up—he duels on behalf of the devil against Ralph Macchio's character. It's a draw until the end, when Macchio plays a classical piece, Paganini's "*Caprice* No. 5." I told Steve Vai that I thought he kicked the classical dude's ass, and he laughed because he actually did both parts.

But Dan Aykroyd had been my hero for much of my life.

He was specifically powerful for me because, first of all, he's funny. *Saturday Night Live* was the beginning of my rebellion as I tried to break out of my own skin as this young kid in the suburbs. *SNL* was the first subversive thing I ever got to experience that felt like it was mine, and then, after that, *Second City TV*. That would be my religion every Saturday: *Saturday Night Live* and then *SCTV*. And then these people started making movies, so I started to feel my religion permeating the world's culture—or at least North American culture.

Beyond all that, Dan Aykroyd was the guy who got me playing the harmonica. I still wear a black hat to this day because of it—his influence is insurmountable. Our band name is a combination of the Blues Brothers and a scene from *Ghostbusters*, a film he wrote with Harold Ramis.

So this guy really affected me in a lot of ways, and meeting him was particularly sweet because he liked the way I played harmonica. A couple of months after seeing him in Los Angeles, Blues Traveler appeared at the House of Blues in New Orleans as part of the *Live from the House of Blues* series that aired on TBS. He joined us as Elwood Blues on "Rock Me Baby." Later, when we did the movie, I heard him practicing because I was playing the harmonica parts for the little kid Buster Blues (Evan Bonifant), so we had to duel, and I still can't describe the honor of hearing him sweat me.

My favorite part of *Blues Brothers 2000* was getting to play "Can't Turn You Lose" with the Blues Brothers band. You get to hear my harmonica solo, and it was the harmonica solo I had always planned if I ever got to play with the Blues Brothers band. So getting to play that with them and even getting to play the kid's harmonica parts were like a series of bucket list items, and it has a philosophical importance because technically my sound is the future of the Blues Brothers. I can take a certain pride about my place in that mythology.

I remember Dan looking at me one night. He was beaming with pride—"Look at what I helped to do"—and I felt really proud that he felt proud.

One of my less successful would-be film appearances was in *Jack Frost*. Michael Keaton played a harmonica player in Colorado in a blues band, and he was late for a gig, crashed his car, and died but came back as a snowman to watch over his family. They were going to use Blues Traveler for his band. As an enticement, I was going to play Santa Claus in this little village where the kids were running amok, whipping snowballs at me and just going crazy, so I'd say "Santa's getting angry, kids!" It was a funny scene, but there was this large, older kid who really enjoyed pelting me with ice. All the other kids were first and second graders, but he was a fifth grader, and he'd whip it in my face, and I'd get really hurt by this kid with every take. So I saved this ice ball when I figured no one was looking and tagged this kid. *Bam!*

I hit him really hard, right in the face, just before they said, "Roll 'em!" He cried out, "Nobody does that to me!" and started attacking me. People had to drag him out while I "innocently" asked, "Is he okay? I don't know what's wrong with the little guy." Strangely I didn't get in the movie. My theory is he was the son or nephew of somebody really high up in the production. So I was supposed to be in that movie, but some little fifth grader stopped me cold. But looking back, I do have to say it was still worth it to tag that little fucker in the face. Santa did get pretty angry.

While I'm on the subject of movies, in 1995 we all had an opportunity to appear in *Kingpin*, the Farrelly Brothers Amish bowling film with Woody Harrelson, Randy Quaid, and Bill Murray. I heard they really wanted to get Hootie. Although we weren't quite as famous, we *were* available. Blues Traveler performs "But Anyway" during the end credits. To this day, if someone hasn't heard of Blues Traveler, that's my best shot at getting them to know who I am: I explain that we're in that Amish bowling movie.

I also appear in the film as an announcer at a bowling tournament. According to my manager at the time, they said, "We'd really love it if you act." But according to them, my manager informed them, "He really wants to act." In December 1995 I flew to Reno to shoot my part.

My most memorable interactions were with Bill Murray. He had this loose piece of hair that was part of his wardrobe, and he really knew how to animate the thing. He could make his hairpiece spin at will, and it reminded me of the bee costumes from *Saturday Night Live*. He also instructed his assistant and me on how to build a cooler for several bottles of champagne using a trash bag and a cardboard box because he said he was going on a big drunk.

The band's scene at the end of the movie meant lip synching to "But Anyway" for an entire day, from right before sunrise until right after sunset. On the set of *Kingpin* I discovered that bit parts are the best to do in a movie because there's no responsibility on you to do anything, but you can yell "Apple box!" or call "That's lunch!" with impunity. At first they look at you all mad, but eventually they just sigh, shrug, and say, "Oh, you guys!" You're sort of extras but you're not extras; you're sort of stars but you're not stars.

That's also how I would describe our time on the road with the Rolling Stones. During the summer of 1997 we opened nine stadium shows for them. Before the very first night at Soldier Field in Chicago, they bought us a case of champagne. The first thing I did when I met Keith Richards was pull a knife on him. I showed him my cool giant knife because I heard he collected them. I also brought him some moss from my yard and put it in a Tiffany box because I heard that apparently they don't gather any. He patted me on the head.

My favorite song of theirs was "Miss You." The studio version has Sugar Blue, who happened to live in Chicago. So I innocently asked, "Is Sugar Blue going to be here? I could play with you if need help with that."

Mick said, "Great, thanks. I'll let you know."

I almost perceived a tone, and what I didn't realize was that Mick had been playing harp on that song live and fancied himself a harp player. He's actually not that bad. I'd put him a notch above enthusiast. They've been teasing him about it ever since.

There's a *Rolling Stone* article in which they discussed the possibility of my sitting in with them and Mick said, "Fuck off." He said I'm a good harp player and then added, "too good." I want to frame that article.

This was also the summer when we released *Straight on till Morning*, the follow-up to *four*, which helped usher in the end of this era. Thompson and Barbiero produced once again, and there was this feeling of tons and tons of money being thrown at it—everything magically cost twice as much because we were the world famous Blues Traveler. I predicted in *Rolling Stone* that we would sell another 7 million records and win another Grammy. The moral of that is don't ask me stuff while I'm making a record because I will think it's pure uranium—although it is still one of my two favorite Blues Traveler albums.

But when that record didn't do what *four* did in terms of sales, we felt like we'd failed the record company. We didn't appreciate then that records happen in their own little moments of time. They tried "Most Precarious" as a single because it was the most like "Run-Around," which I thought was a terrible strategy. A band like us can't go chasing after a single; we need to accidently stumble over a single. If you're the kind of musician who can work by committee with a team of writers, then you probably can figure out the Aristotelian unities that make a single. But for us that wouldn't have been honest; we were the Aristotelian unities of ourselves.

To have lightning strike at all is pretty rare, and to have it strike twice is almost unheard of. But the good part is that we gradually made a fan base, which has allowed us to plug along for decades. And that's how our career has been—a slow and steady arc in which we've created a middle class in rock and roll. When people are having great years, we do okay, and when people are having terrible years, we do okay. That's sustained us. As long as we get to make the music we want and can pay the bills, I'm happy.

Ultimately the live show has been our staple. Throughout the nineties this meant a culmination on New Year's Eve. After our Madison Square Garden show in 1996–1997 we moved out of New York. By the next year Chan was expecting his baby, and he and his wife, Serena, were living in Florida, so he had to be nearby—I think she delivered on the 24th. So on December 30 and 31 we performed at the Pompano Beach Amphitheatre. Because it was Florida, for the black cat's death we went with a *Miami Vice* drug deal gone bad. We hired some Rasta-looking Jamaicans in suits with machine gun pistols firing blanks— one guy was a practicing Rastafarian and did not believe in depicting violence, so we had to talk him into that. Amidst the carnage and bloodshed a briefcase opened and plumes of white powder flew out. We learned to play "Conga," and that was a lot of fun.

The cat's ninth life expired on December 31, 1998, in Chicago at the Aragon Ballroom. We reenacted the Chicago fire, and the cat fell from a balcony. Dave Graham, who was still portraying the cat, had to jump out of a building and fall into some boxes below. He was very excited about that.

So we made it through all nine lives of the cat and almost immediately began thinking about what we were going to do for the year 2000—maybe the cat was going to return like a phoenix rising. But that never happened because Bobby died that summer. That was the last life of the cat.

23

PRETTY ANGRY

In the spring of 1999 I recorded my *Zygote* album. *Zygote* was about me saving my own life. I was 436 pounds and had done nothing but Blues Traveler since high school. The idea was to take six months after the release in September, tour it, and then go back to Blues Traveler.

I knew that Bobby felt somewhat uneasy about this, but when I told everyone in the band what I had in mind, to his credit, Bobby stood up, looked me in the eye, and said, "I think it's the right thing to do, and I'm very happy for you." But I could also tell he was a little scared. I think he sensed the same thing: we were running out of places to go and live our lives the way we were.

What I was looking to do with that opportunity was to create something un–Blues Traveler with my friend Crugie Riccio from high school. He had this really cool punk feel on the guitar but always in weird time signatures, and I always wanted to work that angle. It was a promise to an old friend that we really have to work together—one of a few I would make over the years to follow.

It all got off to a strange start, though, even before the first session. I was trying to move into my little room in Hoboken, and Allen Woody, who I knew from the Allman Brothers and Gov't Mule, was in there, completely drunk, and wouldn't leave. He was a really sweet soul, and they were trying to get him out of the room to take him to the airport, but he was shitfaced wasted and just kept on saying my name over and over again—"John Popper . . . John Popper. We go back . . . John Popper, you sweet motherfucker . . . " He knew I was trying to get him out, and he did not want to leave. He was packed and everything, but he was just sitting in the kitchen, seriously plowed, and did not want to go. Eventually he did, and that was the last time I saw him alive. It was about a year later when he passed. He and Bobby had some of the same impulses. It was really unfortunate.

Once we got started, it was Carter Beauford who saved the album. I'll always love Brendan Hill, and I love Marcus Bleecker, who would be the drummer on the John Popper Project. But Carter is one of the best drummers in the world, hands down.

A lot of the ideas were very rough, and he made them work. I was trying to use dynamics, where sometimes I would use the drums and sometimes I wouldn't, and he was great at just floating there. It was a lot of rough ideas, and I was improvising, but time and again Carter would save the song by making a smooth transition. I had an Irish whistle solo and needed some sort of pocket in the back to try all this artistic shit. I had guitar solos over a 1980 beat-box effect that would work if there were a real drummer making it all breathe, but I needed an amazing drummer so that it wouldn't sound derivative of a thousand other things. He pulled it all out of his pocket as if it were nothing.

It seemed like Carter was in the middle of six other gigs. He was always on his cell phone. They were taking a picture of us for the album, and he was still on his phone, so I told him I wanted him to stay on his phone for the picture because that's how I wanted to remember him for the album.

Just before I recorded *Zygote*, as I was getting ready to begin my long-awaited, therapeutic treat for myself, I also received a call from Allman Brothers drummer Butch Trucks: "Hey man, we're going to do this jam—you gotta come down to Florida!"

You can't say no to Butch; he's a force of nature. I remember we once had this gig in Vegas where he walked right past security and onto the stage. No one stopped him because he's Butch—how do you stop the drummer from the Allman Brothers from doing whatever the hell he wants at a rock show? So he came out while I was singing and said, "Hey man, how are you doing?" He was a little lit and was talking to me like he wanted an answer. I was singing, so after I finished a verse, I answered him, "Hey man, I'm good. I'm just doing this thing right now." So he said, "What are you doing? How long are you here for?" My manager at the time, Scott McGhee, was there and stepped over to talk to him, and I don't know what he said, but Butch's vibe was, *I will fucking kill you if you get between me and my friend here.* And that's Butch. You can't stop him—least I don't think I can—and none of my crew was going to try. So I went to Florida to join the Frogwings project.

Frogwings was all monsters. You had Butch and Marc Quinones—when you bring the drumming artillery like that, it's hard for it to be a bad show. Then on guitars it was Derek Trucks and Jimmy Herring. Oteil Burbridge was on bass, and there's something about a great bassist and the harp because one's so low and one's so shrill. They always end up dancing around each other.

This time away from Blues Traveler had been my big chance to settle down and focus on making an album, and then all of a sudden, "Oh yeah, let's write some songs and make a whole other album while we're waiting." But there was no saying no to Butch, and there was no saying no to Derek and Oteil and Jimmy—those guys are monsters (and I mean that as players because they're three of the sweetest guys). The logistics of that now would never allow such an album to occur. There are too many motherfuckers, and they each have their own plans. I was really spoiled in that all these motherfuckers were hanging around where I could get at them and whip up a project with them.

We went and rehearsed for five days. There were tons of great riffs, and I put words to some of them. One of these was a riff Oteil had written for Blues Traveler years back. I also recall at one point my amp feedbacked right into Oteil's ear, and I said, "Oh my God, I'm sorry." He looked up like he didn't notice and said, "I work for Dickey Betts" and went back to reading his paper.

So we rehearsed, did seven gigs in the Northeast, and recorded a live album, which came out around the time of my *Zygote* album. At the time I wondered whether it was going to be a problem, but they were so different. One is pure musicianship, and one is song concepts. I love how I made two albums. The Frogwings' album has some cult status, and I'm grateful it didn't disappear. That was one of those albums that made me feel like I earned my stripes.

We finished up *Zygote* in May, and a few weeks later I took a little trip to Hawaii with a girlfriend. We were in the hot tub, fooling around, and I started feeling chest pains. I didn't know at the time, but hot tubs are really bad for your circulation. I said, "I've got to go to a doctor and check this out because this just isn't normal."

There had been some time before that when I would be whacking off to porn and suddenly I'd get chest pains and not feel so good. Before it would calm down I would get this shivery feeling and my teeth would start chattering. I'd stop what I was doing and that would calm down and I'd start to feel better, but the porn was still going. So I'd get horny and start up again, and the same thing would happen. This went on for hours; it was almost tantric. It was annoying.

We had some shows coming up, including Red Rocks, so after a Rainforest Action Network benefit at the Warfield, in which Phil Lesh sat in with us, I figured I'd swoop down to LA from San Francisco to check in with my doctor about the chest pains and then head off to Colorado. I visited the doctor, thinking it would be a formality: he'd give me a new pill or something. Instead, he told me I was 95 percent blocked in every artery and had to get into bed immediately. You don't quite believe it when they tell you that, and it turned out there was no way in hell I could make Red Rocks.

They had to give me an angioplasty. They kept me awake, and as they put that steel wire in my heart, it felt as if they were blowing warm air into my innards. It was a very creepy feeling. At that moment the idea of ever having a cigarette again became abhorrent to me. I felt that if I had one more cigarette, I would die.

Red Rocks is a tradition we continue—really the only tradition from the early days of the band—and that's the only time we missed it. People thought I'd died—a rumor spread that I'd had a heart attack. But I didn't have an actual heart attack because they put a stent in my heart and cleared me. A heart attack means that the actual heart muscle is damaged. Because they fixed the blockage before I had any damage done to my heart, I did not have a true heart attack. This might be lost on some people, but the important thing is I still have 100 percent function in my heart, which is what's essential when you're talking about heart disease. They then told me I had to lose weight or else I would have a 25 percent chance of imminent death. It's a weird thing when you're told there's only a 75 percent change of living if you do nothing, and that was a rather scary statistic.

Then the band held an intervention, appearing in my hospital room to tell me, "John, you need to change your life." Chan and Brendan showed up, but Bobby wasn't there. My intervention became the two of them saying, "John, we're really worried about Bobby." He showed up a couple of hours after everybody left and looked purple. His speech was kind of slurred as he told me I needed to get my act together, and that was the last time I ever saw him alive.

I was with my *Zygote* band, preparing for a tour to support this new record when our crew guy Bob Mahoney came in crying and told me Bobby had died. I immediately got in my car, and it became a week of being on call for everybody. They all wanted a hug, and I wanted to hug everyone as much as they wanted to hug me. That's what funerals are like—you've got to howl at the moon with everyone else.

After the funeral we just started hugging everybody—friends, friends of friends, fans. It became a hug off. I was really hugged out and burnt by the end of it. It became too much. That was a really tough day, tough month, tough year. It was brutal.

I just wanted to be useful to people. At the wake Bobby's old girlfriend wanted me to put something in his pocket, which I agreed to do. His brother asked me if I could remove the custom Blues Traveler ring that someone had made for each of us. I did that as well. I was in a daze, and the whole situation was heartbreaking.

Bobby and I were addicts. My addiction was food, and his were a lot of other things—I won't go into specifics because his mom got upset when I tried to talk about his addictions on the air once, and she's his mom—but his addictions killed him and mine almost killed me.

When someone you love dies so suddenly and you see in retrospect how it was leading to that, you want to blame yourself. But those were choices he made just as I was making choices that weren't really good for me that led my band to get me help. We tried getting Bobby help, but that didn't work. We tried to be there for him, but we failed horribly and the reason for that failure is an addict has to do the work himself.

This is where I sometimes feel bad because I knew for a fact that if I didn't get off the road and do something for myself, which became the *Zygote* record, I was going to die. I felt it coming. But I also had a really strong suspicion that if I took that structure away from Bobby, if I stopped our endless touring, he would die.

At some point I chose me. And as soon as the doctor told me I had a 25 percent chance of dying, I knew I had made the correct decision. I recognized, *Oh my God, that decision was real.* It wasn't a paranoid choice in my head; it was a real choice I had to make.

I was going to a shrink who told me I should be trying to do something for me because then you can take that satisfaction and return it to the work. It doesn't mean I didn't love doing Blues Traveler, but at that point it was all I was doing. And I was dying. I was getting fatter and fatter; it was just the way it worked. I hid out a lot and just ate while he just partied. He did all the social butterflying, and I did none of it. We were such extremists in that regard.

We were like Alexander's army—we were looking for more objectives. But we didn't know how to function without constantly being on a war footing and constantly touring.

Brendan and Chan had enough sense of self-worth that they were able to start families for themselves. Bobby and I did not know how to do that, but I knew I wanted it. Bobby knew he wasn't happy, but he was at the beginning of the place where he could start to deal with it. I think he was almost there. It's a function of growing up, and Bobby and I were children as long as we could be.

I think everybody in "normal existence" eventually is confronted with the reality that they can't go on living completely for the moment or for themselves. But for Bobby and me, the band functioned as a place where we could continue to live in that moment. We viewed it as something beyond us, and I don't think either of us ever worked out what to do if our dreams for the band came true.

By 1996 it was clear that the dream had come true, and we couldn't figure out what to do next. From 1996 to 1999 we were trying to have that life, which meant buying a home and being financially stable. And we were dating, trying to have a significant other, but I had no interior life and neither did Bobby. It was something we were both trying to figure out, but while we were doing that, we were busy destroying ourselves.

It's very incremental. You think, *I did this yesterday, so why can't I keep doing it today?* and gradually you get more and more isolated. I knew I didn't want to be isolated. I knew there was something I could do about it, but I wasn't sure what that was. Lord knows I wasn't losing weight. That was something I couldn't do; that I was something I was powerless to fix.

When it came to food or my appetite, it was always, "What can I do given that I have these appetites?" That's something I still wrestle with today. I don't think appetites are bad; it's acknowledging them that's the important part.

Bobby and I knew no other way as adults, and that manic behavior of ours made the band great. But we were built for wartime, and then when there was no war, we didn't know what to do with ourselves.

It's kind of trite to say, but I think Bobby's passing saved my life in a shortcut kind of way. When you lose somebody, you always want their passing to mean something, but really his death was an accident. He did something dumb. He had sleep apnea, so he could choke in his sleep really easily.

I think I would have been much more into drugs had I not taken an antidrug stance. I was worried about Bobby, but I was also worried about the business. I figured that if it's away from me and I'm where the business is, then it won't be around in the business.

I knew that you could never stop cocaine from being on the road because too many people have it (and I came to enjoy it later in life). So I said, "If I see any crack around me, I'm going home."

Two things happened as a result. One, I never saw any crack being smoked on the road. Two, any cocaine use on the road was kept away from me. What that did was to start the lie: "No, I'm not doing any drugs at all." When he would do drugs, I wouldn't know about it. His priority wasn't, "Let's get clean." His priority was, "Let's keep it away from John."

At that time I was considered the teetotaler. I partied and I'd drink and smoke weed but nowhere on the order of my bandmates, so I was still considered the straight one. So any attempt to get Bobby to stop doing drugs just drove him away from our circle, where he would find friends to do drugs with. That's how drugs work. It was a dangerous thing because if you're really trying to help somebody, you have to keep some communication going.

So I became the cop. Chan didn't have a leg to stand on because he wasn't sober, which left me as the sheriff of drugs. This wasn't fair because I did drugs, just not with the regularity that became the norm out there.

Brendan was incredibly disciplined and very loving to his girl-friend, who became his wife. He always emphasized that he had a work life and a private life. His one thing was that he loved to drink, and on occasion he would get crazy and it was pretty fun. Some-times, just to mess with him, I'd give him the nickname Brendan "Blackout Alcoholic" Hill. But he wound up taking that very seri-ously, and if there were an episode where that happened, he'd stop and check himself. And Chan would do that too. He'd party really hard, but he also took care of his body, so he'd say, "I don't feel right. I'm going to stop for two weeks." He'd do that periodically and monitor himself.

Then when Chan got married and had a kid, he changed. Chan always said that Bobby felt like he'd lost his running buddy, and that was Chan's guilty issue. My guilty issue is that I made it so Bobby couldn't talk about it, which in a way drove him further into it.

Bobby and I did not know how to grow from the places we had been for a decade. Brendan and Chan were starting families, while Bobby and I had failed miserably at even considering some sort of a life at home. I had bought a house, and he had just bought a house, but he bought a house in New Orleans, which was a very dangerous place for him to be.

Bobby's move to New Orleans was the equivalent of me moving to McDonaldland where Mayor McCheese was in charge, I would have to put up extra security because the Hamburglar was on the loose again, and Officer Big Mac would come by and visit.

The last gig Bobby played with us was with his childhood hero, Phil Lesh, and Bobby couldn't really appreciate it because he kept comparing Phil to some of the people he had met in New Orleans. Bobby started hanging out with this negative crowd down there. At that time all the musicians would go to New Orleans, thinking it was the music mecca, but then they couldn't find steady work because there were so many knowledgeable, brilliant players. In a scene like that, especially where substances are involved and people are scratching to survive, things can turn bitter. And I think he was sucked in by people who envied his situation. As a result, he didn't get to appreciate his situation as much.

I remember visiting him once there, and his place had people in it all night. There was never any privacy, never any quiet time. Good enough people, but a scene like that really wasn't a rest.

Bobby and I were both self-aware, but we both decided we weren't supposed to live very long. I had it in my head that thirty-seven was the year I was going to die. A lot of the rock stars we had grown up on had died young, and here I was arguably the best harp player in the world, and this band had gotten everything it had dreamed of. So there had to be some horrible thing coming. We looked at it very fatalistically.

The problem with thinking fatalistically is that it can prevent you from trying to take part in your fate. And then it's not really fate; it's something you've affected because of your view of your fate.

After Bobby died, I was looking at my Jimi Hendrix poster and thinking about Bobby and Jimi, how they lived life so black and white—"Do what's good, and good things will come back to you. And screw the annoying parts." But then Felicia said to me that the real courage is that life usually isn't a black or white thing; it's actually gray. It isn't an adventurous or heroic decision; it's cooperation or compromise to get the things you need, and that's actually the true heroism.

We both had these views that we were supposed to die young—"Think about how lucky we are; think about the lives we've lived. It's okay if we don't live long as long as we've lived honestly." And I think Felicia's point is that it wasn't as honest as we might think. It was easier, but it wasn't honest. And truthfully I'm not sure there is any life that doesn't have hypocrisy. You can't really live honestly in this universe. You can live as honestly as you can—I love the *Nightly Show with Larry Wilmore*, you can keep it as one hundred as you can—but sooner or later, when you're on the toilet, it's just not pretty.

Existence requires some sort of coming to terms with the fact that you're a blop of molecules spinning around on a planet, trying to ascribe meaning to things, and the very attempt of putting language together is hypocritical.

Bobby and I were working on the presumption that our lives were so blessed that we couldn't live very long, that we had done too many amazing things. But as I wrote in "Pretty Angry," I basically blinked. I realized that I don't want to die. It was the first time I knew that for a fact, and it took the loss of my friend to show me that death is right here. That was after having an angioplasty and after the bike wreck.

I spent the nineties thinking I might live and I might die, and that became a regular existence for me. Then when you actually lose somebody, it drives home the stakes of that and what it means to people.

"Pretty Angry (for J. Sheehan)"

I wish I drank tequila.
I wish I stayed up late.
But lately when the sandman comes,
You know I just can't wait.
No lately I can't wait.
And we packed up all your boxes.
It's all been hauled away.
I never stare at walls so bare
'Cause something always stays.
Yeah, something of you stays.
And I wanna shout from my guitar,
Come out, come out wherever you are.
The joke is over, open up your eyes.
A heart like yours it never dies.
And I found your keys behind your chair.
I still can see you sitting there.
This isn't funny, don't fool around.
You let me go, you let me down.
And I guess I'm still pretty angry
And I don't wanna be.

I don't know which was the bigger waste of time,
Missing you or wishing instead it was me.
I wish I walked on water,
Pulling rabbits from my sleeve,
Guessing cards and saving everyone.
Oh, I wish I still believed.
Oh, I wish that I believed.
That I could also channel voices,
That I've endured the burning blade,
That I could make some of your choices.
I wish I weren't afraid
Of those choices that you made,
Like I could give you what you need.
So ally ally oxen free.
The game is up and I give in.
So show yourself so that you can win.
Come claim your prize and I don't care.
I still can see you standing there.
How you could leave, how you could lie.
You cut me off in midreply.
And I guess I'm still pretty angry
And I don't wanna be.
I don't know which was the bigger waste of time,
Missing you or wishing instead it was me.
The will to win, the urge to race,
I still can see it on your face.
Thought I'd keep up but only crashed.
I wasn't built to move that fast.
Thought I could match you stride for stride,
But I was on the other side
And holding on to the safety rail
With knuckles white complexion pale.
A cloud of dust and you were gone.
Thought I would catch you later on.
I limped behind your race was won.
But were you racing or on the run?

How you enjoyed, you loved to drive.
And I'm destroyed
Cause I'm alive.
Cause I'm alive.
And I guess I'm still pretty angry
And I don't wanna be.
I don't know which was the bigger waste of time,
Missing you or wishing instead it was me.
I guess I'm still pretty angry
I don't wanna be.
I don't know which was the bigger waste of time,
Missing you.

24

I WANT TO BE BRAVE

Zygote was ten days from release when I found out Bobby died.

Kurt Loder had come to my house to shoot some guns, and this was supposed to be part of a half-hour special about my new record. It turned into a five-minute piece, *Is There Life After Blues Traveler?* They had a shot of me brushing a bug out of my face that they slowed and converted to black and white so it looked like I was having a breakdown. *Entertainment Tonight* did the same thing.

I had booked all of this press for a huge release. In our A&M contract I was allowed to record a solo record and they were obligated to pay for it. They were supposed to eat the loss, but they used the fact that Bobby died as a technicality to wriggle out of it, and in the process I was screwed out of $170,000.

Tom Whalley was the head of the record label. He came out to our *Zygote* band's gig at the House of Blues LA to say, "I want you to know we're killing your album, but have a good show."

You'd think that's as bad as it could get, that that's the final thrust of the sword you could do to a band. But he had one last spike to shove up my ass. The next day he called after having seen us play live for the first time and said, "I didn't know you guys were good. Fuck, I could have really helped you too." And then he said, "Do you know what you should have done with the song 'Home'?" He used his old producer chops and solved the chorus for me over the phone just to prove that *I alone could make your record better but I didn't know you were worth anything. Sorry we killed you, oh well.*

I suddenly had to take all the canceled Blues Traveler gigs and work my band just to pay the bills. I wound up quite in the hole after the record company decided to withdraw their support because they could do so legally after our bass player died.

Blues Traveler was supposed to play in Reno for three to five thousand people for New Year's Eve, and in order to help pay my bills, that gig got transferred to me for the John Popper Zygote tour. I had a horrible flu and had to fight with band to get them to come and do it because they knew the project was ending and three hundred people showed up. That's how I rang in the new century.

There was a sense of disorientation. I wasn't altogether sure what would come next.

It was Chan and his wife, Serena, who were instrumental in finding the gastric bypass operation for me. Chan's point was, "I'm not going to lose another friend by doing nothing."

I had become resigned to the idea that I just couldn't address my weight. I thought it was hopeless, and truthfully, if I'd come to that point five years earlier, it *would* have been hopeless. The technology to do a gastric bypass was brand new and usually involved a very invasive surgery in which they literally sawed you open and tied a knot in your stomach. But now there was a new procedure in which they could do it laparoscopically, so the risk was a lot lower. There was one guy in America, a doctor from Holland practicing in New York, who was licensed to perform the new procedure laparoscopically.

I was willing to do this operation because I thought it wouldn't work, my friend was dead, and I was ready to die. I had that angioplasty a month before Bobby died, and I had a real feeling the end was coming. As I met with the doctors, I discovered there was an entire subculture of really obese people who were just ready to die. The doctors kept trying to talk me out of my fatalistic attitude. I had made my peace and figured it was meant to be. But then they'd tell me, "No, that's insane. You should do something about it. You should save your life."

On the day of the surgery I learned there was a 10 percent chance I might not be able to sing again because of the operation and the way they had to go down my throat. To their minds that wasn't a reckless decision as long as I was trying to live. As they were wheeling me down the hall to begin the surgery, Chan was there and said, "I've got your twenty dollars." He'd owed me twenty dollars for about a year and chose that moment to pay me back. So he put a twenty on my belly, and as they wheeled me away, I was gripping Chandler's twenty dollars.

Apparently I have this ability to endure being cut open, because the surgery seemed to work.

They tell you that you can never eat beef again, so I'd had all these farewell meals, but it turned out I could eat beef and all these other things, but just in very small amounts and not right away. The first thing you do is you vomit up all your food. If I had anything with sugar, I immediately shit myself. Your body undergoes this incredible shock. It's like you have a baby's stomach.

I thought if I smoked pot, that would treat the nausea, but I found that I was just stoned and throwing up. I eventually learned a Pavlovian response to food. I can remember the first time somebody brought in a plate of homemade cookies and I felt this aversion to them and wondered, *Where did that come from?* It was because I had vomited up so many cookies trying to sneak them into my new stomach. I also learned to feel nauseous when I was too full, which is something I should have figured out when I was a kid. But what I learned instead at age nine was that if I just kept on eating, that nauseous feeling would go away.

Then I had to survive the scars and everything else that came from the operation. I lost an average of five pounds per week over ten months. It was quite an adventure, and quite a depressing year.

As I said, having that stent in my heart and then having my best friend die really drove home the fact that I'm going to die, so I was ready for that. But what was weird is that when I didn't die, I wasn't quite prepared for *that* because then I had to deal with all the emotional aspects of not being fat anymore. Because if a girl rejected me, I could tell myself, *It's because I'm fat—she doesn't see the real me.*

But then when I was no longer fat, to be rejected and have it just be because she doesn't like me—that's something most people deal with when they're fifteen, but I was dealing with it at thirty-two. It was that kind of a catch-up where I had to let myself be an adolescent in a way but I could also never truly be an adolescent now because I'm an adult. So it was a really weird time.

I got laid even in my fattest days, but I had to sing a lot for it. This was a real recalibration.

When I was obese I didn't care how I looked, and there was a freedom to that, a liberation. There's an incredible power when everyone knows you've walked into the room just by the size of you. They're very aware you're there. People get out of your way because they can't quite figure you out. But they also make a point to listen to you—"I don't know what his deal is. Let's try to find out." Then when you "look like everyone else"—you know, a human shape—people are trying to tell you what *they're* thinking or trying to assimilate you into what they're thinking.

The band used to tell me that after I lost the weight, I would be in the room and they didn't notice me. It was very creepy to them. It was like when I was four hundred pounds, I was wearing a bell and they just sort of knew where I was.

I also decided to ditch the harmonica belt at that point. When I lost the weight my balance changed. I was light on my feet and felt like darting around. With a harmonica belt you don't dart as much. When I was fatter I would just plant my feet and lumber along, so what did it matter if I had some more things on me? When my body image was a platform, like an aircraft carrier, I didn't mind holding a lot of things, but after I lost the weight and felt like a person, I wondered, *Why am I wearing this ridiculous harness?*

I was hiding behind this belt, and maybe that was the intention all along. I had this hulking body, so maybe I should hide it or put something on to augment it and give it some kind of strangeness. It was certainly useful—I learned to play off the vest—but it wasn't that big an adjustment to bring a case full of harps and work out of it. That adjustment was a lot easier than I thought it would be.

After the angioplasty I was afraid of having one single cigarette because I thought I would die. But I went back to smoking because everybody was eating cheeseburgers from Carl's Jr. at a band rehearsal in San Diego, and they forgot my sandwich, so somebody ran out to the truck and brought me a shitty turkey sandwich they'd picked up at a gas station. I looked at the sandwich, looked at them, smelled the Carl's Jr., said, "Fuck you guys," got the keys, and drove off to Carl's Jr. to get myself a big, juicy cheeseburger. I took a big, juicy, defiant bite out of it and then vomited all over the place. So I said, "Fuck it, give me the cigarettes," and I haven't stopped smoking since.

Still, some part of me thinks like a little kid. Chan used to say, "Life is about steaks and beer," and I'd tell him, "Sometimes it's about Twinkies and grape juice."

I think the most sophisticated I get is barbeque, because there is barbeque that is better than McDonald's, by far. If you've got some real Kansas City barbeque on your hands, then screw the McRib sandwich. But now, with a gastric bypass, I need six hours to eat barbecue.

To eat a rack of ribs I need to be naked in my bed. I can be in my underwear—it's not like I'm going to get sexual with the ribs—I just need to be unencumbered by clothing and to be in a bed. I will play a Ribfest, where all day I'm smelling it, will demand a rack of ribs I've been drooling over, eat half a rib, and I'm done.

So I gotta get the ribs back to my hotel, get in my underwear, and turn on the TV. Then I'll pass out from all that fat and sugar and then wake up forty-five minutes later and say, "Oh look, ribs." So I'll start eating the ribs again and pass out. This goes on for hours. I'm like a lion at a kill, because then a slab of ribs becomes an all-day thing. In the nineties that would have been a footnote in an all-day meal that involved many, many other foods. And really, if I eat a rack of ribs, I'm done for the day if I can get through a whole rack. I don't do that every day or, literally, I'll never be able to leave my room.

What is weird is that after the gastric bypass, I have had so many really obese people come up to me and say, "I wasn't going to do it until I saw that you did it." And then I did feel a certain responsibility as a human being to at least talk about it and share my experience with it as others had done for me.

There was a guy in his fifties; he was 450 pounds and said, "I've come into this waiting room twenty times, and I always chicken out and leave." I talked him into staying and at least discussing bypass with a doctor. And I know what the fear is, that you think it won't work, that you've always held out hope—"I can always get a gastric bypass"—and then you discover you're not a candidate or it won't work and you realize you're doomed.

But the cool part is that it does work. Weight loss is still manageable, and gastric bypass is available. And I know if someone hears that and they're 700 pounds, they'll say, "Bullshit. I'm way too far gone." And yes, 700 pounds is way the fuck down the road, but you can still climb out of that. Seven hundred pounds takes twice as long as what I did. I went from 436 to 238 in ten months, and believe me, I was throwing up. (I gained about 45 back over the next three years, and whatever you gain back over after those three years stays that way.)

It was at this time that I got my one and only tattoo to remind myself to go out and not be a shut-in because that felt like normal behavior to me. That was my comfortable instinct, but I realized that what I needed to do was go out and meet people, hang out with them, and do what was uncomfortable. It was the beginning of a new sociability for me. So I put "I Want To Be Brave" on my chest backward so when I get up in the morning to take a leak I'll look in the mirror, see that mantra, and say, "Oh yeah, that's right." And as long as I remember to do that, my day works out. You have to do the thing you're not used to and leave your comfort zone. And if I remember that I want to be brave, I'm going to try things that don't feel comfortable right away but eventually they become comfortable.

I felt that as long as I was trying to do the thing that was out of my comfort zone—meeting people, talking to people, and hanging out with people I didn't know—then I would be better. I think a large part of this is that Bobby was my conduit to the world; he was my social ambassador. I would go out with him for a night on the town, and now I was going out by myself.

I got the tattoo before the frigging *Memento* movie, but nobody believes me. I remember my dad said it would be cooler if it read, "I Must Be Brave" or "I Am Brave," but I think the braver thing is to admit that I need to be brave, that *I want to be brave.*

Throughout all of this I still am a fan of appetites. I'm just going from one vice to another instead of just focusing on one. I think that one thing I learned after that weight loss operation is that it doesn't have it be one thing. Spread it around—have a bad meal and then get a little drunk and then do a little blow—just don't be cokehead, don't be an alcoholic, and don't be four hundred pounds. I'm all for having a vice, but don't let it be something that destroys you or makes you miss out on doing things. Just be healthy enough to live long enough to do the things you like to do. It sounds simple, but let's assume that the things you like to do are not that good for you.

The truth is that life is kind of a crapshoot and you don't know how long you're going to live. But to use that as an excuse doesn't wash. I'm still not a terribly healthy person, but as long as I'm healthier, life will treat me like I'm trying to live.

It can be a bitch, and I'm not sure what death is like, but this is better than not being allowed to see again or walk again or fuck again or even eat the thing you like again. I know there are some addictions where you can never touch these things anymore, but maybe at that point you can say, "I've had enough of them. I've already done that." You can look at it not as a waste but that you've had your allotment all at once.

So you want to have some good things and some bad things. You probably need to do more good things to support the bad things, but when you do the bad things, they should be completely joyful and guilt-free because you've earned them. That is what I'm going to go to my grave expounding, at whatever age that may be. But that's okay because nobody's really looking to me for health advice.

25

THE BRIDGE

I'm not sure what the appropriate mourning period should have been, but we began talking about bass players within days after Bobby died. It was probably a survival mechanism. It was as though our family was falling apart and the preservation of the band gave us purpose. I know Bobby would have wanted us to keep going, but I still find it bizarre that the way we dealt with our grief was to keep functioning as a band.

The first thought it my head was Dave Wilder, with whom we went to high school. He was an amazing bass player, so I called him up within a few days of Bobby's death and he said, "I've got this gig with this girl in LA named Macy Gray." I said, having seen his other bands, which, though good, were really much smaller, "No offense, but this is a good opportunity," and he said, "No, I think I'm going to stick this one out." I hung up and thought to myself, *Macy Gray, what is he thinking?* Then I saw her on television and got it right away.

I went to Oteil Burbridge at this same time. I might even have gone to him first because he is the absolute best bass player I had ever played with, but he said, "No, I've signed on with the Allman Brothers and I've got to see it through."

Meanwhile Chan was thinking of his little brother. I knew Tad was good and was willing to do what we needed, but what really made it work was that he was different from Bobby. We put him in an audition with three or four bass players. One of them did a good Bobby impression, but that just made us sad because we thought the worst thing we could have done was to try to be what the band was with Bobby in it. It would be us misplacing our reverence for him.

The other thing that wound up being fairly important is that we'd grown up with Tad. We'd known him since the band started, when he was in the seventh or eighth grade and he had seen all the early days of the band, which really made for a seamless tradition, as he was family.

As we were doing this, a lot of very good friends couldn't come anymore. The band with Bobby in it came to mean something very nostalgic to them and reminded them of a time when it felt like their family, so they had to stay away because they missed Bobby. I understood, and there were times I felt that way myself, but we had to be there. And as we decided on Tad we were also auditioning keyboard players. We'd always talked about getting one, and this seemed to be the time. One of the guys was Jason Crosby. I still tease him about this because he wouldn't have had enough to do, as he plays both violin and keyboard—I would have been endlessly fighting him for solos.

We hired Ben Wilson in that process. He was the clear early favorite and never stopped being so. By bringing in a keyboard player, we really committed to moving away from our original sound while opening up some new avenues.

And as it happened, there was still a record we could go make. People were still interested, and we still could tour on it. Within a year I lost a lot of weight, and our story became the story of how we came back from that.

While we were starting to develop the band and build what became the *Bridge* album, we also made a wonderful discovery: Austin, Texas. It became the backdrop for our next chapter. At this time I was in Pennsylvania, Chan was in LA, Tad was in Brooklyn, Ben was in Ann Arbor, and Brendan was in Seattle. So we'd all converge on Austin, in the middle of the country, where it was warm and there was a music scene. We never got to do that with Bob, and it's unfortunate because he would have loved Austin as a place to make albums.

The first thing the five us worked on together was *The Sun and the Storm*, a rock opera we had started with Bobby. Ultimately we put together an abbreviated version that had all six band members on it because Tad and Ben had finished what Bobby had started with us.

The starting point was that Aesop's Fable in which the sun and the north wind are having an argument over who's more powerful, so they make a bet about which of them can make a man take his coat off. The north wind blows as hard as he can and the man holds his coat even tighter, and the sun gets warmer and warmer until the man takes his coat off. That's the moral of the story: you catch more flies with warm sunshine.

In my story they up the ante. The storm says, "I'll take the form of his desires, dreams, and aspirations, and the sun will take the form of true love." So he's battling for true love, and this was a reflection of how I was looking for a balance between an interior life and my dreams of conquest and plunder.

We released it online during the fall of 2000, just before we began our first tour together in October. It was a brutal time because we felt we had to demonstrate to everyone that we were still a live force, which we were, while I was still on the path to recovery from the bypass and at times would be throwing up and feeling ill.

We actually had our first gig in New Orleans two weeks after the surgery. I was on a strict liquid diet of smoothies, and Susan Bank, our manager, accidentally brought me a smoothie with sugar in it, and I shit the bed. That caused me to be so dehydrated that I had to go to the emergency room and get rehydrated intravenously. It was a challenge finding someone to get me to the hospital because everybody was drunk at this bar—I remember Chan was passed out on the pool table.

While we were developing the new five piece I wanted to make some changes in the way the band operated. I didn't want the guys to receive the same dictatorial edicts from me, and for two reasons. First, I didn't think it was the best use of musicians who were really good. And second, it was taking a horrible, terrible toll on me. When somebody on your team dies because of the way you're doing your business, it's a chance to ask yourself what else is going on with your life and really embrace that and deal with it.

Part of that decision was to have Tad and Ben come right in and take a hand in the set lists. For many years this had been Bobby's role, and it could be a rather thankless role, particularly when he had to sit through the complaints of the three other guys who hadn't put in the effort. Still, we had felt that we were in a rut of playing the same set over and over, so we agreed to divide it up. We came up with an anagram: Big Cock Blow Job for Brendan Chan Bobby John.

Everybody had their favorite songs. You can always spot mine because I go for the schmaltzier stuff, which they call my vagina songs, like "Sweet Pain" or "Alone"—they were always in my sets. Chan always wanted a rocking set, whereas Brendan wanted something with lots of power, like "Crash Burn" or "Fallible." And Bobby wanted something as Grateful Deady as he could get it.

I'd come after Bob. He'd always start things off with "Ivory Tusk." That was one of his trademarks because he always felt it was a good first song. Brendan would come after my set, and he'd react by writing the metaliest set he could.

The other thing I did—and this really drove the band crazy—is that I wanted to see how many segues we could do. So I would write a fourteen-song segue and what Brendan pointed out to us is that I would exhaust the band. But what I also noticed is that they'd complain less about a seven-song segue, so pretty soon we were doing five-song segues without any problem, and initially that *had* been a problem.

So as we began ramping up the live show once again, we decided to throw Tad and Ben into the mix. It wasn't exactly trial by fire like the old days, but I think they felt enough internal pressure to keep them honest. Of course we needed a snappy acronym, and after cogitating on that one for a little while, we came up with Big Cock Tiny Blow Job (Brendan, Chan, Tad, Ben, John). Blues Traveler was back in business.

Patrick Clifford, the guy who originally signed us to A&M (he was the one who came out to the Buddy Miles extravaganza at Wetlands) and certainly was familiar with the original quartet, saw the new five-piece and told me, "I see what you've done—you've become a jazz band." I sort of understand what he meant: we take extended solos rather than jamming like a Grateful Dead thing. I think Bobby was a sloppier bass player; he was more about feel than precision, so that enabled us to do really cool personalized feels. But at times he limited us to two chords when we were rehearsing and writing. So we were a band of really great feels and not much harmonic texture.

Bridge came out in May 2001. On that album we were wrestling with the issues after Bobby's death while we were also trying to have some cohesion. It was the bridge to the next thing. We were taking different steps and cautious steps, but earnest steps. That's what I really liked about *Bridge*. Then *Truth Be Told* was us being the band that we are, and *¡Bastardos!* was us trying to grow.

It all started with *Bridge*, which is also where it ended with A&M. Actually *Straight on till Morning* was our final record with A&M because 1998 was the year of the big Seagram's buyout of A&M's parent label Polygram, in which hundreds of acts were dropped. We made it through, but *Bridge* came out on Interscope.

The label president was Tom Whalley, who killed my *Zygote* record and then told me how he would have fixed it, had he cared. He invited Blues Traveler to his mansion, where his servants brought out the heads of his former musicians to dine as he spoke in dulcet tones about what he had in mind for us.

What did he have in mind for us? The privilege of spending $20,000 for two seconds worth of tiger. The "Girl Inside My Head" video from *Bridge* cost us over $200,000 because the deal was that the band would split expenses with the label. We ended up with a half-million-dollar video, and he paid half of it, including $40,000 for the rental of a Bengal tiger that barely appears.

During our previous video for "Carolina Blues" I had to stand outside in the rain alone on a giant steel bridge in the middle of a Louisiana lightning storm. Not only was I on this steel bridge, but it was an aerial lift bridge, and they raised it up even further so they could film me against the sky. I was on it lip synching for five hours while the band looked on from a nice dry window. "Girl Inside My Head" was going to be my payback. I played a hip-hop mogul, and they gave me a bald wig and a gold chain. I got to be in bed with Playboy bunnies in lacy underwear (them, not me, and not real Bunnies, but close enough, including Chan's wife) having a money fight with piles of cash while a machine blew feathers on us. I remember seeing Brendan pulling up a chair and watching, and that almost made it weird.

In the middle of this there was a Bengal tiger gathered around the pool at my fancy party. They brought the tiger out, and it growled like, *Mmm . . . delicious!* When I heard the rumble in its belly, it sounded like it was right above me, and then I learned it could leap across the pool like it was nothing. Everyone on the shoot figured out pretty quickly that this tiger could easily get to any of us who were within fifty feet. Then I realized they weren't telling the tiger what to do; they were asking it. We were supposed to be cavorting like it was a party with beach balls flying and splashing, and the handler said, "Don't make any sudden movements—it upsets the tiger." So what you have is the most timid and tentative cavorting and partying during that scene because we didn't want to piss off the tiger. It cost $40,000 for that tiger, so that was $20,000 to us, and when the video aired, the camera passed by the tiger for less than two seconds.

So that's what Tom Whalley did: he helped us spend some money and killed my solo album. Oh, he also gave the guy from Limp Bizkit an office—he named Fred Durst senior vice president of the label. So there you have it, Tom Whalley. Ladies and gentlemen, the man is a mogul, who can touch him, what a genius.

He left Interscope at the end of the year for Warner Bros. Records. We lasted about a year longer, at which point we owed $4 million to the label. Thankfully they let us go with that money unrecouped. Scott McGhee took over for Dave Frey as our manager in 2001, and getting us out of that debt was one of the best things he did. Imagine owing them $4 million. Dear Lord.

26

HOWARD'S TURN

The first time I heard Howard Stern was on NBC radio. I was used to *Imus in the Morning*, so his rhythm seemed off, and I had never heard radio like that.

Gradually, as I moved to New York and we would be going to bed in the morning after doing gigs all night, he was the cherry at the end of my day. We became huge Stern fans, just like most people in our generation.

Then one day while I was listening Stern mentioned our "Run-Around" video. He was saying, "Imagine you're the manager of that band and you have to tell them they're not attractive enough to be in the video." The thing that galled me was that it was our idea. The whole premise of the video was that other people would shoot it and we would be behind the curtain—the attraction was that we only had to be there for two hours.

The stupidest thing you ever do is your video, and to avoid actually working on this video seemed ahead of the curve to us. A normal video requires about twelve hours of filming a day, and to get that down to two was just brilliant. I wanted to call him and gloat over the fact that "Hey, we knew we were too ugly to be in the video. That was our idea."

It got me so worked up that I actually called in, and as it happened his producer, Gary Dell'Abate, knew Susan Bank, who was one of our managers—they'd gone to school together or something. So Gary quizzed me, "Who is your manager?" And then they he got me on the air and Howard soon realized that I was willing to talk about anything.

The only issue was that he was always trying to turn my volume down because I grew up with seven kids and I had to shout over everybody.

I was so happy to be there because I would always fall asleep to Howard Stern, so I'd have the same dream over and over again that Howard and Robin and I were having a conversation but they wouldn't respond to me. So we were having this great conversation, but whatever I interjected they ignored. This was a recurring dream, so whenever they would talk to me, I was so excited that I conditioned my brain: *You want to cram as much as you can into a session.*

I've had a ball every time I've gone on there. My mom worked in the same building but didn't want him to know because she was afraid he would send someone over to her law firm to harass her. So she made me promise never to tell him.

I met his wife, Beth Ostrosky, before people knew they were dating. We were doing *Letterman,* they hired her to be a chorus girl, and she told me, "I want you to know I'm secretly Howard's girlfriend, but we're not supposed to tell anybody." She said that because she knew me from the show; I was very flattered about that, but I was also thinking that a lot of people probably believe they are secretly Howard Stern's girlfriend. So I said, "That's great," but in my head I thought, *Perhaps she only thinks she is.* As it turned out, she really was.

They invited me to this wonderful New Year's party at his apartment one year, and my fiancé at the time got completely drunk and I had to carry her out of there, so I missed the magician. Marilyn Manson was there. Kevin Smith was there, and my then-fiancée had some sort of sexual confrontation with his wife in the bathroom. Artie Lang and I took over Howard's bedroom, and it became the smoking room.

I wrote "Fallible" as an observation on the Stern show. I tried to explain that to him once, but he didn't see it. It's very metaphorical, but if you look at the lyrics, it's about the Stern show's process, in which they're so honest, sort of like group therapy on the radio. It's about tearing down the veneer of that painted porcelain face. It still stands on its own, though, for someone who doesn't know anything about Stern.

I also wrote a song for him called "Howard's Turn." I ran it by him on the air, but he didn't get it at all. I wish he had.

Still, he invited me to appear in his film *Private Parts*. I had been going on the show quite a bit, and despite the fact that I was yelling a lot, he really enjoyed having me on. I appear in the beginning in a scene that takes place at the MTV Movie Awards. I was standing next to Ted Nugent, and we were talking about guns, of course, and we jammed as well.

At one point Howard called out to the audience who was there for the scene, "Do you guys wanna hear John Popper play the harmonica?" People cheered, so I went out and played, and by his look I could tell he knew how moved I was to be in the movie. I'd put that reaction up there with Dan Aykroyd beaming with pride at what he helped create.

I could also see that Howard really had the presence of mind to think, *Wow, I can't believe we're actually making a movie.* And for someone who was so gigantic in my eyes and in the eyes of so many to be aware of how lucky he was, that's the thing that makes him unique. I've always felt that way, and to have Howard think that way as well really struck me.

When the film finally premiered I was on his show with Conan O'Brien, and Howard did something really sweet for us off the air that I'd finally like to share.

It's important to remember that in the late-night wars of the nineties you were either Letterman or Leno. We were Letterman, but Leno was certainly an opportunity you didn't want to sneeze at, so we'd do our best to walk the line. Everybody on both sides would tell us there was no late-night war, but there was. And we knew they were going to tell us there was no late-night war, and we knew we still had to walk that line. If pushed, we were always David Letterman people, but there was a time when Jay Leno was the bigger rating, and the record company wanted us to go on there as well.

Throughout all of this there was always Conan O'Brien. We liked Conan, and he wanted us on his show, but because he was NBC, that would ruin our Leno play, and because he was based in New York, that would ruin our Letterman play, so we'd always avoid going on his show. He kept getting screwed, but the way I dealt with it, because he was a nice guy, was I would accuse him of not letting us on his show. I'd write him letters: "Dear Conan, why won't you let us on your show?" Once I also sent an entire box of cupcakes to his crew, daring them to eat the cupcakes, attesting that I had not tainted them with some sort of virulent strain of stomach flu, and everyone loved the cupcakes.

The first time I actually met Conan is when we were on *Saturday Night Live*. I had a giant security guy named Raul who was this six-foot-nine biker-looking guy with a huge ponytail. He looked very intimidating and called me boss all the time. I was with my friends at the after-party and said to him half-seriously, "Raul, go out and bring me somebody famous." He came back dragging Conan O'Brien, who was in a tuxedo and looked very confused. I said, "Why won't you let me on your show?" It became a thing.

Later, when I was at Howard's movie premiere after-party, Howard called me up to talk on the air. Conan was sitting there too, so I asked him, "Conan, why won't you let me on your show—is it because of my political ideas?" I began accusing him of towing the NBC company line and suggesting that he wouldn't let me on because I was a Communist. I was just riffing; it was all nonsensical.

Eventually A&M said we could do the *Conan* show, which we had wanted to do, but because of politics, we had put off. I think the late-night war had cooled. So Conan came up to me and said, "You know the funniest thing about that is that as soon as you left, Howard took me aside and said, 'Why the fuck won't you let Blues Traveler on your show? They're nice guys, they try really hard.'" Apparently Howard delivered a lecture on our behalf to get us on Conan's show.

Howard doesn't know that I know this, and it was the nicest thing. I would like to use this book as an opportunity to thank him for that. Poor Conan was getting shit on both ends because I was trying to think of a creative way to not deal with the fact that I wasn't allowed to be on his show.

In 1997 I had a conversation with Howard that landed me on *Celebrity Deathmatch*. I was at the MTV Music Video Awards in 1997 when Fiona Apple gave her "This world is bullshit" speech. I was one of the presenters; I was giving an award to Beck with Dermot Mulroney. Everyone else got copy, but they didn't write copy for Dermot and me; they forgot. So I said, "Don't worry, I'll wing it." This would not be a winning solution for Dermot, who would wind up having little to do and instead would be relying on my "wit."

So as I was standing there, wondering what I was going to say, Fiona came off stage after having given that speech. I didn't see the speech, but she said, "I can't believe I did that. That was the dumbest speech." And I said, "I'm about to fuck it up. They don't even have a speech for me," and we bonded over that. Then her boyfriend at the time, David Blaine, the performance artist, came over and said, "You were perfect, baby." It was such a cheeseball pimpy way to say that. I kept it to myself, but I thought he was all wrong for her.

So I listened to Stern the following Monday, and she was on, defending her speech. I was at home and thought, "Man, they're railroading her." So I called in and said, "Hey Fiona, don't let them back you in a corner. You told me you were drunk and that you didn't mean it."

And as soon as I said the word drunk, I heard "Ooohhhh . . . "

It turned out she was nineteen and wasn't supposed to be drinking. And I was like, *Oh God. Now they're off the speech and into her drinking.* I just threw her into the fire.

So I sent her a Bundt cake because that's an old rule of thumb: nothing says I'm sorry like a Bundt cake. No one can refuse that apology.

That became the premise for a feud, and a month or two later we were opponents on *Celebrity Deathmatch.* My first line was "Nice to be here, I guess." That was my persona, a well-meaning, easygoing, slightly indecisive hippie who was going to come in and sit on your picnic—"Sorry, did I just sit on your picnic? I didn't mean any trouble. Sorry I just squashed your thing on the Stern show."

But back to the MTV Music Video Awards. Poor Dermot Mulroney. I sent him a sweater for leaving him out in the cold because my "clever improvisation" was "I can't believe they didn't write me any copy." Then I said a bunch of incoherent babble like a lunatic, which was fine because Fiona Apple had given such a worse speech.

Dermot did send me a thank you note for the sweater. But I never did hear back from Fiona Apple about the Bundt cake.

I also had an issue with Chris Robinson on Stern in 2001, when we were the two guests and he wouldn't come out until I left.

He had developed this thing, which I kept to myself for a long time. I felt I had been reasonably nice to the guy, but at some point in October 1999 I was sitting in with Warren Haynes and Gov't Mule at the Fillmore—this was a giant jam session in which they brought out Gregg Allman, Audley Freed, and some other players—and Warren told me that Chris Robinson wouldn't come on stage until I left.

This was long after they'd done H.O.R.D.E. with us. At that time they were doing a lot of drugs—the only other one in our band who was doing that was Bobby—and they said in an interview that the only person they could hang with from Blues Traveler was Bobby, that he was the only cool guy in the band. Brendan is convinced that they stopped liking us when we did a version of the Rolling Stones' "Miss You" when they sat in with us and we ended on an upbeat, so they lost respect for us. This is exactly the kind of thing that makes Brendan a cool guy in a way that the Black Crowes may never grasp, and by that I mean the worry. In another article they said we were corporate. Maybe we were corporate, but it *was* a business; the band was also a corporation, and we were there to work.

The first time I spoke to him he was including me peripherally in a conversation in which he was saying that when he's recording, he needs the lights dimmed and there needs to be a giant candle melted a certain way. I kept thinking, *God, I like the lights on when I'm singing; otherwise I'm going to fall asleep. I don't like all the cool ambience; I want to see what I'm reading if I need to read words. I want to feel like I'm awake and doing something.*

The Crowes' style was more to do repetitive blues solos rather than the school we came from, which was from the bebop guys. I was a Coltrane student with the modal approach I took on the harps. I was trying to extend the solo, and they found me kind of noodley.

But that never explained to me the decision he made to never be on stage when I was there. When Warren told me this, I said fine and I left the building because why do I want to be around if somebody doesn't want me there? I'd already played, so I left.

Then the next festival we played that the Crowes were at, he wouldn't come out of his trailer until I left. We were always parking next to the Black Crowes, so it was kind of annoying. Oddly they had a Winnebago and we had a tour bus—maybe that had something to do with it? I never wanted to go outside because why would you want to go outside when there's somebody who just loathes you out there?

After that Stern appearance people would come up to us and say, "Fuck the Black Crowes," and we'd make a point to say, "No, they're a really awesome band." "She Talks to Angels" is one of the greatest vocal deliveries ever, and I never really had a problem with them.

We were in airport bar in 2006. It was Chan, Tad, and me, and one of them saw Chris. He was sort of hiding, trying not to be recognized. They said, "Go buy him a beer." So I did, knowing that he was cornered and had to wait for a plane, and he was like, "Hey John. How's it going? I'm just dealing with stuff after the divorce." He stuttered on the word divorce. He seemed smaller, like the wind had been taken out of him, and he wasn't as feisty. We did some gigs with him later when he didn't seem as adamant about me not being there. Some part of it made me sad; I almost missed his anger.

Back in the day when they couldn't stand us I don't really think it was us. I think they were doing a lot of heroin and their whole world was pissing them off. It was such a dark cloud with them—"Everybody sucks. . . . These people are terrible. . . . *They* don't know rock and roll." And some time later I was backstage, and Marc Ford, who was no longer with the Crowes and was not partying like that, said about someone who was playing, "These guys are pretty good." I kind of lit up.

For me there was negativity about them I never understood. I think they lumped us in with a time they were going through, when things were not really good in their world.

About a year before Chris Robinson and I were on Stern, I went on there to thank Howard for helping me lose the weight. I ended up taking off my shirt, which was a big deal—it was something I never did. I also got three grand for it.

I didn't go on the show intending to take my shirt off, but I figured that they might ask me, so I was ready with a number if they wanted me to. The key was to pick a number that Howard wouldn't balk at but was the most money he was willing to give me. I had heard some people ask for five thousand to do something embarrassing and they got denied, and I heard some people do something embarrassing for two thousand, and I felt that they could have gotten more, so I felt good about the three thousand.

I really have to credit Howard for pushing me. My thought at the time after Bobby died was that I was going to die too. My best friend had died, but I still had all of this press booked for my solo record. I had commitments. I was on Stern and talking about what happened, and he said, "I'm worried about *you*. I'm worried that *you're* going to die." It was very confrontational but in a very loving way. And that was a real tough interview to get through.

Roseanne had a new talk show and had me on, and she did the same thing. Having someone confront me like that about my weight, I couldn't get away from it. Fame had been a way to hide, and they turned it on its ear because it became how they were going to confront me.

Oprah also wanted me to come on her show as someone she was going to help lose weight. The thing about Oprah, though, is she didn't want me on as the guy from Blues Traveler, just as a regional musician. She didn't really know who I was, so that was going to make it even worse. Plus, it was too scary; I didn't think I could do it.

But then I decided to get the bypass, and Howard kept in touch with me about that—again, in a very public way. Then when I had lost 150 pounds, I went on the air with him. I knew they were going to weigh me, but I didn't know they were going to ask me to take my shirt off. That was a big thing to me because taking my shirt off was something I never did. The cash made it all the sweeter, but the truth is that if it weren't for Stern, I wouldn't have lost the weight in the first place.

27

THE PRINCE INSIDE THE MICHELIN MAN

My imagination was always a real boon when it came to songwriting and other creative endeavors, but it became a real hindrance for my romantic life or the facsimile thereof.

I was in love with Sarah, the girl who played alto sax in the high school band. One day during senior year I had called her up and revealed my feelings to her, but she told me she didn't feel that way about me and just considered me a very good friend. So then I became her confidante, her Duckie if you will (*Pretty in Pink*, anyone?).

Still, in her yearbook I taped a key to a little treasure box that I put on her doorstep. Inside the treasure box was a note professing my undying love for her. I had also enclosed a locket with a glass slipper that I'd gotten from Disney World at precisely midnight—I'd had to wait around because Disney World closed at midnight and I wanted to be there at that moment to buy her this glass slipper. The box also contained a tape with a song I'd written for her called "Honesty and Love." I did the vocals, harmonica, keyboard, bass, and guitar, and I had poor Brendan do the drums for this four-hour session. By the end it started to sound like "Piano Man" with fifty verses.

She was going off to Switzerland to study structural engineering, and we would remain friends and exchange letters. I swore to her I would never give up loving her even though she didn't feel the same way about me.

Sarah would set the pattern that would keep me socially cloistered, which was putting a crush or an unrequited love in a bubble. I would formulate a love affair in my mind, and rather than disturb the bubble, I would keep it a secret. Sarah was the source of songs like "Alone," "100 Years," "Sweet Pain," "The Best Part," and most if not all the early acoustic songs where I would play guitar. She represented the perfect love that I could never have for some reason.

I think a real part of it was that I was very obese and felt that she was failing me because she didn't see the prince inside the Michelin Man.

It took over a decade and the help of a shrink for me to acknowledge that I wasn't obsessing over fat girls. I was looking at healthy women. So that was on me. Why shouldn't any woman I judged incapable of seeing the real me instead seek out someone who looked vaguely healthy. I should have wanted to look vaguely healthy.

I wooed Sarah over a period of eight years. She was in Switzerland and then came back and saw that everyone was singing these songs that I'd originally written and sung just for her at gigs we were playing at Nightingale's and Wetlands. This is when she started to take me a little more seriously.

Our first kiss happened at a diner where the waiter kept coming back to our table asking us if we wanted more ketchup. I mention this because it was extremely odd how often the waiter came back to interrupt us as we were having this pivotal moment it took eight years to arrive at. You might think I am saying this to embellish the story, but I am not kidding. As soon as I said, "I'm still in love—" the waiter swept in and asked, "Are you sure you don't need more ketchup?" Then he came back again and again with the same damn question. Was the waiter secretly in love with Sarah? I'm not sure; they didn't seem to know one another. But finally after we had the all the ketchup we could possibly have at the table and we assured the man after much discussion that we indeed had enough ketchup, we got back to our discussion eight years in the making about how finally she felt the same way.

I still don't know if he was putting me on.

When we finally sealed the deal, it only lasted a month. I think it was because I had put her on such a high pedestal that she thought she couldn't live up to it. After all, I had written eight years of songs about this woman and this magical time. Now we were beginning an actual relationship that was almost impossible to live up to. I finally broke up with her, but she wanted to end it as well. The last straw was when she said, "Why can't you just be dumber?" I'd heard that one before because I'd found that a lot of women just wanted to control me.

I was virgin until I was twenty-one. The first girl I ever had sex with saw us at Nightingale's and brought me home to get back at her mom. When she found out I was a virgin, she said, "I'll have sex with you, but it's just this once." I looked at her and said, "I think I can handle that."

The next day she called me to let me know that she'd be going away for the weekend, and I thought that was odd for just once. But then she came to the Lizmar Lounge the following week where we were playing and said, with a jarring urgency, "I have to talk to you." I thought, *Oh my god, she's pregnant* (or in my weaker moments, *Oh my god, she has herpes*). But instead she said, "I'm in love with you." So I figured, *Okay, I guess this is normal.*

But then we went to her house, and I assumed at least I'd get sex out of it, but we just talked about what a bitch her mom was. When I decided to break it off with her, she went fetal on Second Avenue, sobbing. So I had to rescind my breakup order just to get her off the pavement. Two days later she dumped me, and that was my first adult experience with women.

I've thought about mentioning her name, but this was the microcosm of a long, torrid, horrible relationship all compressed into a week. And we only had sex once.

I would start to meet girls through being in a band, but all the while I was secretly in love with Felicia. I would formulate love affairs in my mind, and rather than disturb the bubble, I would keep it a secret. She was the source of songs like "Run-Around." It was me trying to confront her with my love for her well after she had a boyfriend. The worst part was that through it all I suspected she just didn't feel the same way that I did.

Carolina was this passionate Italian girl. She adored me and I loved her, but I wasn't in love with her that way. I remember her punching me square in the face because we just had sex and she said, "I want you to know I will wait for you." And I said, "That's good, because I don't know . . . " What a thing to say to somebody. She was like, "What did you say?" I tried to explain myself rationally, but then the "fuck yous" started, and she full-on punched me in the face and gave me a bloody nose. So I told her to go upstairs and I waited downstairs and then drove her to her train. That's what that song "Carolina Blues" is about.

I also wrote "Yours" about Carolina because she was so passionate. A few years earlier I saw that Beethoven movie *Immortal Beloved* and wanted to go write a song that was passionate. Looking back, Carolina was very good to me, but I kind of treated her like shit, although she ended up treating herself like shit too—she loved to be a pariah.

Around the time we were starting to get on *David Letterman* I had a brief fling with Claire, who had been dating Dave Graham as well Eric Schenkman and, I believe, Dave Precheur for a second. We had developed a strong friendship, and I finally got the nerve to act on it at Wetlands after they aired our appearance on *Letterman*.

At the moment of our very first kiss Tom Gruber, who worked for Dave Graham, walked up and started to kiss the both of us, which kind of ruined it. (Tom was really hard-working and dedicated but almost too dedicated.) Perhaps that awkward beginning was a foreshadowing. We lasted about three months. She was one of my very first sexual experiences along with Carolina and the unnamed crazy girl.

I had so many coping mechanisms during this period that kept me out of actual, healthy relationships. For instance, I employed faux intimacy, where I would share so much about myself that I would scare off women. Or I would have these feelings that were pretty much a bubble in my head—I would fall in love with people from afar and hold these huge crushes on them without actually living it.

After I broke up with Sarah the bubble needed to be replaced with a new goddess upon the pedestal. This would gradually become Felicia, who played violin and joined Blues Band as our earnest but terrible bassist. She was a friend of mine, someone to whom I could piss and moan about my unrequited love for Sarah, and she was really brilliant. and I think she liked the attention, certainly the friendship. I would write songs about her, and along with the songs about Sarah, these became the bulk of our work in the early days.

Felicia became my very best friend, my confessor, and, eventually, a crush that would become a blindingly powerful love in my own mind. She was utterly brilliant and was quite a guide for me in the early days, as she seemed to have no end of advice for me and a sense of wanting to take care of me. I even found the fact that we were not acting like we were attracted to each other as respectfully keeping the secret of my unrequited love. That's the beauty of such a ruse: by not acting on it, you are making it that much more real, because it still exists as a silhouette's darkness does against the light.

She was always willing to accompany me to events like the Grammys, and in her mind she was going somewhere with her friend, but in my mind I was thinking, *Finally I get to take Felicia to the Grammys* or *Finally I get to take Felicia to the Howard Stern movie opening.*

Walking down that red carpet at the *Private Parts* premiere, Felicia became terrified by the screaming throngs and wanted us to get through the red carpet as quickly as possible. I think that was the chief difference between us—I needed the crowd in a way she could never understand.

I couldn't help but notice a wave of sympathy from Felicia as I got more and more obese. I think there was a point where she was beginning to humor me, not knowing what else to do. And she did value the friendship we had and still does to this day. But at some point I had to confront her, and it did not go well.

Felicia inspired most of the Blues Traveler love songs from *Save His Soul* through *Bridge*. This also was true of any song in *Zygote*, where "Once You Wake Up" was my coming to terms with Felicia not being in love with me. I found that the most honest songs that I wrote during that period were ones where I expressed and explored unre-quited love, and I think Felicia was the perfect model for that.

Eventually as a result of Felicia's rejection of me as a love interest and my corresponding rejection of Carolina as a love interest, I would come to have a catharsis. I decided that I wanted to have these experiences and feelings for real and that the only way to do that was therapy. It was about developing my own life. After twelve years, all I knew of my identity was Blues Traveler. I had to develop my own identity, and it was in there somewhere. I had a lot of work to do in establishing that identity outside of the band, and the shrink was helpful in my doing that work. They don't do the work for you; they're more like line judges while you work it out. They keep you honest. So in order to get to a place where I could have love, I had to start with me.

This is what led me to my *Zygote* album and also a brief but positive relationship with Tiffany, a really cool girl I met at shows—she was with me when I had my chest pains, although we didn't last much longer than that. Tiffany represented life after big crushes and unrequited bubbles, and though the relationship was short—it didn't go six months—at least it was real, probably the most real relationship I'd had to that point.

Then after Bobby died and I lost the weight, it was a very different life for me. I couldn't recognize the guy I used to be. I see pictures even now and remember consciously being there, but I can't to this day imagine what it felt like to have three of my friends help me out of a chair or to discover a barbeque sauce stain on a part of my belly I couldn't even see. It's an amazing thing your brain does—selective amnesia, I guess—but I started to see myself more as a sexual being and, therefore, other people could too.

That's when I met Delana. Chan's wife, Serena, knew her; she was Serena's sister's nanny. Delana was a breath of fresh air, about thirteen years younger than me and was there at the time when I was remaking myself, so it was easy for me to embrace something new, as she came to represent. We had a four-year relationship, the longest one I've ever had. She was the one who led me to move from Pennsylvania to Washington State in 2004; she had a connection there. I proposed to her on the last day we were at my house in Quakertown and totally caught her by surprise. I faked her out because she thought I was going to propose the day before. Here's a life lesson: never let a girl drive just after you give her an engagement ring because she'll stare at it, and you'll drive off the road.

Ultimately it was too destructive a relationship. We had a lot of fun at first, and I still care a great deal about her to this day, but Delana was really allergic to alcohol, and when Bobby left she became my new codependent. At times she would put herself in dangerous situations, which would terrorize people. And now that I couldn't use food the way I once did, I discovered drugs and alcohol.

A year after we moved she broke up with me. I think also the fact that she needed a live body in her bed to cope with what she was dealing with from her past was incredibly important and sort of a dealbreaker. She just became too lonely. We were six months from getting married. She helped me find a house and then moved into my guesthouse for a while, so it was amicable. I think she wanted to prove to her mom that she could live a conventional life, but her version was to marry a rock star, so it really wasn't that thought out.

After we broke up I did an Air Force Reserves tour overseas with the New England Patriots cheerleaders, and I instantly fell in love with Amber. Not much happened there, although she used me to get out of a relationship. We became friends, but there were always a few guys after her; eventually it became clear she was stringing me along. Still, in the first five days I knew her I wrote five songs. There was something inspiring about her. Perhaps it was her noncommittal nature or perhaps it was the mystery of hoping she'd be tamed if I just wrote one more song. I haven't heard much from Amber; I hope she's well. Her father was a New England Patriot, her husband was a New England Patriot, and if she has a son who grows up to be a New England Patriot, then I think she'll have pulled the hat trick.

It was through Amber that I met Kristen. She was another cheerleader and became a friend on whose shoulder I would cry about Amber. We were friends for a year and half and then began a real relationship that lasted a year. That fizzled out because I was gone a lot and because her dad was only four or five years older than me. She was sixteen years younger than me, and I think that messed with her head. That one really broke my heart; it was a tough one.

I think that after Kristen I didn't feel so much like a kid anymore. With Felicia it was more in my head, and with Delana, Kristen, and even Amber, this was me going out in the world and getting my heart broken. When you're fat and you get your heart broken you can say, "Oh that was because I was fat." When you don't have that excuse anymore it becomes about you. That's something even a fifteen-year-old learns, but for me it was much later. I think I got tougher or at the very least learned that real relationships are harder than a storybook thing. I was thirty-eight years old, and it was weird that it took me so long to realize that. I became more jaded at least in the interest of my own survival.

For the next four years I was doing my best to play the field. I met some interesting women, like Joy. I knew I liked Joy on the first night we met when I fell down a flight of stairs while we were holding hands, and instead of letting go of my hand, she chose to fall down the stairs with me. From that point we cared about each other, although the romantic aspect didn't last very long. She's still a very good friend to this day.

My next real shot at a relationship came in late 2011 with Caitlin. We met after a gig in a Vermont bar, and a few buttery nipple shots later we had a kiss and decided to see where it would lead. We had a good time, but she had her own life in Vermont and couldn't leave, and I just didn't have it in me to move to Vermont—part of that old and jaded thing—but I value that relationship.

About a year after Caitlin and I broke up I would meet Rachel and again try living with someone. She needed a place to stay, so I had her come live with me. She was cool, and it was kind of a light thing, where we had an open arrangement.

It was during this period that I had an incident with a Vegas prostitute that made the news after she roofied me and stole my Rolex. My manager had some party, and I drank way too much whiskey and then went back to my hotel, where I got it in my head that I wanted to go to the bar and get a drink, but I'm not quite sure what really happened next. I remember a young woman coming up to me in the bar; I have some sense of being in an elevator headed up to my room. The next thing I knew I was in my underwear, not having done anything, and my wallet was empty and my watch was gone. I wasn't looking to buy a prostitute, although my arrangement with Rachel would have allowed it. I eventually pieced together that I must have been roofied. I went to the police but never got my watch back, although it was insured, so that turned out okay.

I have had a few encounters with prostitutes over the years, and they have not gone especially well. The sexiest part of a woman is her enthusiasm, and that's what you lose with a prostitute.

On our very first tour of Europe in 1992, when we pulled into Amsterdam, everybody was talking about how they were going to get one of those women in the windows. In response, I went on and on about how I would never treat a woman that way, that I could never purchase a woman for money, and I ended up being the only one who went—everyone else chickened out.

I wandered over, and on the way I stopped in at one of those coffee shops and had three space cakes. As they were kicking in, I saw this lovely Austrian woman in a window. I lingered too long, and she said, "That'll be 25 guilders if you want to come in." I thought, *Why not?* and 50 guilders later, I left. From there I went to a live sex show, where I witnessed sights I'd never even imagined, including the longest penis I'd ever seen—it curled around like a monkey's tail.

Then, as I was walking back to where I thought the hotel was located, I noticed the woman in the window I had just been with. So I gave her a casual wave, being very sophisticated, and she stepped out of her window, ran to the door, and informed me that I had left my passport behind and that she'd given it to the police.

She told me how to get to the police station, but I got completely lost until I finally stumbled into one and said to the officer behind the desk, "Excuse me, I hope you'll bear with me because I'm high on one of your many legally obtainable hash cakes, but I was enjoying the company of one of your legally obtainable prostitutes, and she said that I left my passport." The cop instantly ordered me to get the hell out of his building. That's when I realized that just because these things were legal in Amsterdam, they weren't necessarily socially acceptable to everyone.

The fun part was the next day, when we had a gig at 5 p.m. in Belgium. So first I had to walk back to my hotel, which I kept thinking was right around the corner because I was really high on the legally obtainable space cakes, but it was actually on the other side of town, so it was a long walk back.

Everything opened at noon and closed at three and was scattered all over town: the US consulate, a passport-worthy photographer, and a police station. I had to go to one place to report the theft, go to the next place and get a form, and then go to the photographer before circling back with the picture. It was very close, but we did make into Belgium in time.

I think I finally realized I'm really not a prostitute guy years ago in LA when I ordered an escort service, and this woman came to the door and asked me, "What turns you on?" I made the classic mistake of saying what nonprostitute people say, what a normal healthy person would say about someone he's having sex with, which is: "What turns me on is really what turns you on." So oddly I spent $800 talking until 4 a.m., but that's really not why I called her. I just didn't have the nerve to tell her that.

A number of years later I was in Vegas and was single. I had mentioned to one of my managers that I wasn't good at getting prostitutes, so without my knowledge, they tried to help me out. I met this girl who was hanging out, and she seemed to be paying attention to me, so I bought her breakfast. She asked if her friend could come along with us, and I said, "Sure," and I just hung out with them. The next day the band told me that they had hired her for me, but I just didn't realize it. That was lost on me, and really that's me with a prostitute.

Another time a girl I was dating hired an escort to dance for us in our room. The dancer was not there to sleep with me, but she seemed to like me and took me aside. So I looked back at the girl I was dating, and she said, "Go for it." I was pretty drunk, so I said, "Ohhh, okay." It turned out she was just testing me. But, as I later explained to her, I just don't take tests well.

As for the roofie incident in Vegas, shortly after I reported it the story was all over the news. I couldn't quite figure that out until I realized that the first guy I spoke with and said, "Oh yeah, I got roofied" was the person who was the head of the Las Vegas press, and suddenly it was all over the wire. I didn't really mind because it's good to come clean about things like that. What you don't want to do is have a secret life. I think a secret life is much worse.

When Rachel had moved in, to keep things on a pseudo-independent level, we agreed that she would primarily live in the guest house when I was gone. This way she could bring all of her stuff and I didn't have to move any of my stuff.

When I began dating Jordan, who is now my wife and the mother of my daughter, before it got very serious—and it did get serious fast—we felt it only fair to tell Rachel, and that was a painful experience.

At the outset I had promised Rachel that if she moved to Washington, I would guarantee her a place to stay for at least a year. Some people thought my home life was a little strange because Rachel kept living in my guesthouse after we broke up but I stopped charging her rent. She had wanted to pay rent when we were together so she could remain independent, but after we broke up I said, "You just take care of the house and my truck while I'm off on tour or in the recording studio."

After Rachel found a place to live and met her current boyfriend, the timing seemed to work fairly well for Jordan to come move in with me. I'm still friends with Rachel and wish her well too. I've been pretty happy in that I've been able to remain friends with most of the women I have been serious about. I wish them well (and offer apologies to any who weren't mentioned here).

I do think that these experiences have had a tangible impact on my songwriting. One of the things that I think I can contribute is dealing with how bumpy life is and how hard it can be and then expressing how we find strength from love. I do have some catchy rhymes, but I think that's the meat of it.

I don't think a song can really work when all it does is express how everything in life is just great. The exception, of course, is that song from the *Lego Movie*, and who sings that? Toys sing that.

I think Chris Barron is one of the best songwriters around. He can come up with something catchy and brilliant in the same song. He can write you something about dishwashing detergent that will make you think, and that's kind of fucked up but it's a good thing. His song "How Could You Want Him (When You Know You Could Have Me?)" is one of the best confessions in rock and roll—to say that for all of my parading and confidence, I'm really expressing this pain that you rejected me. His favorite line is "Saint Christopher lives on the end of a quill," and that's a good line. He loves the pretty stuff, but it's the confession that's the thing. All of it builds to where he is forced to say it out loud—"How could you want him when you know you could have me?" The singer still can't believe it. The version they did on the record is pretty good—they added a little more guitar and put thought into it, and it's still a great song—but I'll always prefer the spare confessional that I heard in the take on the demo.

My own earlier stuff was a lot more naïve because my love experiences were from my perceptions of heartbreak—I would hide from that without having tried it. When you're hiding, love can be this very sacred thing. You can build it into this shrine, and it's a very beautiful shrine, but it's not a real answer; it's not a real response. It doesn't love you back. You're just endlessly struggling to express this. There was a naiveté to my earlier stuff that people enjoyed because I was willing to run head on into the fan blades.

But really being in love demands being there when they suck, and contentment is a fleeting emotion between vomit or poop or bad breath. The reality of a relationship is that it is never going to be this Cinderella story because where does that exist other than in a Disney premise?

Disney premises are great. We've all lived for Disney premises, but you have to know the difference. I was so naïve and unpracticed that I couldn't see the difference, and that kept me alone and, therefore, writing more of these songs. I kept making that tradeoff: my solitude is my gift. And that's dumb, something a young guy does.

But if you manage to get in the experience that other people have, which is the experience of life and settling down and having a real love relationship, then whatever observations you make are going to be more real.

To be a songwriter, you have to live in the real world and pony up your naïve enthusiasm. But to hide and then pony up your naïve enthusiasm is kind of cheating; you're not really earning it. If you earn it, I think it'll resonate better.

I think an earned naïve enthusiasm, one that has survived reality, is one that strikes a deeper chord. At least hopefully. I suppose that's my naive enthusiasm talking.

What I have learned for sure through my relationships is that it becomes a problem when people think a song is the definition of a relationship. You have to remember that a song is just a snapshot of a moment you're feeling, that it's not the sum total. A song is like a sitcom with a happy ending that only lasts a half hour.

28

SHOWING MY RANGE

I made VH1's 100 Most Shocking Moments for sitting next to my friend and smoking some weed while he drove my car. People often think that's a gun story, but it really isn't.

Before I explain what happened, though, I will share another gun story that's actually about guns. I'm not so proud of it, but it actually happened and caused Dickey Betts to run away from me, which was a shocking moment in its own right.

When you have friends in your crew rather than professionals, as we did in the early days, you really do whatever you can to motivate them, especially when you're not paying them anything.

There was a point when I happened to be the only sober guy in my band, and I'm including my crew, so I became accustomed to a certain level of physical intimidation to get things going.

We were at a show opening for the Allman Brothers Band in 1992, and I couldn't hear anything again. I figured I had to try something extreme, because in those days I needed to throw a new kind of temper tantrum every day to get my crew's attention; otherwise, they'd just nod and smile and wouldn't do a damn thing. I once threw harps at my monitor guy in order to make my point.

But this time I brought a derringer with me onto the stage. I had taken the bullets out of it, but looking back, this is still something I regret deeply. As a gun guy, this was the most abhorrent thing I have ever done. I motioned to Grant in my crew to come over, stuck this unloaded derringer in his ribs, and growled, "It's loaded. Give me more fucking monitors or I'll kill you."

Looking back in amazement, he went and gave me more monitors.

As it happened, Dickey had done something with a live gun a few years earlier. I found out about this because there was this rumbling within the Allman Brothers tour, within his crew—"He did what?!"— and I had to go and apologize to a whole lot of people, and rightly so. I remember telling Dickey Betts, "Did you hear what I did yesterday?" He responded, "I can't talk about it" and ran away.

Grant should have said, "okay" to me and then turned and walked out of the building and maybe called the cops or something. But, amazingly, he gave me more monitors.

These days I consider myself a responsible gun owner and would never pull that kind of stunt. Without acknowledging guilt, let's say it's possible that I once smuggled a gun into Canada, but if so, even that was a relatively minor offense and was overshadowed by a drug bust, which is the exact opposite of what would land me on VH1.

When we opened the stadium dates for the Stones in 1997, the tour included two shows in Canada, which meant a border crossing on September 30. The previous time we had played in Canada, about a year and half earlier, they confiscated my crossbow and gave me a $60 fine.

So this time I (hypothetically) decided I would have my vengeance by smuggling a handgun into Canada. It was barely a gun; it was a pen gun. For about two weeks people were allowed to buy one from American Derringer. It's a single-shot .25 caliber pistol that looks like a tire gauge. You unscrew the barrel and put a round in it, and then you screw the top back on. It's a half-inch barrel and is built for spies; it's supposed to be a last-ditch weapon, but if a spy pulled it out, he'd probably be killed because it's not going to hurt anybody.

So (perhaps) I put the barrel in my shoe and the rest of it in my stuff and smuggled it into Canada. I really just wanted to be able to say I did that (if indeed I did do it, no need to rankle our friends to the north— did I mention that my tour manager was turned away at the border because he failed to acknowledge he had been arrested for setting off illegal fireworks . . . in the fourth grade!). It was (theoretically) a little secret for myself to say I did something bad, but then lo and behold, a short while later, I discovered that Bobby was busted for cocaine at the Winnipeg airport. Of course the press had a field day because we were opening for the Rolling Stones tour and twenty years earlier the Toronto police found heroin in Keith Richards's hotel room, confiscated his passport, and detained him for over a month. In Bobby's case he eventually pled guilty to possession and received two years of probation. As I told him, though, "Remember, drugs are felonious, guns are not."

I suppose that point was reinforced in some fashion on March 8, 2007, when I was returning home to Washington from Texas. It was moving day, and I was legally transporting fourteen guns in my car. That's what made the news, and what's funny is that everyone thinks I broke the law because I had guns in my car. When I explain, "No, it was for weed," they usually respond, "Oh that doesn't really matter."

My friend was doing 111 miles an hour, and as soon as we saw the cop running to his car, we pulled over. We felt bad because we knew what must have been going through the officer's head when he pulled over the car: "Will I ever see my family again?"

I had the guns, along with a Taser, a switchblade, night-vision goggles, a public address system, and a siren. My car also has a secret compartment, and I had put the weed there. But once you put the weed in the secret compartment that you have constructed, you are officially smuggling drugs. I didn't know that, so they seized the car, and many thousands of dollars later, I got it back.

When they brought me to the station, they wanted to know why I had a police siren. What I told them was "in case of a national disaster because I didn't want to be left behind." The real answer is if there's an earthquake, people are getting the fuck out of my way. That's why I have a police siren in my car. The night-vision goggles are just cool and happened to be in my car.

But for that I made VH1's 100 Most Shocking Moments. I beat Elvis meeting Nixon—and he was packing two guns in the White House. I beat Leif Garrett running over his friend and crippling him for life. I was just sitting next to my friend in a car, smoking some weed.

The next day I was about to go the airport when I received a call from the ATF. I had a stalker, and she called the ATF after it was reported that I had been arrested. She told them that she was afraid for her life. So they wanted to come over and see what I was doing. I told the agent I needed to get to the airport but showed them the police reports we had on her—it's always wise to document your stalkings—and they let me go. Funny side note: she ended up stalking the ATF guy for a while.

When I first got into the limo there was a .44 magnum sitting there. Apparently the owner of the limo company wanted to sell it to me because he heard that I liked them. So while I was playing with this cool .44 magnum (it has interchangeable barrels), all over the radio I heard "Our top story: He didn't want to be left behind!" The quote was blaring up and down the dial. After I arrived at the airport my phone rang, and it was Ted Nugent—"It's a travesty, man. They're trying to railroad you." He invited me down to his machine gun ranch in Texas—I hadn't realized that machine guns are raised on ranches—apparently they milk them or something. But I guarantee you it's free range.

Anyhow, I was at the airport and everyone was looking at me like they caught me masturbating. It's weird being known for something you weren't trying to be known for. The kicker is that when I went through the metal detector, I forgot that I had a metal container full of weed in my coat. But it didn't set the thing off. It was as if God said, "You've had enough, son," patted me on the head, and sent me on my way. I've always heard the Lord protects the stupid.

Oh yes and the drug charge—it was actually just a misdemeanor for possession—was dismissed after a year passed without an arrest.

I suppose I should acknowledge that I did go to jail once for holding a gun, but it was actually a cap pistol. This was back when I was nineteen and was home from the New School. My friends Dave Wilder and Crugie Riccio who were in the band the Disturbed (not the Chicago heavy metal band, the Princeton punk band) were making an album in Philly, and I had nothing to do, so I went with them in Crugie's van. He had a mohawk and leather jacket, and Dave was a thin little kid with frizzly hair. I, of course, looked like a maniac with my sideburns from that era. Crugie had a cap pistol in his glove compartment, and as we were talking, I'd twirl the cap pistol on my finger. Occasionally I'd point it at Crugie's head and demand that he take me to Cuba, and over the course of the drive I'd wave it out the window, not thinking because it was a cap pistol. I had long since put it on the dashboard when we hit a pothole, and all of a sudden we see the lights of a police car. We figured he was pulling us over because we had a flat tire, but suddenly three cop cars surrounded us and we heard, "Get out of the car now and go on your knees!" Then I saw the cap pistol on the dashboard and realized what had happened. I forgot I was nineteen and not nine, and the police had received reports that someone was waving a gun out the window. They arrested us for terrorism, and we sat in a jail cell for three hours and then let us go because we had no priors.

I also was arrested once with a wooden samurai sword. Back in high school we broke into the Princeton reunions, which is what you had to do when you were a high school kid because they were all gated off. So one time I was at a friend's house with a practice samurai sword, and I hung onto it when we decided to break into the reunion because I liked the way it felt. So when they caught us for breaking in, I had the fake samurai sword, which in retrospect may not have been the best decision and could have made the situation appear more alarming than it actually was. I eventually explained myself, and there was no major fallout from that incident, but sometimes I just don't know why I do the things I do.

But as for the incident in 2007, what really what came out of it was that people were treated to a photo of my guns lined up on a card table in some conference room. Ever since then, people will sometimes come up to me and ask me how many guns I own. A gentleman never discloses exactly how many weapons he has, but I am certainly aware of the number.

My friends say they never worry about me because I don't have a million rounds of ammunition. I'm not really bunkered in. I think guns fascinate me the way shoes or golf clubs fascinate people who are into shoes or golf clubs.

A really cool gun you can trick out is a 1911, the .45 automatic World Wars I and II sidearm. You can polish the barrel so it cycles better and makes the trigger like butter. It's the same way that somebody cuts an angle on a skateboard's axle if they're into boarding. It's that kind of a hobby to me.

I don't hunt because I go to the supermarket, so I find that hypocritical. As a kid I went with my dad to New York on a pheasant hunt. I shot a pheasant and was so proud that we were going to eat it, like my older brothers did. But my dad was too sleepy to help me clean it, and I ruined the meat. I ruptured the shit sack and then cried because I just murdered a bird.

A few years later my dad took me on a deer hunt. You sit behind a stone wall, freezing, and you're not allowed to shiver because the deer will notice you shivering, and you can't give your position away. Deer in the woods sound like squirrels dropping acorns, and for eight hours there were a shit-ton of squirrels dropping acorns but no deer. I wanted to do two things when I was done: shoot every squirrel I saw and buy a deer, tie it to the ground, and shoot it. I realized that wasn't a good hunter's spirit, so that was when I stopped hunting. But I do respect people who are really into it.

I've let people hunt on my property who feed their family through it. The key to a hunt is that you actually have to use the meat; you can't just kill something for no reason. If you are using the meat, then there's a sacredness to it.

I was talking to Alicia Silverstone and got her to admit that if I harvested an elk in that fashion and substituted it for beef, and used every bone, sinew, and hide, I'd be more humane as a meat eater and as a user of animal products. It is the one way in my heart I would acceptably take an animal. Every knife and gun would have a bone handle and all of the hides and antlers would be used—that's the only way to do it.

But I love weapons of all kinds, including swords, spears, atlatls—any kind of weapon has an aesthetic that is superbly efficient. It has to be because it's designed to take a life as if your life depended on it. So there's a beauty to the curve of a saber, which had to work as well as it could because the other guy was trying to build a saber that was better than yours.

I own a Civil War–era cannon that can shoot cans of dog food a thousand yards. I only have six acres of land, so I haven't fired it since I moved to my current house. You can see my cannon on Google Earth, though. I feel like Fidel Castro: you can see my artillery from space.

It's a rough-barrel cannon so you can't put real munitions in there. The balls would rattle around and explode. It's good for tin cans, though. I could have spent another $15,000 for the rifled barrel that would shoot projectiles a mile away, but I don't need anything shelled that badly. Of course, that would give me a much more active role in the PTA. If you're a member of a local community and you have an artillery, they have to listen to you just a little bit more. It's called gunboat diplomacy, and it'll work in your neighborhood.

There's something about tracing the evolution of firearms that fascinates me, but I also like to have some form of a modern version. So I have a few assault rifles, and they are the niftiest, coolest weapons that I can get my hands on, with all the doodads and bells and whistles. They're locked up and everything, but they're also ready if shit goes down, although I'm not really planning for shit to go down.

I'd say in an apocalypse I'd last about two weeks because I'm not the healthiest dude in the world and I don't know how far I could run. I suppose my best bet would be to load up my car, drive to a convenience store, take that over, map out the location of the next convenience store, and just convenience store my way to the wilderness. I am basically part of a grid, and eventually someone bigger and tougher would come and take all my guns.

My attitude is that I'd have to make friends with people who know how to chop wood and catch rabbits because all I can bring is a lot of firearms and a fast car. What else am I offering other than a unique psychological perspective? I could play songs, but the most valuable person in our society is still a plumber because everybody shits. You need a plumber, and then when the apocalypse hits, you don't even need that guy—you need a hunter or maybe an electrician. Sometimes people sing, sometimes people listen to other people singing, but you can't guarantee a meal if you're going to live by performance.

So by and large my guns end up collecting dust in my attic because I'm on the road so much. I used to bring all of my gun-hating friends to my house to shoot because they all secretly love to shoot guns, even if they don't want to have one—"I still want them illegal, but that was fun." And then I had ten guns I had to clean, they'd spent all this ammo, and it was annoying.

At this point I'm not just indiscriminately buying guns. It's a treat to buy a gun. I think at one point my accountant made me sell a gun before I bought a new one, but eventually that got swept under the rug. I sold the accountant and got a new accountant.

One of my biggest challenges is keeping all of my gun licenses up to date. When I got into carrying, people told me, "You don't want to do that; it's a lot of paperwork." And my answer was "If that's what it is, if it's a matter of paperwork, I'll take that challenge. I'll jump though the hoops." I'd rather have a gun permit and not need it than need a gun permit and not have it.

I just need to be reminded when it's time to renew and what that requires. The states won't send you notification if a permit is up—that's your obligation. So I have somebody in management whose job is to keep me legal. If I didn't have management doing it, I'd hire a lawyer to babysit all of my permits and see where I'm at.

That's the thing: they want you to think it's too hard so you'll give up. And that's what will get a curmudgeon like me to fly all night to get to Rhode Island to make it to the permit office in the hours they require, just to keep that permit active in a state tinier than most people's back-yard. And really, how often will I be in Rhode Island during the four years before it expires again? But if I'm in a state that requires a permit from that state and I don't have that permit, then I'm an idiot.

They approve you before you take a photo, so I always like to have a look on my face that would make a rational person ask, "Would you give this guy a gun?" All my permits look like that. I try to look confused or extra happy. The USO once refused to accept a photo where I had hammed it up a bit too much. We were on the way to Bosnia, and they wouldn't allow it, so they had to use a picture off an album.

In the early days we worked some dicey places, and just knowing I was packing helped. In Chicago we worked a couple of scary spots, and I'd be hanging with the Chicago PD. They'd show me theirs and I'd show them mine—that was allowed. Back then I didn't always know where I was legal, but I don't let that happen today.

You have to be a jailhouse lawyer and go state by state to weave this web of reciprocity. Texas and Florida permits are respected by most everyone, but there a few states that need their own permits. For instance, all of New England has its own laws.

Hawaii has an islander tradition where they don't like guns and that's marrow deep, so the rule is if you own a gun, you have seventy-two hours to register your weapon at the police department and fill out a form. Usually I'm not on Hawaii for three days, so it's not such a big deal, and more often than not, I don't bring a gun to Hawaii.

The one that got away from me was California. I actually got residency in Santa Barbara; it was in this little shithole. My bass player's old girlfriend would sit for my dog, and she was a beach bum or ski boarding bum, depending on the season, and she also wanted to live in California. So she lived in this shack and I kicked in some rent so it was my place too, but the police thought it was too shabby for a gun permit. It was all discretionary.

I find they're often looking for some little thing: "You didn't fill in your application right. Even though it's been expunged, you said you've never been arrested, so you lied in your application."

"But because it has been expunged, I'm allowed to say I wasn't arrested."

"No, you had to tell us that you were arrested and that it was expunged."

Then they explain that if I withdraw my application, they won't deny it. If they deny it, then that would get into the system and they would have to explain that I lied on my application, which could lead to a revocation of all my permits. It's like the DMV for guns.

Every time someone starts talking about the Second Amendment, they start sounding like an asshole. It's an absolute right, but I get little squeamish about celebrating it because it's a right to defend yourself with deadly force. So it's not something to high five about.

I see that right as similar to the right to have an abortion (which technically isn't but should be a right). It's not a moment for happiness; it's a right to deal with something tragic. And I believe people are adult enough in adult situations in an adult society to deal with the consequences of their actions. I hope that I never, ever have to use a gun to protect myself. So far I've never had to shoot anyone and I've never had to threaten anybody with a loaded gun.

My brother, who's a lawyer, says, "You've got to admit—it's just a lark." And that is sort of what it is for me, a hobby gone awry. But I also believe that I can't run; I've been in some dangerous situations; and I've felt better being armed.

But to espouse the Second Amendment like it's something everyone needs education about is a little presumptuous of me. If you respect the right to have guns and the right to love guns, you have to respect the right to hate guns. The only reason to use deadly force is if you don't want to die—I look at it as my I-don't-want-to-die spray—and you have to be prepared to live with the consequences.

If we're going to vote and pay taxes, then on some level we're trusting each other to be adults. I think it's an adult thing. I have to be able to trust that my fellow man is able to deal with deadly force. That's what you're doing, being trusted by your society.

Most permits prohibit you from showing your guns to people, because that creates terrorism. You're not supposed to be wielding them. If you have a gun and start brandishing it for no reason or to win an argument, that's just dumb. You have to look at it with responsibility. There's something to be said for the discipline of a samurai who never pulls out his sword.

29

TROUBADOURS
AND MOON SHOTS

In 1991 I wrote in my tour journal, "Life is short if you go by albums." I find that oddly wise, considering I was only twenty-four years old and we'd put out exactly two albums.

I think what I meant was that we'd devote a year or eighteen months to each new album cycle. First we'd gear up and develop material, then we'd record it, and finally we'd support it with a tour. That album would become our focus for so much longer than the actual time we spent in the studio.

Now I view albums in terms of eras within the larger trip we have taken as a band. Looking back on them, even those that didn't work as well, still have something to say in the conversation about that journey. And that to me is what making albums is all about.

Bridge really reflected a new formative era for the band, and I respect its sincerity. On *Truth Be Told* (2003) I felt that the new version of the band had found its stride. It was our current incarnation's early high point and an accurate reflection of what we were doing.

This was the time of true optimism because *Bridge* had carried with it such a heavy burden of the transition of the band into this new era. With *Bridge* there was a question of who is this band going to be, and that question wasn't fully answered. With *Truth Be Told* we had enough touring under our belt—we had done so on our own terms and we'd done well at it—that we felt confident enough to stay who we were and we were enjoying it. It was a very happy time. We were excited about what was coming, and I felt that this new version of the band had found its stride.

The songs on *Truth Be Told* remained fearless and innocent. I think after that point we started to wander and search for some new ways to make albums, although we weren't even aware of it at the time. But in 2003 our system that had worked since the beginning of Blues Traveler was still effectively functioning as far as satisfying us artistically.

Working with Don Gehman was a huge treat because he had done so many albums I didn't even know I liked. There's one song on there, "Unable to Get Free," that was actually inspired in some melodic ways with its minor chord progression by an old Barbra Streisand tune, "Woman in Love," that, it turned out, Don Gehman had recorded and engineered. I discovered this while we were talking about it. I referred to this Barbra tune as far as the emotional pang I wanted my voice to hit, and he said, "Oh yeah, I did that song," which in itself blew me away.

What Don Gehman came up with was us sitting a room, ready to record, and working out the little details of the song as we were rolling, and I don't think that any other producer had allowed us to do that before. Usually we would rehearse and rehearse and rehearse and get some sort of a sketch of the song down to a very accurate place, but what Don Gehman was offering us was the respect that the tape would wait for us, that we would work in a timely fashion and that the ideas were valid. That was a very important thing for us to take away, and it really added a fun and loose feel to a lot of these songs.

I think we got a little lost on *¡Bastardos!* (2005). I was really smitten by these cheerleaders in my social carousing and writing some especially sappy stuff. I was also trying to be like Picasso—I'd just come in and scribble. I wanted Ben to take over and find his voice, as he was the newest guy in the band (we'd had a longstanding relationship with Tad, as he was Chan's brother after all), so there was a lot of pressure on Ben.

Meanwhile our management couldn't find a record deal for us, and we couldn't even find a producer. We were going on faith because we wanted this album to come out in 2005. We eventually decided to part ways with manager Scott McGhee. In the midst of this we lucked into Jay Bennett, who was still recovering after getting fired from Wilco following their record *Yankee Hotel Foxtrot* (you can see some of what went down with Jay and Jeff Tweedy in the documentary *I Am Trying to Break Your Heart: A Film About Wilco*). Jay, rest his soul, was in a very shaky place. I left it to him to produce the shit out of the album, and I liked that approach because we hadn't done it yet; it seemed very new to us. So *¡Bastardos!*, which some have found to be an overproduced album, was the product of us shifting the sound a little more onto the keyboards, at least in my mind, and also trying to make what we could out of a slightly injured producer and an uncertain course.

We soon landed new management with Charles Attal, and the good people at C3, and a new record deal with Vanguard. Still, *¡Bastardos!* did take on the feeling of a stop-gap album. For the first time we were feeling a little unfulfilled.

I wanted to do something different on *North Hollywood Shootout*. Three years had passed since *¡Bastardos!*, and part of the reason for that is because I thought we'd gone as far as we could making albums the way we made them, where somebody would bring in a riff and I would write words and shape the song to that riff while the other guys were working on the next song. This became an endless assembly line of songcraft that started to blur into one thing. The results started to seem as though we were writing the same song over and over again. I think once you get settled into an artistic process that becomes efficient, it also comes with the danger of being unoriginal, at least to your mind.

There were still a lot of strong songs on *North Hollywood Shootout*, but the premise I'd adopted in order to make this album different wasn't working. Instead of our assembly line, what if I were the absolute slave driver going back to the nineties, only with a sane approach in which I didn't have to bully my way into being the lord and master of the music? We would mutually agree as rational adults that I would be overseeing the music. What I was hoping to do was wield the whole band like a pen. The problem was that the pen began asking, "Why are we doing this?"

I wanted to be czar of the record, but instantly our producer Dave Bianco put himself between me and the rest of the band. He seemed to get my premise when I talked with him alone at the beginning, but right away he tried to insert himself into the process. I don't blame him for this because he's an artistic mind as well. I had intended to be there the whole time, but he talked me out of it. Instead, I would show up at night, and they would show up during the day, so there were two camps going. The reason is I sing better at night, and he wanted me to be there to perform, but it was at that moment that my idea started to fall apart. I also found that before I became czar, I could write whatever lyrics I wanted, but after I became czar every lyric was scrutinized by every band member. This drove me crazy. It led to a watering down of the lyrics. "You Me and Everything" is the American cheese Kraft Single of our writing career.

I became disheartened. I felt that I had failed the guys in the direction I was trying to take us. The producer definitely didn't get what I was trying to do, and as much as the band tried, they couldn't turn off their brains or their creative ears, nor should they have to. If I were working with dependent mindless robots, it might have worked. But I wouldn't wish that on anyone. When you have autonomy over thinking people, it's never autonomy unless you want to stifle their creativity, and why would I want to do that?

So it was a frustrating experience, but it did lead me to the Duskray Troubadours, which has affected the way I am doing things to this day.

Duskray was actually my second solo project of the decade. In 2005 our old crew guy Bob Mahoney had an idea for a jam session out west with DJ Logic, who I'd played with before and is a cool guy and a dear friend, and Rob Wasserman. Who doesn't love Rob Wasserman? Something about the bass, harmonica, and DJ really worked. As I mentioned earlier when I was I talking about Oteil Burbridge, I think it's because the harmonica is so shrill and the bass is so low, and it was just this no-brainer that sounded new and interesting.

When we were back in New York where Jason (DJ Logic) lived, I talked to him about keeping it going. I knew we couldn't get Rob, but

I figured that when Blues Traveler was off, we could hire Tad to do the bass part. I also had an old friend from high school, Marcus Bleecker, a drummer, who had also been in Mr. B's band, the *Whiplash* band (he was the first drummer I saw who received the type of abuse depicted in the film), and I had always wanted to do something with him, a theme of mine, apparently, of going to people I've known ever since I was a kid.

This new band borrowed from the Wasabi, the band with Arnie Lawrence, Blues Traveler, and Spin Doctors, and the Authority in that we never rehearsed. One advantage is this requires very little work for the band as long as everyone keeps their minds open. Marcus was a jazz drummer, and with Logic's precision there was a wonderful breathing effect, while Tad and I knew how to work together melodically.

We were essentially playing together for beer money when we were approached by Jonathan Schwartz from Relix Records about putting out a record as the John Popper Project Featuring DJ Logic. We didn't want songs per se, but we knew we would need some for the album. So we created jams, and our producer, Craig Street, really made something out of them. To his credit, he was dealing with a bunch of coked-out, drunken fools, and he somehow took a bunch of jam sketches and created real song structures. He was not just a brilliant producer but he also put up with so much shit from me because at that time I thought you were supposed to have tension with your producer. He was an unsung hero.

When we toured in support of it, before each gig we had a few shots of Patron Silver, chilled. We'd only do ten dates at a time because if we did any more, we would have died. It was absolutely madcap. I remember some of it. The jams were good—we'd get into some really good zones of noodle.

It was that collaborative nature I remembered fondly as I thought about my next project, which followed *North Hollywood Shootout*.

I had remained in touch with Jono Manson ever since the Nightingale days. He moved to Italy for a few years in the mid-2000s because his music was doing fairly well there. Occasionally I would join him, and we would busk around the country. By the end of the decade he was back in Santa Fe, where he had settled after he left New York City in the nineties. We'd been talking forever about doing something together, but there had always been a Blues Traveler thing I had to deal with.

We began talking very earnestly in 2009 because *North Hollywood Shootout* had drained me so much. That year we started collecting songs and discussing our approach, and in 2010 we made the album. It felt rejuvenating to write some Americana songs and not be pinned to the expectations of being in Blues Traveler.

Jono has a little studio in the Chupadero Mountains, and I got into my car and drove down there on New Year's Day. It was a beautiful ride from Washington. If you take the right roads, it really clears your head. I'd known some of the players since the Nightingale's days, and it was a fun album to make, just perfectly framed in that American sound that is the Southwest.

Every player, by his style, reminded me of a dime novel cowboy, and we were holed up in Santa Fe, so it really took on that vibe. We made the album we wanted to make, and it had a real soul to it. But what I especially enjoyed was sharing the writing, which brought things out of me that I wasn't used to getting out of me.

I came to appreciate the process of taking my vision and making it coincide with the vision of other people I respect. That's how you create true vision. Nobody knew what the color blue was until two or three people discussed it. Before that, someone said, "This fire engine is blue," and someone else said, "The sun is blue." Then they got together and decided, "No, the sky is blue. We're all calling that blue." And that was the beginning of the color blue.

It also felt really satisfying because, as this project came together, I had put my own money into it, hoping I might get a record deal. I had that much confidence in it, and this allowed me to cut through all the bullshit of having to sell it to somebody. As it happened, our new management, Charles Attal and C3, had just hired Dave Geller and Mat Whittington to come on board, and they were excited about finding a label to release it. We agreed to meet and talk about it at SXSW in 2010.

When I was at SXSW I saw Bill Murray, and he gave me the biggest pep talk about Duskray. I was nearly in tears. I was looking for blow and mentioned that to him. He said, "You could do that, *or* you could appreciate what's around you. Have you ever been here before?" And that kind of stopped me in my tracks because he was right.

From there I told him what I had hoped to accomplish with the Duskray Troubadours album and what I had on the line, and he really got it. I started to explain how I wanted to bring this new approach to Blues Traveler, but he got there ahead of me and told me, in essence, that I was fighting the good fight. Then he spoke about a time he had seen Blues Traveler in Cape Cod on the spinning stage and kept going on about my drummer—that really made me happy because Brendan doesn't get enough credit.

Bill told me what I needed to hear and in such a way that I didn't get distracted thinking that everything he said would end in a punch line. It was all really deep and meaningful. It gave me a renewed confidence that I was on the right path.

When I first saw him, he was sitting with Woody Harrelson and Matthew McConaughey. I walked up to them and asked, "Are you guys here to whore yourselves too?" At first Matthew seemed to take offense, saying, "I'm not whoring myself." Then Bill interrupted, "Hey, can you play 'Red River Valley' on the harmonica?" I did, and that's when McConaughey recognized me.

Eventually we went back to Woody Harrelson's room at the Four Seasons. I was with DJ Logic, and Bill dropped us off at the hotel. Logic had this cast on because he had broken his ankle or something. So Bill sat in the trunk of the SUV—it was just so awesome. I took a picture of it and told people that we'd kidnapped him, locked the car, and gone skinny dipping, but when we came back, there was broken glass and the car was gone, so I just went to my hotel, packed, and got the hell out of there. But all that really happened was that he gave us this cool ride.

There were a few of us in the room, and we were probably making a racket because at some point we heard *Boom! Boom! Boom!* on the door. The musician's rule in this situation is to do any line that might be on the table and then leave because security's here and you're being thrown out. It was then that I learned about movie-star power because Matthew went to the door and took charge: "Good, I'm glad you guys are here. I'm going to need you to stand point—it's going to be about two more hours." And sure enough, I heard, "Oh right away, Mr. Mc-Conaughey." So we got to party two more hours with a guard.

We then took the party over to C3's management offices because Mat Whittington and Dave Geller were still trying to impress me and didn't understand that their boss, Charles Attal, would have murdered them had he known that John Popper was bringing a bunch of movie stars and other people over to their offices to have a party. But seeing as the C3 offices were right next to the Four Seasons at that time, the convenience was undebatable. I remember seeing this punk-rock chick, who was operating the elevator and working for C3 in some capacity, acting very unimpressed until Matthew McConaughey and Woody Harrelson stood on either side of her. Then she turned to royal jelly. When I finally left, I may have seen various people snuggling on rugs and other folks doing various things on executive desks that I still cannot fully attest to as fact. Suffice it to say, Dave Geller and Mat Whittington were in some trouble the next day.

At the end of the night I headed over to the Radisson, and Matthew had to catch a cab, so we walked out together. I had handed him a harmonica earlier, and he asked, "You're giving me this, aren't you?" When I answered yes, he smiled and said, "Well, all right, all right, all right . . . "

Although SXSW was fun, it was more about meeting Geller and Whittington, and it wasn't long before they had some interest from Stu Fine at 429 Records. Stu was a longtime Blues Traveler fan and Jono Manson fan going back to the Nightingale's days, and he wanted to us to do exactly what we wanted to do, which was a rare situation.

Drawing in part on the confidence I gained from my conversation with Bill and my experience with Jono and the group as a whole, I took the Duskray idea to Blues Traveler and said, "We've got to do this with our band." I imagined that they would enjoy it as much as I did because they were on the same hamster wheel as me, in which it had become an assembly line and we were writing the same songs.

The band at first was reticent because they had not tried this idea, and I should have taken that into account because when I started the idea, I was a little reticent as well. But I knew they would come to love it. The Blues Traveler idea would be a variation on the Duskray idea.

Instead of going to friends of mine who were songwriters, we would find professional songwriters we had not worked with before. But I still believed that the theory would hold strong and get us out of our assembly-line approach.

So to C3's credit, Mat Whittington went out and found writers who we'd never worked with, like Ron Sexsmith and Alejandro Escovedo. I saw Carrie Rodriguez on the Austin music channel, made a call, and we found her. We also had Aaron Beavers from the band Shurman who was also part of the Duskray Troubadours project. We even squeezed a few friends like Chris Barron and Jono Manson into this roster of cowriters. We would go into a room and collaborate on songs. Everybody in Blues Traveler is such a hit man on their instrument, and I think that took us in a cool new direction on what would become *Suzie Cracks the Whip*.

Sure enough, the second this process started, the band took to it instantly without being told what to do, bringing many of the ideas further than I could have taken them. That was the difference between *Suzie Cracks the Whip* and the right process and *North Hollywood Shootout* and the wrong process. I wasn't in charge of coming up with every idea. The band intuitively took ideas far beyond any expectation I could have, and it made for a happier feel and a more natural feel on the album. Something fresh had been restored, and that was the triumph of that album.

When I first brought the song "Cara Let the Moon" to the band, I told them I didn't want a drumbeat behind it. I had written it while on tour with the Duskrays, hearing a piano and nothing else. The song was about a conversation I had with a bartender outside the Brooklyn Bowl, who was nineteen (I don't know why she was able to be a bartender). I found her attractive but realized she was a fan and her father was even a bigger fan and she was in Brooklyn because she wanted to get into the music business, the same way that we'd come to New York and wound up in Brooklyn. I felt a kindred spirit with her, and it struck me that her at nineteen and me at forty-three could reach such a similar feeling when we think about music and Brooklyn and that scene. I wanted the song to be an Irish dirge that you could imagine someone singing at the turn of the twentieth century in a Brooklyn bar. That was the premise of the song.

They fought me on my idea for the song's arrangement, but I didn't want it to become this midtempo ballad to make it "fit" with the album. I've had songs in the past get to that place, where I'd fought alone and the song became ruined. This time our producer, Sam Hollander, backed me: "John's 100 percent right." As soon as he said it, the band started to give it a chance, and it got on the record that way. Sam, by the way, went all the way back to Nightingale's as a fan, where he also was a big booster of Jaik Miller (Xanax 25), who got him to come see us and who passed away while we were making the record.

When we play "Cara Let the Moon" live, it's supposed to move on its own, like I'm singing intimately with a piano in a bar. When we pull that off in a huge crowd and I get to thunder my voice and then get super-tiny, we take the crowd with us—it's a new dynamic level we can hit. I like it in the set because it allows me to get powerful without yelling over some drums and convey this ability that I think I'm good at. It's just another set of legs to stand on, something else in the arsenal. The key is having that sonic break from the drums, which allows me to take the tempo anywhere I want, including really long pauses like they would do on Broadway, and it's a very useful tactic.

Suzie Cracks the Whip was about taking us out of our comfort zone so that we could become comfortable with some new approaches. It all began when I took a drive and made the album with Jono and collaborative writing got my full attention. Then in 2014 we took that concept even further.

Suzie Cracks the Whip was the prelude to *Blow Up the Moon*, where we not only cowrote but also recorded with other musicians. I think most humans don't have the ability to see what's great about themselves. The process of collaborating fully with all of these people allowed us to see something new about ourselves.

I also owe credit for *Blow Up the Moon* to our new management, UD Factory. When Scott McGhee took over as our manager in 2001, I remember thinking, *Blues Traveler goes to Hollywood*, because he had an arrangement with Mike Ovitz, where Ovitz was creating a mega-super-entertainment megalopolis, and it all fell apart just as we signed. So now Scott, who had promised us all this access to media, was in the lifeboat with us. He did a great job getting us out of our record deal with all that money unrecouped, and I credit him for our

Thinnest of Air Red Rocks DVD and our *Behind the Music* appearance, but after that it was time for a manager who really knew about touring.

That's what we found with Charles Attal and his outfit C3, because this was just as he was getting the Austin City Limits festival going and was in process of acquiring Lollapalooza. That was a really exciting relationship from 2006 to 2008.

In 2010 we discovered that our accountant, who had signed on with us around 2006, had been propping up loans to support other loans, so we were in the hole for a huge chunk of money. We owed money on loans we had taken out to support our touring machine. We were earning enough to pay it all back, but we kept taking out loans for convenience, to time a tour, and then that money would get spent on the next tour. To make up for this, we started playing a large number of casinos. That's okay, but when all you're doing is casinos, you should start worrying. It was an attempt to keep us running as a truly nomadic band, but I think we took a lot of gigs that were high in volume but didn't add up over time.

Our accountant declared bankruptcy, and we had to get a new accountant. We didn't realize how much trouble we were in for a year or two, and the climbing back to make it right was daunting. The key was to not lose our heads, and gradually we climbed out of that hole. It would take a lot to make us tour efficiently and also to pay down the debt we had accrued. This all came as a shock to us, so around 2010 to 2011 we began a big housecleaning. Charles Attal stuck through 2012 to 2013, when we finally went to UD Factory and Seth Yudof. They seemed to know a lot about records but were definitely green about live touring bands. That's where Lani Sarem took the idea of a collaborative record that initially started with the Duskray Troubadours album and then added her own twist to the sessions.

The brilliance of her idea was in pairing Blues Traveler with bands that you would not likely associate us with, like 3OH!3, Dirty Heads, or Thompson Square. We've spent so much time establishing who we are, so what can we do with that? We have a sound people can recognize, and now we can flip it on its ear and put it next to some other sounds. Hopefully that all merges, offers a nice contrast, and yields something worth hearing. So we can try something country with

Thompson Square, do a reggae or ska thing with Dirty Heads, or some electronic music with 3OH!3. It all expands on *Suzie Cracks the Whip*, where we were writing outside of our comfort zone.

The old Blues Traveler is still there in our live show. But this is about writing in a way that keeps it new. This new writing does translate live, and the melding is interesting.

In 2014 the American Society of Composers, Authors and Publishers sued Pandora over online royalties, and I went on CNBC to talk about it. My position was that it's always been about a gig. John Philip Sousa refused to record, and his point was that if someone can buy a record, they won't need to hire a seventy-piece orchestra to play their birthday party. But the fact of the matter is that you still want John Philip Sousa's band because it's so much fun and you want to hear whether John Philip Sousa can sound like he did on the album. And that provides enough work for John Philip Sousa, who couldn't possibly be in the home of everyone who wants to hear John Philip Sousa.

So streaming music makes everyone aware of us, and if we're any good, it makes them want to hear us live. Then if we have a strong live show, they'll hire us back, and that's always been the business.

We were able to participate in a wonderful, magical time when making a record actually earned us money. We got to taste a little bit of it, but most of our career wasn't that, so when the record business shrank, we were already expecting it to shrink for us.

If you look at any generation, any time period, there are people who want to see concerts. Music just matters that much to people, and I'm very grateful for that.

The Duskray Troubadours album, *Suzie Cracks the Whip*, and *Blow Up the Moon* are nothing like each other. Yet they offer a formula to prevent us from falling into a rut—I think that's the biggest problem when you're in an old band and want to continue to take people on a journey. For me the more opportunities to get weirder, the better. That's what I'm after—on *Blow Up the Moon* we wrote "totes amazeballs" into a song lyric.

When you make your first album, you think you've done it, but what you learn is how to really make an album. Then you build on that with each album.

The professional gig of making an album is living with the difference between the perfection in your head and the reality down here on Earth. While we're making an album, I always imagine up. I never think, *This album is going to be terrible.* I always think, *This album is going to be perfect.* Then we do the album as perfectly as we can in the time given, the situation, and the context we're in.

The important thing, though, is that we keep hearing the possibilities and still carry that hope of perfection.

30

CORPIES, STEROIDS,
AND CONS

Blues Traveler is like a baseball team. We have to be sharp, and the only way to be sharp is by playing with each other and getting sharp, and there's this crazy arc that happens every year.

We need to be slightly weathered so we can read each other's minds but remain into it and excited about the new things we discover while we're playing. Eventually, when we're tired and it starts to feel like Vietnam, that's when the season's over and we need a vacation. Like a baseball team, we've got to be playing and intuitive, and knowing what the other person's going to do only comes from having tons and tons of gigs. It can't happen any other way, at least not for a band like us.

Some bands approach it like studio guys, where they can just step into it. I've done situations like that, and it can work. But for the band who we happen to be, with guys who met in high school in New Jersey, it really requires a little blood on the field. We became a formidable live experience, and that only comes through formidable live experiences.

The discipline in my particular job is to accept mistakes and incorporate them. Improvising musicians make mistakes all the time, and the challenge and the glory is setting those mistakes on their way to being the right thing. If you fuck up a note, you do it again only with a relative change in the chord progression, responding to the chords that are happening but making the same mistake, and suddenly you've started a pattern and it's a melody. Mistakes are wonderful.

In my natural state, when we're on a bus, it's three gigs on, day off, two gigs on, day off. So we're working five gigs a week, and if I do that, I can do it indefinitely. If we do more than that, if I do four in a row, then suddenly my voice starts going. Five gigs a week is a good maximum clip, but throw in a TV show, throw in some promotional thing on the radio, and it all gets hinky and I have to start hitting the steroids.

I think it was in 1989 when a doctor first told me that I needed steroids. My response to him was "Isn't that bad for you? Won't it give me superhuman strength and make my balls shrink?" And he said, "No, those are anabolic steroids and these are anti-inflammatories, which are very benign steroids. You only use them when you need them, and you get a six-day dose pack."

It's actually very common to take prednisone when your vocal cords get swollen. Before the first time I went to a doctor for my voice, it got to the point where I started coughing up a little blood. I remember when that first happened; I didn't flush the toilet so people could see that I coughed up blood because I'm such a hypochondriac that they've learned not to listen to me. So I went to a doctor, and he said, "Oh yeah, you're straining your voice. Eventually you'll get a polyp or a node." They can laser them off now, but you can't make a sound for ten days, and back when I was first singing, it was a new science.

The prednisone shrinks the tissue but it also makes it hard to fight off infection. You also can't forget that there's a reason your vocal cords want to swell up—it's for their protection. So if you go too far, you'll tear your vocal cords into spaghetti. But if you keep it on a ten-day regimen, and then you stay off of it for ten days, it works like a charm.

As we've changed management I've had occasional bouts in which I've been singing for too many gigs in a row. But as long as I adhere to my schedule of five gigs a week, with a day off in the middle, I'm fine, as long as I get eight hours of sleep. The secret to keeping your voice is your ability to sleep.

I've also learned to say no. There's always a great gig to take you out of your vacation or take you beyond your line of safety. It's always something cool, and it's always a shit-ton of money. Saying no is always the hardest thing, and I've learned to do it begrudgingly because I want to play all the gigs. But it's also necessary or else I'll do some damage and end up on the sidelines.

These days I break the year down into three seasons: spring, summer, and fall. In the spring you're raring to go; you're like a grizzly bear who woke up out of hibernation, and playing is food. All you want to do is play. Then you get together, and you're so rusty and sloppy. Everybody's making rookie mistakes. The guys aren't syncing up. Everybody's winded because they're not used to exerting themselves this way. But what you have is plenty of enthusiasm.

And over time you start to iron out the mistakes. Muscle memory returns—the longer you've been doing it, the muscle memory is there, even if the actual memory is not. It's a weird contrast.

So by midspring you still have the enthusiasm but you're starting to settle in, starting to get good. By late spring you're starting to push it further, but you get a little tired because summer's coming.

You've armed up in the spring, so by summer there's a little rustiness, but you get sharp really quickly. That's the best time because you've got the maximum enthusiasm and maximum sharpness and weatheredness, and you're like a finely humming machine that rolls through August.

Somewhere around the end of August you're starting to get a little tired; you're pushing it. You need a break because you've been on since April. Everyone gets tired and start missing home—the food on the road is bad, the drugs are boring, the conversation is repetitive, and you've seen every show on television on that stupid satellite that keeps freezing in the middle of the punch line. You start wanting to slow down, but then it becomes a test of your courage and fortitude. Then a great second wind comes in and you start to use war metaphors a lot more—"The campaign is almost over, we've got to push on through. . . . We've got to break them before they break us."

By mid-September you've earned yourself a two-week vacation. and although it feels good to be home, now you've got to saddle up again and go back out there. That's when I feel like the men and the boys separate, because it's only a man who saddles up in September. It's starting to get cold, which, as a singer, affects your voice, but it affects everybody—your bones get achy, especially as you get older.

So there's a week of enthusiasm, and then you're back to Vietnam. But you know what the job entails and that you've been through it before. By the time you finish, everyone wants to kill everyone, but then Thanksgiving arrives and you go home and sleep for a week.

By the time I finish I can't even walk right. All that matters is the refrigerator, the television, the bathroom, and the couch. I don't even make it up to my bed. It's on the third floor—why go all the way up there? I'll just get hungry and have to go to the bathroom.

And that's the way it's been for nearly thirty years.

The three-season year is the best way to go about it. You try to put a two-week vacation on the end of each season, so basically you tour for two and a half months with two weeks off. That's a comfortable way to go about it, although I'll admit it doesn't always go that way.

There was also a time when we had four seasons: we had winter as well. That's for the hearty because it can be brutal. It's freezing butt-ass cold, and whether you work with your fingers or your face, the cold has a way of exacting a lethal vengeance.

After being home for a week or two, you eventually peek your head outside and gradually become a human again. I'd say it's around the end of that first month when you want to play again. All is forgiven, but now you don't get to play. Then January shows up, and you really want to play. By February you're raring to go, and by March a few gigs come in, maybe some corpies, and you get real restless for the tour.

Corporate gigs—we call them "corpies"—are really just frat gigs; it's just that the guys have graduated and now have access to larger money.

It's the same group of guys who saw us in college and hired us for a frat gig—"Hey, I represent a group of guys. We've got some money together and want you to come play for us." Then twenty years later the same guy is the VP of some company and is in charge of getting their entertainment for their company—"Hey, I represent a group of guys. We've got some money together and want you to come play for us."

If somebody's willing to hand you a chunk of money to do what you do, I think it's awesome. I see it as something you've worked hard to develop. It shouldn't be your only thing—every good band needs to go out and be working against a hard ticket—but if that's all you do, then you're missing an opportunity.

Sometimes the person buying the talent misreads what the people want. We wind up playing for a huge room with twenty people who are all in tuxedos, eating fondue, and we're playing a rock show, and it clearly doesn't go with what they're after.

One time we played a lung cancer benefit, and everybody had ridden their bicycles to get to this place, and we had to stand outside and smoke while in full view of everyone—it was just an odd way to celebrate lung cancer awareness.

Sometimes we'll do a corpie that involves us meeting people more than playing, and that's weird, but it beats digging ditches. If people are psyched to pay us for our company, I find that odd because we won't massage you, we won't suck anything other than our own instruments, and what you see is what you get.

Sometimes we'll play somebody's birthday, and they want to sing. We've had some good experiences with that. It's for their family, so I don't see any reason not to let them. They're going to get the most charitable and kindest audience they're ever going to find, and sometimes they can actually sing. It sort of takes the pressure off of a show when you know that it's their party, and as long as we're not asked to murder anyone or take part in a religious cult or any sort of sexual congress without our consent, I'm fine with it. If we have a ticket-paying audience who has to put up with it, then it's different.

I'm easy. No job is too small, no fee too big.

We feel the same way about playing political conventions.

As a band we don't endorse political parties. The band has been largely Democrat, and I generally go Republican, and we came to an agreement a long time ago that we would play either convention as long as we're paid. The Republicans would always pay us, while the

Democrats would wonder why we weren't donating anything. So we tended to play the Republican conventions because the Democrats would tell us, "We don't really need you because we have Michael Jackson and Sheryl Crow, here and they're paying us to come." Although recently the Democrats started paying us.

We would say no to something if we had strong beliefs against it. I just don't think that making your political stand should have to interfere with making your living.

I'm not there to represent their political leanings or stand for what they're trying to extol. I would never play a "pro-life" event—that is an actual political issue, and by showing up there, you're saying you're "pro-life" (or "anti-abortion," if that makes you feel better).

Glenn Beck wanted us to play something, and none of us wanted to do that. It didn't feel like just anybody was hiring us. Glenn Beck is somebody who's making a point whenever he shows up. Even *I* didn't even want to do that one. It seems like there's something dangerous about his worldviews. He's absurdly militant.

But if you're playing for a bunch of people who are having a party and have a bunch of money, then I'm like the dancing girls. I'm part of the prize winnings to whomever can afford it.

31

DON PARDO
AND THE TROLLS

Shortly after the great *Saturday Night Live* announcer Don Pardo passed away in August 2014, Jordan, my then girlfriend, now wife, was hanging out with someone who had a question for her: "I don't make any judgment . . . I just want to know what John said to make Don Pardo that upset."

She didn't know what he was talking about, and *I* didn't know what he was talking about. It turned out there was quote about me that someone had posted online:

> My least favorite episode of *Saturday Night Live*? September 30, 1995.
> Blues Traveler was the musical guest. The singer was a real creep.
>
> —Don Pardo, from his autobiography

At first this made me really upset. What did I do to Don Pardo? I loved Don Pardo, although I only met him one time—we just showed up on the day of the show. It started me thinking, *What could I have done to Don Pardo in that moment?*

The mind plays terrible tricks.

274

Maybe I shoved him, maybe I ate the last donut, maybe I asked him how his family was and his mom had just died. Maybe he thought, *I'm seventy-five years old. I'm sorry I've been doing this job since you were six years old, so leave me alone, you creep.* Maybe he imagined I was doing all sorts of disturbing things to myself in my sad little apartment while he was making the *Saturday Night Live* announcements.

I also know that I don't act normal around famous people, and *Saturday Night Live* was so important to me that maybe I kissed Don Pardo's ass so hard that it became annoying. I know that I approached him like a dweeby fan.

I have genuinely admired Don Pardo for decades. So if there's anything I regret it's that I was so corny when I met him. What I said to him was "I know this doesn't make sense, but I need to tell you 'I will fight the good fight.'" Then I saluted him, and he said, "Go forth." My interaction with Don Pardo took all of forty seconds, but because he said, "Go forth," I left thinking that he got it. Hopefully he did, but this made me rethink it.

We hosted the season premiere of *Saturday Night Live* that year after Prince canceled. We actually had to cross an old friend to make that appearance. We went to high school with Michael Showalter, whose sketch comedy show *The State* had been on MTV for a couple of years and was going to debut on CBS. But because we were doing *Saturday Night Live*, we couldn't do their CBS special. Their show aired, CBS decided not to pick it up for any more episodes, and to this day I think some of the cast members are unhappy with us. I completely understand how they would feel that way, but we were all in our twenties, and to get an offer to play a show we'd wanted to do since we were kids and might not ever have a chance to do again— there really wasn't a choice.

My thought going into it was, *Here I am on* Saturday Night Live, *and it's probably the only time I will be here.* So I wanted to do everything that I'd always wanted to do. Part of that was to have an interaction with Don Pardo. Another part was to sit in with the band at the end while everyone is waving. I'd heard the saxophone do that for years, ever since I was six, and I'd always wanted to play on that—it's a nice blues song that goes to that major third. You have to pursue those chances. It's like if you have an opportunity to have a cigarette in the White House, you've got to do it.

The key is you need to find that line where people are letting you do things and enjoy that moment without insulting anyone terribly. If there's an insult, you want it to be a Grey Poupon insult, where they've got some nerve for being insulted. Then it's kind of even—"Screw you, I'm having my *Saturday Night Live* moment." But Don Pardo, he'd been there for every show, so I could see how that could have been lost on him.

Then I remembered something else that happened that night. A few years earlier Sinead O'Connor had held up a picture of the pope, tore it up into little pieces, and said, "Fight the real enemy." Well, I had this idea that at the end of our performance I was going to rip up a picture of a jellyfish and say, "Fight the real anemone." I thought that was clever and was really excited to have a chance to do this on *Saturday Night Live*. I thought it was nothing but harmless fun, so I sent someone out to get a picture, but word got back to Lorne Michaels, who called the head of our record company, Al Cafaro, and down through the ranks it went until it got to me—"They don't want you to do it; they don't want anyone to mention that episode. Do you want to make an enemy of these people? It might be nice to be able to get on the show again." So I said, "Fine. Give me a hundred bucks and I won't do it." Immediately they gave me a hundred dollars, and then a little light bulb went off in my head: "Oh my God, they'll just give me money." And that started a new thing that went on for a few years while *four* was hot:

"Hey we got a lot of press for you."

"Great. Where's my hundred dollars?"

So I would get a hundred dollars all the time, and they had no problem with it; they let this float. All except one insecure guy in the Midwest who tattled on me. So eventually they had to stop doing it, but even then, a lot of them would still sneak me a hundred dollars.

After the album peaked, though, I remember one guy came up to me somewhere outside of Philly and said, "John, there's a couple of press guys out there. Give me a hundred bucks and I'll make them go away." And I thought, *Oh, the jig is up.*

But I couldn't figure out how Don Pardo would even know about any of that. Then someone told me that Don Pardo never even wrote an autobiography. So although there's a comical aspect that I don't want to let go of—I almost wish that Don Pardo was somehow insulted by my absolute worship of him—I have to acknowledge that all of this probably started with a Twitter troll.

I've always been quite willing to interact with our fans. It's really cool when people like what you do and are nice to you. Twitter has been quite an experience because that was when I discovered people who don't like me. And that has catered to this part of me that wants to go and mix it up with some middle school kids.

I think the first time I got Twitter assaulted was when we were at Bonnaroo and I wanted to sit in with Dave Matthews, but they said he wasn't having anyone sit in with him. Then these Twitter people said, "No, he's totally having people sit in with him." I felt like I kind of got the run-around—if you'll excuse me—from Coran, his manager. I wouldn't use the pun, but there's no other way to put it.

So I think I said, "It's disappointing to be old. I miss the old days when I could just jump on stage and do it." And 50 million Dave Matthews fans Tweeted, "How dare you!" and started laying into me. I was feeling all this anger and was trying to be funny. But eventually, as you get comfortable with Twitter, you realize that everybody has a "Fuck you" saved up their butt, and that's kind of the currency on Twitter.

So I've learned about Twitter trolling from the trolls.

It helps if you call someone a racist or a fascist and get them defensive: "Wait, how am I racist?"

"If you have to ask that question then you really need to learn."

The thing you have to remember about Twitter, though, is that it's Twitter—it means absolutely nothing. Unless you actually start spewing hate speech, there's really nothing you can do wrong on Twitter.

You can say something and later explain, "I was being completely benign," and you can imply something unbenign while remaining completely benign. I love Twitter for that reason.

Twitter is not an effective form of communication. If you're interested in having a conversation, then Twitter is not for you. But I look at Twitter as a way to practice one-liners. You have only a few characters, so try to say something as surreal as you can.

I name search because I want to find the guy who says, "John Popper sucks," and then start fighting with him. They usually can't believe that the guy from Blues Traveler is fighting with them. That to me is really turning it on its ear—I love that.

So we battle on Twitter, and if they're childish with me, I'm childish with them, and then we develop a camaraderie and you are forming a communication that has a rhythm to it. Eventually, if the guy says something truly funny, I like to think I'll laugh at it.

We all want to do a prank phone call. I don't blame them for that. We all want to harass a celebrity if we have nothing to do, but I *am* one, so I get to harass the harassers. As long as that doesn't make me a belligerent bastard.

By setting up a Twitter page, I'm saying, "Who wants some?" Except I didn't set up a Twitter page; I use the band's page. If I had my own Twitter page, I'd be hunted for meat. But I get to hide behind, "It's not me, it's the band's position that your mom sucks." Then I've got a little leeway and try to play these things as best I can.

Tad has some things to say because he actually works our social media, but no one else from the band will get on Twitter, so they're kind of at my mercy. To be fair, I don't think I Twitter properly, but I'm lucky I joined a band that is more social media inept than I am. Except for Tad, who really just wants content.

One time I got into an argument with someone who worked for BuzzFeed. It started when she and a few of her friends were trying to recall the interview on *Behind the Music* where I was discussing being so obese that I started having chest pains while masturbating. The odd thing was that ten years earlier, being honest about that was helping people, but now it seemed to be some sign of weakness or something to be laughed at. I was trying to go along with the joke, so I told them it turned me on that they were so interested in this. She answered, "You can't even rape your hand," and I responded, "Nothing funny about hand rape . . . unless the hand was asking for it." The next thing I knew, "Rape advocate John Popper" was all over BuzzFeed.

That had been my best attempt at being jovial in that context, and a fight then broke out and it all degenerated into me calling her the c-word. To my mind this entire exchange just illustrated the stupidity of everyone involved on Twitter in which we get into fights with the middle schoolers in all of us and also with actual middle schoolers.

In the middle of this Roseanne chimed in, "Hey John I haven't talked to you in a while." Then she must have noticed everyone was saying "Cock, asshole . . ." and I didn't hear from her again for a while. She just got out of the way. It was hysterical.

We all take ourselves so seriously on Twitter that at times it can become a place to have an adolescent-style fight. We're really worried about what words we're typing, as if those words have the power to destroy, and in this case what word was being said? The female variant of the word cock. Completely useful in England, by the way, and English people Tweet, I just don't get it. The whole point is that Twitter is not a place for brilliance; it's a place to be mediocre. That's the great equalizer of Twitter: you have 140 characters, and you're not as clever as you think you are.

Another time I said, "I am so pro-choice that I think a mother should be able to kill and eat her baby until it can physically escape from her, like a lioness in the wild. Good luck starting that lobby."

You can't read the tone of my sarcasm, and this "pro-life" magazine (or again, "anti-abortion," if that makes you feel better) put out a headline: "Blues Traveler encourages mothers to eat their babies."

And there was an organization that was having a festival and they fired us from the gig at the last minute because of that. I'm not really allowed to say too much about it because they gave us half the money. I wanted to fight it tooth and nail because I can't stand it when people tell me I can't do stuff, and I was in the area already, so I was tempted to stroll in there and try to sit in with somebody. But my managers bought my girlfriend and myself a nice dinner, so I let it go.

I had said the same joke on Ricky Gervais's Twitter feed, and all of the pro-choice people started asking, "Are you saying pro-choice is murder?" So I caught a bunch of shit from them too.

And the moral of that story is the abortion issue is a hot-button issue. Or that it's just not as funny a joke as I think it is.

However, I couldn't stop with the Twitter jokes: "But they're so delicious. I could eat them up, especially when their fontanel hasn't hardened. I just pop a straw right in and drink it like a kiwi." I said I would remain "soylent" on the issue.

And I know it's a stupid little joke. But that is what Twitter is for. People who go on Twitter to express true ideas are morons because you've got 140 characters, and what do you hope to express in 140 characters? Is this the new game that the only true thoughts are in haiku? Is that really how we're going to express things to each other?

"You suck balls." "No, you suck balls." I am the guy who will sit there and debate who's actually sucking balls. I think it's important for people to know that they, in fact, actually suck balls. And I'm willing to sit there like their bartender or their therapist and prove conclusively through patience that they do indeed suck balls. I will stick with them and hear all of it until something good is on television.

The only thing that bothers me is when really nice people from really nice places just want to say, "Hey, I really liked that song," and then they have to see, "No, you suck balls."

I won't shy away from a good troll battle, but I don't want to subject the nontrolls to the ball-sucking declarations.

Ultimately, though, we all kind of suck balls for being on Twitter.

32

SAFETY PATROL

I feel that going on a USO Tour is like getting a free ride to the moon without being qualified to fly a spaceship. You're watching all these young kids deal with stuff that didn't even occur to you to deal with when you were their age—honor and saving each others' lives and facing death willingly, not to mention a host of technological processes. These guys are the only people I know on the road more than we are, and they really don't know when—or if—they'll go home.

Every single one of them I met who was wounded was pissed off because their friends, their brothers, were at the front and they couldn't be with them. They didn't care about politics or who the president was; they were upset because "my friends are back there and I'm here."

I went to the Walter Reed Army Medical Center and listened to a lot of the wounded, and some were mad because their corporal died and they didn't and where was the fairness in that? These are things way beyond my experience, and I'm watching people process this. All I could do was listen.

The third year I finally burst out crying. I was at Landsthul Regional Medical Center, where they fly the wounded directly from the battlefield in Afghanistan and Iraq. This guy had one arm left—their tank had blown up and a gun turret flipped on top of him—and he couldn't reconcile how the guy inside, who he considered a better man, didn't walk away while he did. I was trying to engage him and just started sobbing. He had to crawl out of his bed with one arm to hug me, and that made me feel worse.

They told me it's a normal thing, but that was the last time they had me back. I think they decided that after three years I couldn't take it anymore.

Whenever I've been overseas, the troops just wanted to know that somebody back home cared. I could have been the Crazy Eddie spokesman.

Our first USO tour was Korea and Japan in 1998. I just wanted to do my part if I could help in some way. It's something I'm really proud of, and I recommend it.

In 2002 we went to Landsthul. They explained that the average turn-around is forty-five minutes, so sometimes people were there only forty-five minutes and sometimes they came straight from the battlefield before heading out to Walter Reed stateside or wherever they needed to go.

Then they told us that some Green Berets who had been in a firefight had just arrived, so we ran down the hall to see them before they left. We had no idea what we might see, how horrible it might be but we raced to it. I remember thinking, *Why am I running to see this?* It turned out that they were all right, though, they were just covered in dirt, but I can't imagine what that's like for them: one minute you're engaging the Taliban, and then there's Blues Traveler—how surreal is that? They still had shit on them from the battle and looked dazed.

I'm not sure whether they were necessarily fans—I think they were—but they were happy to have anyone come see them and know what they were doing and be proud of them. I really got that feeling whenever I would go overseas. They want you to know that this is the best helicopter in the Army because it's their helicopter and that it runs right. Every time we visited a vehicle, we received a little speech about how it worked.

When you're visiting the wounded, they just want to know they're not alone and are appreciated. They just wanted to see a civilian of note—or any civilian, really. If everyone received the same tour I did, they would appreciate what's done on their behalf. You really do see some of the best people ever. I've never approached being honorable the way they do, and their whole day is built around that.

I talked to one woman who was a helicopter pilot and asked her what it was like when people were shooting at her. She said it's all routine; you're doing your job and then they shoot at you, and suddenly you take it really personally—"You're not going to keep me from seeing my kids again." Think of that. It's easy as an anecdote to go, *Wow*, but when you're living that way, seeing your kids is now a fight between you and someone you've never met before who is trying to kill you and now you're trying to kill them. It's unreal.

In Afghanistan I was in a MASH hospital, and there were these mountains over my head. Every once in a while somebody would say, "shush" and then "all right." People had their guns on. I walked into the hospital, and a local guy had stepped on an IED and gotten some glass in his brain. So the doctors invited me to put a mask on and come in. The thing I'll never forget was his friend in the waiting room, this really old man with a turban. He looked like Osama bin Laden's grandfather. He saw people come up to me for autographs, so he knew I was somebody, and I could tell he was scared of me. That's how I was meeting people from Afghanistan—they were in a state of abject terror. And I was terrified of him as well. There we were, afraid of each other. To me that's how it was being over there in terms of the local people, mutual fear.

When we first went to Bosnia in 2002, the guy who took us on that tour with the USO was Captain David Mills. He was going in for SEAL training, and he was a badass. We didn't see or hear from him for years, and it got to the point where we were afraid to ask what had become of him. Then in 2006 I went to Saddam's palace and he walked up to me.

I believe that if you're a VIP, you're not in any real danger. I've been technically shot at, but what that means is that miles away someone was trying to hit us with something. When the plane lifted off, we took some small arms fire, but it was so far away that it just bounced off the side like a BB gun. We could hear the dings; they sounded like pebbles. We took off in a corkscrew motion so they couldn't really get a good shot at us, but when that happens you are aware that people are trying to kill you, which is a strange feeling because that doesn't happen in my daily civilian life.

Another time, at Camp Victory in Iraq, we were on stage practicing, and someone tried to hit the stage with a mortar. I guess they saw something shiny. In a weird way we were bait, because after that, I heard the .50 cals being shot from a helicopter, and then I didn't hear the mortars anymore. Somebody flew out to kill the people who were firing the mortars, and we got to hear that. We were listening to sounds of war while we were getting ready for the show.

The closest was when I was in Saddam's palace and an IED went off. It was all serene, there's the Tigris River, and suddenly I heard a *Boom!* maybe fifty yards away over in a city block. It sounded like three m80s combined. My first instinct—this is me in combat—is that someone was practicing. No, it was a real IED, but I wasn't in the perimeter, although I was in earshot and it was enough to make me jump.

Another time somebody was shelling the base, and I came out of the PX with some Lucky Charms. Everyone said, "shhhh," and I stood there for a bit, and then we were good. I felt safe because I was in the center of the military, being very protected.

If you think about it, had the Blues Traveler guy or the six New England Patriots cheerleaders been blown up or hurt in any way, policy would have changed. So there was a real interest and effort to protect us and make us feel protected. Incidentally, if you ever do go into combat, try to bring six cheerleaders. It lends a surreal aspect to the whole affair, and there's nothing like going into any place with six cheerleaders in uniform. The seas part, people get out of your way, and I can't attest to this, but I have a feeling the enemy never hit us for a reason.

We got to ride around in Stryker vehicles through downtown Bagdad and sit up top. People were waving, and even there I felt safe.

Later on I ran into these big SEAL-looking guys, and they said, "If you want, we'll take you on a run with us." But that got stopped.

In Afghanistan the impression I got was that you never know where it's coming from. We were at the base of the mountains in this MASH unit we were in. So when soldiers had their guns on, you had the feeling it was because they really needed them.

In Iraq the captain said to me that they had a good idea where they were going to be attacked. They set up IEDs on roadsides and intersections and learned how to anticipate that and up-armor their vehicles to have an acceptable amount of damage. In Afghanistan that never happened because there no infrastructure to guard; it was just little village after little village.

I learned all this information about IEDs, and then *Stars and Stripes* sat me down for a television interview to demonstrate how informed people are who come to visit. I gave this incredible, erudite twenty-minute lecture on what I had learned. I was knowledgeable because I'm a weapons guy, so I could explain it properly; the problem was that every time I should have said IED, I said IUD. The guy filming tried to stop me, but I was just on a roll. It was my best most informed self, I was speaking to *Stars and Stripes* broadcasting, and explaining, "Yes, an IUD could go off at any point and if you're driving by, a handkerchief or a can could be a sign of an IUD." They just couldn't use it because IUDs are dangerous if they do go off, but in a completely different way.

In Bosnia I learned a couple of things about my crew, in particular that they could find weed anywhere. I came into the barracks where we staying and could smell it and told them that they could get arrested for stuff like that—"This is the military; it's not the same thing." Alcohol wasn't really allowed on the base, and with the smell, it was ridiculous.

One year the Air Force got worried that we were too drunk and rowdy, so they assigned us a chaperone. In the playfulness of having a chaperone, we said, "Oh, so you think you can keep up with us, huh?" He responded, "Oh I intend to." But what he wasn't counting on was hanging with Chan. I think we were in the Azores and the Pittsburgh Steelers were playing, and it was two in the morning and Chan was really counting on the Steelers to win, and we'd all had a lot to drink. And this chaperone started showing me death moves like how to slit a man's throat and was playing with this knife I had, and this was clearly bothering Chan a bit because he can tell the guy's intoxicated. We have wheels up in three or four hours, so we knew we were not going to get any sleep, everyone's going to congregate at the plane, and we're really good at going without sleep and meeting at the plane because it's like bus call.

This guy had a lot to drink, and we clearly drank him under the table because he was nearby but unconscious while Chan was getting so upset that the Steelers had lost that he started throwing glass bottles around his room. I was walking to my room, and just as I turned to go in, I could see MPs coming up the hallway. I said, "Okay, good night," shut the door, and got ready for bag drag—you have to have your bag ready and put it outside your door so they can bring it to the plane.

We all made it perfectly fine, except the chaperone couldn't find any of us because we all beat the guy there—he was twenty minutes late. And he looked like an old undershirt that somebody had ripped off in a hurry. The man looked like used laundry. He didn't last long; he was replaced pretty quickly.

Another time we were on the tarmac of some place we had flown to, and Fisher, from our crew, rest his soul, started snapping pictures. The next thing we know the crew was surrounded by MPs. I'm not sure whether they told us, but it's common knowledge that you don't take a picture on a military runway because that gives potential terrorists information they can use about where things are that they might want to blow up. So we could not leave with that film. Fisher was arguing, "That's my camera—I have pictures on here." And the MP said, "I know." Fisher became so upset that the band had to go over and talk to the MPs. The master sergeant recognized me and was a harmonica player, so the way to get Fisher and essentially all of us out of jail was that he came and sat in with us that night.

In Qatar (we were never allowed to refer to Qatar as Qatar—it was always "Location Three"—something to do with international diplomacy), I got to go out on a mission, but there was nothing in Qatar. It was technically a forward area, but that's where the brass were, so nothing was going to come and get them. Later I saw some pictures and realized I had been wearing my reflective belt that you need to wear in the camp so that you don't get hit by a car. Apparently no one told me to remove my safety patrol belt. And I was safety patrol in the sixth grade so I knew how to wear the belt. Standard issue. All you see in the picture is my belt, but I did get to wear a uniform and hold a gun.

When I was there I was too shy to take a dump in the regular bathroom with the stalls. The brass got wind of this (excuse the pun) and gave me one of the two private toilets in the entire theater. A general somewhere had one and I had one. It makes you feel special and also like the biggest pussy ever. That's me in combat.

There has been discussion of us going to Guantanamo Bay. Some might say that we shouldn't play this place because it goes against the ideology of what American stands for. I understand that point of view, but I feel like it's a shitty posting for solders who are trying to do their job wherever they're sent on behalf of us, so I would go and play for them. Also if my government's doing something horrible, I would want to see what conditions are like. It's a crazy time we live in, and I want to be present when stuff goes down. Not seeking trouble but not running from it either.

In 2004 I met the New England Patriots cheerleaders during our first day in the Azores. There's something in common between a hot chick and a fat guy—we're both judged on our appearances. I would see the shit they would get—soldiers would look at them and see the cheerleader in *their* high school—"You're probably a bitch, aren't you?" And they'd just be trying to be nice to a bunch of soldiers. The cheerleaders would listen, and it would make them cry.

I realized that as a fat guy where I'd be judged on my appearance, I had developed a thicker skin than them. They weren't used to it, but they should have been; they'd get it all the time. It was a weird bonding thing.

There was a band bus and a cheerleader bus, and I told the guys, "Screw the band bus—I'm going with the cheerleaders." I was like their goofy older brother but with pervy designs. Maybe I went too far, though, because after begging and begging, on the final night I was able to satisfy some meager fantasy of mine and get two of them to kiss. The downside, though, was that the next morning my camera "went missing," and it had some really cool images of myself in a war zone (including some with my security guy, Oscar, who'd been my security when I was on tour—he got to come along as well, and it was really a high point for the both of us). Still, both an infatuation and an actual relationship came out of my USO experience with the Patriots cheerleaders. It's like a Danielle Steel novel if you have a tryst with a cheerleader in a war situation. Everyone's dressed like Wonder Woman, and there's explosions and romance and all of that stuff.

Another memorable moment took place when I was in Iceland at a high school class at a Navy base. That's when I first heard, "You might not know who this is, but your parents . . . " It was early in the morning, and I was not in top condition. I hadn't wanted to do this class, and that was God's little kick in the ass: "Oh you're feeling bad, so try this on." And it snapped me out of it.

The thing that struck me, though, was that when I told them the most basic thing about improvised music—just play the thoughts in you head, play anything you imagine—they were so blown away, like I had once been. And I remembered how valuable it had been when Roy Eldridge, one of the greatest trumpet players of the twentieth century, came to the New School and said, "You know, we'd just get high and play." I was like, "Holy shit! That's what I do!"

I just told them every platitude I could: Close cover before striking. . . . Do not remove tag under fear of prosecution. . . . Cross on green, not in between. . . . Always check your references . . .

I began to wonder: At what point do kids not know who the hell you are because, at the time they know who the hell you are you're almost a kid yourself, so you don't feel like anybody knows who the hell you are anyway.

By 2005 they were thinking, *That's the guy who lost all that weight* or *That's the guy who was in that bowling movie*, which as I mentioned earlier is what I tell people who don't know who I am. I'll say, "You know that movie about those Amish guys bowling? There was that band at the end and that was me."

Then they'll ask, "What was with the sideburns—was that a costume?"

I'll tell them, "No, that really was me."

This was in Keflavik, Iceland, just outside of Reykjavik, in December 2005, the second coldest place I've ever been. The coldest was Green Bay, Wisconsin. I bought some Taco Bell a block away from my hotel, and by the time I got back, it was frozen solid. I have not experienced cold like Green Bay, not even in Iceland.

33

SHRIVERIANS
AND LIBERTARIANS

I met Bill Clinton twice when he was president. The first time was on December 17, 1998. It was the night before the House of Representatives began their formal debate over his impeachment and the day after he ordered air strikes against Iraq, purportedly because Saddam Hussein had defied UN weapons inspectors. Some people thought that the reason he had done this was to provide a distraction from the impeachment proceedings. I remember driving there with my manager saying, "To the White House!" as if we were going to get to the bottom of it, as if I was Bruce Wayne and Dave Frey was Dick Grayson.

I was there to perform as part of the A Very Special Christmas concert to benefit the Special Olympics. It was preceded by an event hosted by Eunice and Sarge Shriver to promote the concert and the organization, which she founded. I have to admit that I did not know this or quite know who she was when I first met her.

We were at a photo shoot for the event. Gwen Stefani was there, and Sting was there. I was following Gwen Stefani around, and Gwen Stefani was following Sting, around and Sting was kind of following me around because he wanted to tell me that "Dustin Hoffman works out to your music." I said, "No freaking way!" He said, "Yes, I was on his yacht and asked him, 'What's this horrible shit?' and he said, 'Blues Traveler.'" And I was like, *Wow, Sting just abused me in a joke!* I was the butt of a Sting joke, and I loved that.

Sheryl Crow was talking to Eunice, and I remember saying to myself, *She was opening for me, and now she's at the White House again—how do I do that?*

Then Eunice came over to me and was very sweet in a way that was clear she didn't know who I was and I didn't know who she was. I thought she was Sting's mom. When we took a picture, I tried to get her to wear an elf hat. She said in a very classy way, "I don't think so."

And later they told me that she was JFK's sister and that not only was she running this event but that she also started the entire concept of the Special Olympics.

Afterward she wrote a letter to each person, but she wrote mine to my manager, Dave Frey, thinking he was the entertainer, thanking him for his talent and artistic creativity. And then Sarge, who himself was the founding director of the Peace Corps under JFK and served as George McGovern's running mate in the 1972 election, added a note at the end, talking about me and my harmonica. You could see the save. It was the most adorable thing, and I had the letter to Dave Frey framed.

From there I would go to other events of hers, and she was so sweet to me. The next time Eunice referred to me as John, and it was clear she knew who I was. We had a really great time together, and anyone who knew her knows what a huge heart she had. She was one of the genuine articles. You hear about noblesse oblige, and she's from that school—they really are, that whole family. They genuinely feel a dedicated obligation to better the situation of the entire world around them, and that indeed is a rare thing. Eunice and I met on such equivalent terms—neither knew who the other was—and we became really good friends.

I would say to them I'm not a Democrat or a Republican; I'm a Shriverian because they really cared so much about doing things for other people. It's one thing to say it, but to see it in action really blew me away. They would do nothing but stuff for other people, and in the process they had a ball in the form of bringing people together and having a party. I've seen their sons Bobby and Mark do it too, and they remain dear friends.

It was during this reception that I approached Eric Clapton and asked him whether he would sit in with me during the concert. I couldn't believe I asked him, but I figured I had to. The fact that I was there at the White House already placed me in that situation of improbability, so why not?

He said yes, and then other people started to ask him. I wound up making a lot of work for him, but he didn't mind. He told me later, "It's like I'm running the show," and he liked that at the White House—that's a fun place to be a musical mainstay. I think he had a ball doing that.

That night, when I did my song with Clapton, a version of Canned Heat's "Christmas Blues," I had been told in no uncertain terms that the president would not sit in with me, that at no point would he be playing saxophone, and we were not to ask.

When I met Bill, I wanted to look into the eyes that were the center of all this controversy and scandal. I wanted to see what kind of person lay behind those eyes, and he just seemed exhausted. He seemed almost asleep at the wheel, just happy to be alive. But I was blown away—he was the president, after all. Hillary, however, seemed wide awake and very aware of what was happening. There was an intensity to her. The contrast was quite stark.

The night ended in style, though, when I picked Bill Clinton up off the ground in front of the Secret Service and nobody shot me. The music was over, people were all hugging, so I figured I'd pick up the president and see what he weighed. I did, and he giggled like Barney Rubble.

I guess by that point the Secret Service knew who I was. I'm a gun guy, so I had been talking shop with them all day. They taught me how to do things Secret Service style, where they hold their pistols close to the body and then push forward into an isosceles stance. Good stuff to learn.

One time my bus driver was driving a gospel group to the White House. A few days earlier he had taken a gun from a meth head who was trying to sell it to him at a truck stop for twenty bucks. He did the right thing, which was to give the guy twenty dollars, then take the gun and throw it under his bus. He forgot about it, as his intent was to disarm a meth head, but during the security check they found it. He got detained, and they asked him what other bands he had driven. He said the word *Blues*, and before he could say *Traveler* they said, "John Popper." So the Secret Service knows very well about me. It's nice they're aware of me.

The second time I met President Clinton was two years later at the same event. That time I would play with B. B. King, Stevie Wonder, and many others. I arrived on December 13, 2000, the day before the Very Special Christmas event, and that turned out to be the day Al Gore made his concession speech to George W. Bush. A number of the musicians went over to the vice president's mansion for an impromptu performance, and I joined them. Al's daughters were so kind. I felt bad because I had voted Republican, but they said, "We know. That's why we're glad you're here." I never forgot that, and it moved me. I think that's important, because it's easy to preach to your choir. It's the people who preach to the other choir who are the badasses. That evening the Gores decided to let it go and have a celebration for the campaign they had run, the people who supported them, and the country as a whole. I played with Tom Petty and Jon Bon Jovi, and Tipper Gore was on the congas with me. It was an amazing night.

That evening was also the first time I played with Stevie Wonder. He was up there at the end of the night and called out, "Hey Blues Traveler guy!" The problem was I didn't have my harmonicas.

Earlier in the day Susan Bank, my illustrious manager, was sightseeing, having her Jackie O moment. In doing that, she left my harmonicas in the broom closet, wherever the freaking broom closet was. They were the only set of harmonicas I had. The opening band had a few harmonicas, so I borrowed theirs—they only had three or four of them and they were all gross with spit all over them, but that's what you do if you're a harp player—they should have a T-shirt that reads, "Harp players will put anything in their mouths."

So Stevie Wonder called me up, and they're doing a vamp in the key of F, for which I would need a B-flat harmonica, but I didn't have that key. So I had to climb on stage, tap him on the shoulder while this big jam was going on, and say, "Hey Stevie, it's me, the Blues Traveler guy—I don't have that key." And he called out, "Wait a minute," and he stopped the whole thing. "What key do you have?" I said, "Well, I guess I could do it in E," so he yelled, "E!" I was livid. I went up to Susan afterward: "Did you see what you did? You stopped Stevie from getting his funk on." I felt terrible.

Then the next evening I performed with B. B. King. I had met him on *Letterman* a couple of years earlier when we played "The Thrill Is Gone." B. B. was great because he always made people feel welcome, and he was of a generation who shouldn't have anything to do with me. After we did the song on *Letterman* he asked me, "How come I haven't played with you before?" And in my mind I thought, *I did it again. I fooled another blues musician.*

So they teamed us up again for "Back Door Santa," which we both thought was a wildly inappropriate song to do for a president. Who was vetting the material? We both thought that was a strange and pervy song to do in front of any president, let alone Bubba.

But the two of us took the stage, the curtain opened, and nothing was happening. So I looked out there, and the big chair was empty. Then he came running out of the bathroom with the Secret Service following him, so I took my chance and said, "Mr. President, you don't have to run. We'll wait for you—you're the president." He responded, "I was just going to get my harmonica." At that point I knew I was officially Americana because the most powerful man in the world knew what I did for a living.

When I spoke with the president that night I was trying to think of something clever to say, like, "Don't let the door hit you in the ass," without getting kicked out by the Secret Service. If you go too far, someone will eject you bodily into a prison cell or the street, at least. But I still I needed to say something cute and partisan in a friendly kind of way.

So I walked up to him and said, "I want you to know, you've humanized the presidency, and I think people will look back at you very fondly." And in my head I was asking myself, *What the fuck just happened?* But when you meet the most powerful man in the world, you want him to like you. And he'd been nothing but nice to me. They are very charming people, all of them.

It's like when I later met George W. Bush with my fiancée at the time, Delana, who hated him. Bush said to me, "You better marry this girl before she changes her mind." And then she got all gooey: "Ohh, Mr. President."

But Bill was moved by what I said. He gave me the double hand-shake and the lower-lip bite. It was really cool.

What I didn't expect was that Hillary would be moved. That was the scariest part—her concrete smile, that face sort of cracking. To see her get moved was a very strange sight.

Later on, after the night was over, I was riding up on the elevator, and it was just Jon Bon Jovi and me. He turned to me and grumbled, "F'ing bastards stole the election from us." I had three or four floors left and thought, *Do I tell him I'm a Republican, or do I just humor him for a few more floors?* So I looked at him, shook my head, and mut-tered, "F'ing bastards."

The truth is, though, that my experiences have really made me a centrist. I very much believe the Clintons and the Bushes are really trying to do the same thing as the Shrivers, which is to find solutions to help people.

In October 2014 I was at an event for Chelsea. Hillary was there and was really nice. Brendan brought his daughter, who was about seven, and she saw the guy from *Grey's Anatomy*, McDreamy, Pat-rick Dempsey. I had worked with him on something, so we were talking, but she was too afraid to ask him for an autograph, and then he walked away. But Hillary Clinton got him out of the audi-ence and made him take a picture with Brendan's daughter. That was pretty cool, and she seemed to know all about Princeton and our lives and really identified with me, and I have to say she did show her political stuff. Unlike Nancy Pelosi, I feel like I could have a discussion with Hillary Clinton where there would be some middle ground.

I feel that way about the Clintons. You can't hate them, because I think that to be president, on some level you have to understand peo-ple. I think even Richard Nixon knew how to relate to somebody. Cer-tainly Hillary's got those chops—I think she knows how to relate to people on some level, and that's what a president does. When I met

George W. Bush and George Bush Sr. I felt the same way. You've got to love them all because they're your president.

We're always going to be smarmy because we're the first world and we're idiots and we waste things. We're a dreadful nation built by pirates who stole other people's land. There's no justifying us, save the fact that our country belongs to everyone in the world. That to me is our saving grace.

This is why we can't stop allowing immigrants into the United States because that's what we're made of. The one redemption we have is that this country belongs to everybody because we stole it and the only way to make that right is have it be for everybody. This nation, above all other nations, has to do that.

The game of politics can be confusing. I think that's the problem with our system. Everybody wants to have a sound bite and a nutshell, and when you try to be a true-blue Democrat or Republican, you miss out on being a human unless you're just trying to get your brand of cereal across. I think neither side has it figured out.

I'm liberal on social issues, but I also see gun rights as a social issue, and I think you should be free to do whatever you want. I still lean Republican on monetary and military ideas. I guess that makes me something of a libertarian, although libertarians tend to be isolationist and utopian, which makes me not quite a libertarian either. Still, I figure libertarians are open-minded; they're the Unitarians of politics. Usually when something has "arian" in a suffix, that means they're open-minded—Unitarians, Libertarians, librarians. But oddly Aryans don't, and the only difference with them is sometimes a Y.

The problem for me is that Libertarians right now under Ron Paul are pro-life.

I went to a Libertarian rally, and there was one pro-choice Libertarian who spoke. He said, "You could say that being Libertarian was a pro-choice thing if you look at a mother's womb as a property rights issue." And he was booed. It was terrible—they were booing a fellow Libertarian who was merely suggesting another way to look at something that really is kind of unknown. It just showed me that the group is a cult of personality that turns on whatever Ron Paul says is the definition of Libertarian.

At one point I got to have a meal with Ron Paul and asked him some questions about isolationism, which he seemed to support. I asked, "How can you do that? How can you just leave Israel to its fate?" And he said, "If we take the cuffs off Israel, you'd be amazed how well Israel handles its own job. Israel will wreak hell when it needs to." That's more reasonable than I thought, but it's still just a little naïve for me.

There isn't a party that defines everyone, and I think everyone's catching on to that. I think that before, people were uniformly one thing or the other. But something that can't be denied lately is the way Republicans have been tearing themselves apart. It's a sad thing to see, but I'm hoping it's one of these replenishing things, where what will emerge is a valid conservative argument.

Can the Republicans modify their agenda? They've got to let go of the gay marriage thing and the abortion thing. You're interfering with someone else's lifestyle. Abortion may be debatable, but gay marriage—really? Marriage is a ceremony that was invented in the Middle Ages to make sure everyone knows this is who I'm screwing and I own her.

I think the abortion thing is a problem for Republicans because the church is in on that one too deeply. I think there's a real dilemma with the social issues, and that loses it for them. At the end of the day, do you vote more for social issues or for money? I think you try to vote on money, but the act of voting itself implies some sort of idealism.

At times it all comes down to us vs. them, and *we're* clearly right and *they* clearly aren't. I thought I had outgrown that in elementary school. It's the first rule of living on a playground—you realize, *Wow, maybe they're people too. Maybe they have a good idea.* So then you deprive yourself of half of the good ideas out there. This is where somebody funny would come in and say, "More than half."

I suppose I'll go back to Winston Churchill who said the only thing worse than the democratic process is everything else. If we can come up with a better form of democracy, I'm interested, but I kind of like the arguing. Even when I'm losing the argument, I feel the most comfortable.

That's what struck me about Occupy—once they started requiring hand gestures, they became elitists because you needed to know their vernacular. So then it became how hip you were and how much you knew on the inside before you could communicate with them.

While I was growing up my dad was Republican, my mom was Democrat, all the girls were Democrats, and all the boys except one were Republicans. But then there was some fluctuation of issues: a sister might be more conservative on something, a brother might be more liberal, and every Thanksgiving there would be this huge debate that would go around and around. I think that was a good way to grow up because nobody seemed right.

That's how a society should function: where nobody is completely happy because that's life. That's why we have teeth and nails—we have to chew and tear things. If everything went our way, it all would be applesauce.

I've always held that the answer's in the center. Even my band agrees they might be Democrats, but they've become conservative Democrats. And if I'm a Republican, then I've become one of the most liberal Republicans I know, and that's because we know we need the other side.

It's a very hard place to be when you don't know which party you belong to, but I think that's the reality of things: we want it to be us-them, Army/Navy, Yale/Harvard, crips/bloods—pick your team and have it be that simple. But nothing is that simple, the answer is always in the murky middle, and that isn't a fun story—people want Darth Vader and Luke Skywalker.

I sometimes think that if after *Return of the Jedi*, when they've destroyed the Death Star and Darth Vader and the Emperor are dead, that Han, Leia, and Luke Skywalker will initiate a totalitarian regime that's just as bad. They'll call it the Helping Republic, but it'll be just as brutal—they'll make Ewok hunting legal with no rights for Hutts. Maybe Jabba the Hutt is the most noble of Hutts and we just don't understand the Hutt mentality, but they're slimy, they have horrible tongues, and they're fat, so kill 'em all.

I have Libertarian leanings because ultimately I want to be left alone since I believe in my moral conscience and I'm willing to trust other people's moral consciences, by and large. The problem with being a Libertarian is that it becomes a utopian exercise, where you fantasize about a world in which everybody can handle it and does. I see every other party as an overreaction to the people who can't handle it, who always seem to be on the other side. I think the Democrats wring their hands too much and the Republicans put on blinders a bit. Both are ways to avoid reality, and reality isn't something I think the public would vote for. But I am not concerned about legislating for a crazy person—crazy people don't follow the rules anyway.

The other answer is to do nothing and let people fend for themselves. I don't think that's right either, but I just know for a fact—at least in my bones—that there is nothing worse than a government-run program. Hopefully because Obamacare is a fact of life, it'll get better, but I look at what's going on with the VA, and I'm not impressed. I would rather have things suck than have things suck while an official comes and tells me that I missed my mandatory dental appointment.

34

HOOKS

As Blues Traveler approaches our thirtieth anniversary, I'm not sure whether I'm surprised or not. We're a high school band that had no reason to quit, and I can't quite imagine doing anything else entirely.

I am looking forward to some new adventures with marriage and fatherhood. I have a wonderful partner in Jordan, and we are going to build a wonderful life together with a new generation of Poppers. God help all of you.

At this point in my life I wasn't expecting to have a kid, but as I approach fifty, I really feel I am ready. I think I never would have been the good father I'm hoping to be if I hadn't devoted my energy to my career when I was younger. I would have thought, stupidly, *Man, the kid's holding me back.* But now I think this is the next thing for me. I am just discovering this feeling of, *Wow, I gotta be a better me.* I can do what I want, but I better mean it. I can go off and slay my dragons, but I better bring home some dragon meat, whereas before, my thinking was, *I didn't get anything off this dragon; I'll get the next dragon.* You can still tilt at windmills, but you better bring that shit home and build a windmill in your yard.

Lately there have been some changes in my professional life as well, in particular that after a quarter-century of dutiful service, Gina decided to move on. I think she wanted to do things on her own, which is funny because she was doing things with us on her own, but she felt so much like family that it didn't feel that way to her. I get that. She wound up running the Central Park SummerStage. Although we all knew she could do it, what was a wonderful surprise was that all those years with us did count toward her professional résumé that she could use to get the job. She finally gets to do what she's good at and stay home in New York and develop a life of her own. We love her so much and are so happy for her.

I think I've been through more craziness with her than with any other person—the motorcycle accident, incidents with the police, my weight issues, Bobby's death. Hers is the only number I have memorized. I don't know my own phone number, but I know Gina's number because in an emergency, she's who you call.

Her titles would change over the years. At one point she got sick of the road and wanted to work in our office with management. Because she was Gina, management understood her value and let her come in—she was still interacting with the fans through our mailer. Then eventually she wanted to get back on the road at a time when we needed a real tour manager, and she stepped up and did great.

Finally, after twenty-five years, she wanted to be a tour manager and now a production manager on her own terms, and it does my heart good to see her out there doing that.

Gina started unprofessionally with us and became a professional with us, and sometimes you want to take that out and see what you can do with it. That's why I like to go and do side work. I have this problem in my band in which we've know each other since we were seventeen and get into fights like seventeen-year-olds do and don't get to see each other as the full musicians we are.

I think that's why I enjoyed recording and touring with Jono and Brothers Keeper. Scott Rednor was in Dear Liza, a group that our original crew member Dave Precheur managed for a few years. They were a good bunch of guys who grew up in the town next to Princeton. Scott moved out to Colorado and eventually came to own the Shakedown Bar in Vail, where he put a band together with some guys who play with John Oates. They were one of these really great cover bands, and then Jono and I went out there and I told them about my Duskray Troubadours experience. So we ended up taking the same approach, with them as a power trio focal point, for what became the Brothers Keeper album, *Todd Meadows*. It turned into a five-way writing seminar, and Jono and I were brought in to effect it.

Then, in January 2015, I went on tour with them and was reminded just how pricey it is to run that kind of operation for a band who's starting out. We were in a glorified bread truck, and because I didn't fit into any of the tiny bins, they had a floor bed for me. Scott brought some of his wife's patio furniture pillows and we put some sheets on them. At my age and with my knees, that was *fun*.

I had started seeing Jordan seriously by then, and she wanted to come along. I wasn't sure if she could, but she toughed it out. I'd never take a girlfriend on tour before. Not only was it flat-out fun, but as the band kept getting hungrier and hornier, I had that all taken care of. Plus, Jordan was a real asset. She sold T-shirts, and a lot of the tour felt like going back in time to the good old days. It was a great blast from the past for me, but I knew I could not do it longer than a month because I would be dead. I'm too old for this shit. I'm Danny Glover all over that.

Given that experience, though, I suppose it's only fitting that my wedding to Jordan took place in the midst of a mad scramble while on tour. With our daughter, Eloise, due in November, Jordan and I had wanted to find a date when we could get married before the baby came because we figured that once Eloise arrived, there would be an absolute monopolization of our time between the baby and work. In September we were together on the East Coast, on tour with Blues Traveler, and although we thought about New York City, which is important to both of us and we have friends and family nearby, we couldn't get a marriage license in time. But we learned that in Virginia you can get a marriage license and get married on the same day. At first the timing seemed somewhat sane because we could do it the day before Blues Traveler played in Maryland. I was also going to sit in with Bill Kreutzmann's band Billy & the Kids at the Lockn' Festival in Virginia on that day off in Virginia, but it seemed like it could work.

But on the day we were to be married, a tropical storm swept through Virginia. Lockn' was postponed, and the Billy & The Kids gig moved to Charlottesville. So now we had to sort out the marriage license and the marriage ceremony in the middle of Charlottesville with no warning in the middle of a storm.

I said earlier that you don't ever want your fiancée to drive when she gets a new ring. Well, another lesson I've learned is when your bride-to-be is determined to get a wedding license and then make it to the sheriff's office in time to meet the justice of the peace, then strap in, because she's going to drive at a breakneck pace. It was quite reckless (although no necks were broken in the process), and she did all of it. I was afraid for my life many times.

Of course, we were late because of the traffic and the hazardous weather conditions, but we made it—barely. Then while Jordan changed into her wedding dress in the car, I waited outside in the torrential rain because we didn't want to see each other before we got married. Luckily it all came together, and Jordan Popper was beaming.

From there it was straight to the Billy & the Kids gig. Again we were behind schedule, but somehow we walked in with a few minutes to spare. The gig was really fun because I had forgotten what a great drummer Bill is. He plays like two drummers all by himself—it's a really cool thing to see. They had me sing "Hard to Handle," which I found amusing because it's Chris Robinson's big song.

Then when we came out after the show we discovered that our car had been towed. So we had to figure out where it was, find our way there, fork over $100, and then get in our car and drive two more hours to our hotel in Lynchburg. We finally arrived, beyond exhausted, and who is in the hallway talking real loud at the end of this surreal night but Chris Robinson himself. He was in the middle of a story, and I was interrupting him because I was walking through with our luggage. This was the first time I had seen him face-to-face since the airport, and he was perfectly friendly. I didn't quite recognize him at first.

I explained we were newlyweds, and he offered his congratulations, but Jordan and I needed to get to sleep. Of course, when we walked in the room there was a steak dinner my family had bought and a bouquet of flowers. We tried to enjoy the steak, which apparently was the finest that could be found in the state of Virginia, but could only muster one bite apiece. We were too tired to eat, let alone have a real wedding night.

The next day was September 11, and I had agreed to open the day at Lockn' with a version of the "Star-Spangled Banner" alongside some first responders before driving off to the Blues Traveler gig in Maryland. Due to the previous day's postponement, there was a lot of traffic we had not anticipated. Again Jordan was behind the wheel, driving like she had the prior day because perhaps I gave her some crap about it—"See, we shouldn't have squeezed a wedding in there." But finally we made it to the police escort. We hustled in, I played the "Star-Spangled Banner," shook hands with the first responders, and expressed my appreciation for all they do.

Then we had to drive another four hours to the Blues Traveler gig in Maryland, where we met my parents and my brother for our first proper dinner as newlyweds. After supper we hurried to the Blues Traveler show, where Jordan tossed her bouquet and we ate the wedding cake the band provided, which read, "Congrats on getting knocked up and hitched!"

From there I got on a bus and drove away. That was Jordan's wedding—rushing to gigs and then me getting on a bus and leaving. I have to give her credit—she was a trooper the whole time and did most of the driving. That is not what every woman dreams about, and I'm really grateful she still said, "I do." I think we even snuck some fast food in there.

I should mention that Lockn' was special for me not only because of what took place but also because it was founded by my former manager and H.O.R.D.E. partner Dave Frey along with Pete Shapiro, who took over for Larry Bloch at Wetlands and has since opened Brooklyn Bowl, Brooklyn Bowl Las Vegas, and Brooklyn Bowl London and reopened the Capitol Theatre in Port Chester (he was also the animating force behind the Fare Thee Well Grateful Dead reunion shows).

I remember being proud of him for continuing what Larry Bloch was doing, but it was later, with Brooklyn Bowl, that he really impressed me. With Wetlands he had a model, but with Brooklyn Bowl, Pete put in his own flavor. The first thing I noticed is that people could bowl and see the band, which reminded me a bit of Wetlands, where you could smoke downstairs and still hear the music because the sound was so good. Brooklyn Bowl is geared toward the audience experience, and that's something Bill Graham would have appreciated. Pete is always concerned with everybody having a good time, and he takes on the same characteristic that the Grahams did in that he's never really relaxed because he wants to make sure everybody else is okay. He's always working on some cool aspect of the show, so I'll see him moving through, he'll check in, and then he's off on something else. I would give $5,000 to see him sit still for three hours at a given show, but he could never do it; he has too much going on up there.

He told me about this really elaborate plan he had for a zip line from the hotel across the street to the band room at Brooklyn Bowl. I said, "Good luck getting that through zoning," and he had this look in his eyes like he was going to do it.

I think some of the reason he took the Brooklyn Bowl concept to Vegas was to see what other applications it had. We finally had a chance to play Brooklyn Bowl Vegas, and that room is really fun. I know what he has in mind there, and it's a really cool idea.

I feel like he's the heir apparent to the Fillmore tradition. That's my view of Pete. Bill always had this bug up his butt about modern-day concert promoters. He believed that when they see people, they see dollar signs. Their enemy is the fire code—"If I can somehow get a legal precedent that allows me to cram two hundred more people in there, then I'll win that much additional money." It's all about getting them in, getting them out, offering very little entertainment beyond the band itself, and then selling them an overpriced T-shirt of inferior quality.

What Bill always wanted to do in contrast was to consider the entire show an experience. When audience members come into a place, it should feel like their place. It should be comfortable, and it should have really nice fixtures and a really good staff who know what they're doing and know how to take care of everyone. The staff has to be disciplined, and it's all to make the experience entertaining.

I think Peter has taken that to heart, and he's taken that very seriously. He looks at a show and thinks, *If I were an audience member, how would I feel about being here?* I think that is a rare thing. Bill would be really proud of him.

As for life on the road with Blues Traveler, my biggest gripe now is that because of our longevity, when we play live gigs we end up being custodians of our various eras. I feel like a museum curator in a way. It can become harder and harder to do new things because we also want to include the old things and only have an hour and half or two on stage. When I'm making a set list I try to include one song from every album, and we can still just about do it.

I remember that when we opened for Jerry Garcia, his crew told us, "Don't play any of that heavy-metal music you guys always play." That was the first time I ever heard our music referred to that way. I didn't know we were heavy-metal music, but we were speed demons, so I could see where, if you were an old hippie, you'd think it was heavy metal. Of course, the heavy-metal guys thought we were hippie music. Every genre thought we were something else.

We won the New York Music Award for best blues band, which was hysterical for me. What I noticed when we accepted the award was that there were all these different factions of musicians—rap, metal, folk-rock, prog-rock, and even electronica—and they all seemed to know us and had respect for us. There were probably some really deserving blues musicians who wished we would die, but it was pretty fucking cool.

I've always felt like we were trying to straddle a fence. Back when "Run-Around" was huge, all these twelve-year-olds would come to our shows, and the hippies would tolerate them (barely). The twelve-year-olds would be bored by the rest of what we were doing, which the hippies were all into. Then we'd do two songs, and suddenly the twelve-year-olds would be the vocal majority, with these little kids screaming, and all the hippies would be horrified. They would later tell me that it felt like we were leaving them.

The twelve-year-olds had no idea about any of our other songs. But those twelve-year-olds are now in their thirties, and they've listened to us since they were twelve, so we've become their institution. We were sort of the hippies' institution before that, but these were the hippies who were around in the sixties, who adopted us at the tail end of the eighties. There was an audience who left after Bobby passed away, but we also have an audience who started listening after Tad and Ben joined the band. So we'll get these weird clusters of fans. We're this band of several identities.

I was really struck when Emma Stone had a lip sync battle with Jimmy Fallon on the *Tonight Show* and she chose "Hook." *Rolling Stone* reported that she had managed "to make Blues Traveler the coolest band in the world again." Then I responded in kind by donning a feather boa to lip sync my version of her "Knock on Wood" performance in *Easy A*. We probably lost the title.

The band fun. played some of "Hook" on a radio appearance when they were asked to identify "the very first piece of music you bought with your own money." I was genuinely appreciative (even if fun. may be the least fun way to spell fun) because they were really trying to be nice and say they liked the song, but they got the words wrong. I wanted to complain, but who was I going to call? And then I started feeling like I should be muttering to myself and shaking my fist, complaining about the trouble with kids these days and telling them to stay off my lawn.

I'm sort of put in that same spot when people ask for my opinions about other harmonica players. I never want to be one to say "too many notes," even though there are plenty of talented harp players who are faster than ever. I'm thinking of people like LD Miller or Will Freed. I don't want them to come to me to vanquish or to be vanquished. At times I think they have some trouble with melody, but rather than too many notes, I want to say, "Take those notes somewhere." I want to set a good example, though, so they get there on their own. What these kids really need is somebody who gets it and says, "Yes! Play weird!"

If I had chance to talk to myself when I was a kid, I might have something to say about "Hook." I wrote it when I was twenty-five when I liked to make the point, "Look how high I can sing, everybody! Look at me! Look at me!" I had no idea that for the next twenty years I might like to go back in time and punch myself in the face—"Do you understand what you're going to be doing?" I'd probably respond, "Shut up, old man! You're not my father!" and I'd get into a fight with myself. (Given the weight trouble I had as a younger man, I think I could take the younger me. The key is to sweep the knees. If I sweep my younger knees, I think I'd have a real advantage. Of course, younger me would probably know that older me would do this and would do something to protect the knees and attempt to fall on the older, more bone-fragile me in an attempt to crush my ribcage. But I would know that I really love my testicles and would try to stab my testicles with my thumbs jutted out like some sort of makeshift shiv. It would be a very close fight, but I think I could do it because older me knows more.)

One rarely has a chance to go back, although in 2013 I did have the opportunity to make amends with Stevie Wonder after the incident at the White House in 2000 when I brought his jam to a screeching halt because I didn't have the right harmonicas. He invited me to be part of his benefit show when he performed all of *Songs in the Key of Life*. The only tricky part was that this was one of those rare times when he didn't want me to solo; he wanted me to play the low harmonica section that he played on a chromatic harmonica thirty-five years ago. I didn't know that part, but thankfully Frederic Yonnet, this incredible harmonica player from France, was there. It turned out he was a fan of mine and said, "I hope you don't mind, but I took the liberty of isolating your part on a file for you to hear." I said, "But I didn't get *you* anything!" So he made it remotely possible for me to play the part. I was so thankful that it wasn't like the old days, when we'd think, *Oh you're such an enemy, another harp player.*

Still, it was going to be a challenge for me to do the beginning, even after we fought through it. india.arie (what is it with these kids and their damn lowercase?) had kissed Stevie when she came out, and there was a little imprint of lipstick on his cheek. I saw the imprint and pointed it out to Frederic. I figured I'd keep things light, and there was a pause, so I got on the mic and said, "Who doesn't love this man? Who wouldn't kiss him? Who wouldn't kiss this man?" The crowd started clapping and then cheering, so I walked over to the piano and kissed him on the cheek. He loved it and fell over on his stool laughing. Then the crowd really clapped, and I whispered in his ear, "You know they're really clapping because I just took all my clothes off." Then we started the song, and *he* tanked the beginning, so that was how I saved my own ass.

Afterward Bobby Shriver told me that they were doing music at a friend's house and invited me to join him. I went along, but I only brought one harmonica, an obscure key, because my attitude was that I was done for the night.

It turned out it was Renée Zellweger's house. It was like I was having a dream in which I was at a party, only everybody at the party was somebody famous: Tom Hanks, Rita Wilson, Johnny Knoxville, Nia Vardalos, Ian Gomez, and plenty of other people I recognized by face but not by name.

John Stamos was there, and of course, he wanted to play the drums, but I only had one key, which was a flat. None of the dabblers could play in a flat, but we wrestled out a blues so people could get their money's worth. Then this little thirteen-year-old girl asked whether she could sing one, and behind her was her nebbishy dad saying, "Would you mind if she maybe sang one?" I said, "Sure," because now I'm the lord of the living room, and her nebbishy dad, as if he were cast for the role, was Albert Brooks. I said sure, and people told me it was so nice what I did for her, but all I did was say okay. She sang Etta James's signature song "At Last" a cappella because none of us knew how to play it, and she rocked the room.

I was talking with a crowd of people when Tom Hanks walked by, so I said, "You're amazing, by the way." I've been a Tom Hanks fan since *Bosom Buddies*. Then I think he called me a phenomenon, but as he was saying it I couldn't quite hear him because I was getting tunnel vision—he wasn't Tom Hanks anymore, he was . . . pick your favorite character from a Tom Hanks movie, that's who he was. For me he was Captain Miller from *Saving Private Ryan* calling me a phenomenon.

It was one of the my favorite celeb hangs, and what was really great was I had brought my sister, who lived six blocks away in Santa Monica and had moved to Hollywood to be an actress and had written a screenplay or two. For her it was like I dumped crack down her throat and then chased it with a speedball. And, I have to admit, it felt that way for me as well.

These days, as we play new music festivals with an increased frequency, I find they're a good source of celebrity sightings and new musical collaborations, and I never tire of either. The Southern Ground Music & Food Festival in October 2014 offered ample helpings of both.

It was there that I ran into Bill Murray for the first time since he gave that pep talk at SXSW. I once again thanked him for it, but then I caused him some undue alarm when I began talking to him about my impending heat stroke. For all I know Bill had just smoked a whole bunch of pot, which may have exacerbated any anxiety that I caused. I've come to acknowledge that I can be a terrible hypochondriac and that the way I combat it is by obsessing about passing out. I try to make it worse than it actually is so that when I get on stage, it actually isn't that bad. I've inherited this hypochondria from my father, who wants his tombstone to read, *He was a terrible hypochondriac and in the end he was right.*

It turned out that it wasn't that bad, far from it, and it also marked my first appearance with the Zac Brown Band. I wasn't all that familiar with their music, but when I walked onto their bus, they were in the midst of some bluegrass tune. It was obvious that they all could play. It was fun to see that Zac himself is all player rather than just someone who is supported by good players. I sat down, opened up my harp case, and jumped right in—when you've got musicians that good, you can do that.

I wound up doing a few songs with him. One of them was "Piano Man," in which he played the actual Billy Joel part, which I can do, but I figured I'd play something weird around it. So I did it in a more classical musical style—it sounded all fuguey. He called me a show-off, and then we did the third one together. That was the acoustic set, and later I came out on the electric set with Luther Dickinson for "Can't You See." It felt like we were taking the Nestea plunge into something I had never done before but still felt familiar. It was like falling into a new family, and it was an easy, cool thing to do.

In August of 2015 I sat in with the Foo Fighters, where I experienced a similar level of comfort and connection. We were getting ready for a one-off H.O.R.D.E. show that took place in Detroit (as a possible test run for the future), and I was in town early, so I went to my first Foo Fighters show. At this point I've learned to bring harmonicas with me. I learned from that experience playing at Al Gore's concession party—if your harps are in the broom closet, you're going to have to tap Stevie Wonder on the back and ask him to change keys, and that's just not what I am going to do.

It might have felt a little presumptuous that the Foo Fighters would ask me to sit in, but they're a bunch of players, they like to have all sorts of experiences, and they're easygoing guys, so that's a recipe for having my harps with me. I called Lani, my manager, who had to call some crew guy to get them off some vehicle and rush them to Deer Creek (or whatever that Noblesville, Indiana, amphitheater is called these days). Sure enough, the Foo Fighters said, "We want you to sit in," and they worked out some blues riff.

It was cool to see how in tune Dave Grohl is with the audience— there's such a love affair there, and he gives them everything he can.

He was playing with a broken leg, and that offered an interesting contrast from my own experiences. Back in the day my crew would shovel me into my little wheelchair and then dump me into this tall, swiveling chair—that was the height of my chair technology: it swiveled. His chair was forged by artisans from the Aztec tradition, and there was a lot of chrome and lights and a big FF on it. It would slide back and forth on a track and flames would shoot out of it. Mine swiveled.

Watching him sit there, I was reminded how once a show I would pretend I could stand up for the first time, even though I was just standing on the other leg—"I've been healed!" He would do that too. You just can't beat that gag, no matter what technology you have.

I also really enjoyed watching his daughters, who must have been five and nine, just loving their dad onstage and then putting "Kick Me" signs on the crew's back. I think he gave them each a job. At different times each would run out onstage and present him with a coke. It was just so much fun to watch and made me excited for my daughter.

When I went out to play it was really a no-brainer because I knew what I had to do: just grip it and rip it. It was one for the bucket list because we move in the same circles a lot of the time but we'd never actually met each other, let alone play together.

But even as I try new things like that, it feels good to maintain some traditions as well. Although we gave up the New Year's Eve black cat ritual after Bobby died, one tradition that continues is Fourth of July at Red Rocks, which we've been doing for more than two decades.

I love the place, but it's brutal for a singer. It's so high up in the air that my voice drops an octave—it can be physically challenging. We write set lists for artistic reasons, not altitude reasons. I used to get oxygen but I found that it dried my throat out if I took it during the show. Bugs will fly in my face or in my drink. (That's what happened in 2013 when TMZ posted a video of me spitting up on stage, calling "party foul" on myself—I was about to drink a shot while we were performing in Florida, and as it reached my mouth, I noticed a giant insect in it.) There can be freak weather—one year we were getting sideways freezing rain, and I said to the audience, "If you can take it, I can take it," but they all had brought rain slickers and I hadn't—so it fucked me up for the rest of the summer and I got a vocal thrush that had to be zapped.

I know how much the audience loves it, though. It's a spectacular venue on any night, but on the Fourth of July, it can be quite a light show with all the fireworks in the surrounding towns. There have been times when I have heard the crowd spontaneously cheering and wondered, *Did we do something cool? Let's do it again!* Then I realized they were looking behind me at the fireworks that just started or finished, so my ego would get deflated. But what we also get is all this energy pointed like a funnel right at us because we're at the bottom of this natural amphitheater. It's amazing.

The "No Woman, No Cry" we did there in 2003 with Ziggy Marley (which appears on the *Thinnest of Air* DVD) was one of the banner moments of my life. We played it with the son of the source of that song, who sings a lot like him and looks a lot like him and certainly knows that song and that music. And I had this delivery I had been working on, where I was really late on that second verse. Frank Sinatra often did it that way, and I was late on the line because I was so deep in the pocket. That made Ziggy crack up. It really tickled me.

I have had a ton of moments like that, when I get lost in the music and the crowd takes us there. That's the reason why we all do what we do.

People often ask me what music means to me, and it's really hard for me to describe. It's like air, and it's hard to appreciate air. You need air to live, but you don't celebrate air.

But what I *can* celebrate is my audience. And if you've read this far, then you're a member of that audience, so I'd like to leave you with this. I wrote it on Jam Cruise in 2015—there may have been some mushroom chocolate involved—to celebrate what we've all done together and how I feel about you after all these years. With the deepest admiration and awe let me again emphasize that I never could have done any of this without all of you. You've shaped my experience and perspective. Without you out there to receive my thoughts and ideas, they never would have taken flight. But together, all of us can sail.

Our connection has meant more to me than any of the cool things I've done, the money I've made, or the art I've helped create.

I came from a place where I was entirely isolated, and now I am able to share myself and my music in such a wonderful, surprising way. The lyrics below try to explain how much you as a collective mass or a single ear for me to bend have really saved my life and helped to give it meaning. I owe you something that I will never be able to repay; I can only appreciate it, and I assure you, I never take it for granted. I never take *you* for granted . . .

"Owed from the Aspect"

A chance again to diatribe,
You'll go along if you've imbibed,
My mannered tones of dire cost,
& if something gets translated lost,
Again I seek to hide the same
as though we've never stopped our game
and all the tidings I could bring
Have never really changed a thing.
Dependent on each other we
kept infinite the "you and me" that never really set us free
. . . or too lonely was the place we'd be . . .
(Chorus)
But for all I've ever tried to tell you,
I just couldn't seem to say how much I care,
and speaking as the aspect that befell you,
. . . You've come to mean (be) my (very) universe out there . . .

For all the right or wrong I'd done,
I had to share it with someone.
The true the lie the in between,
their implications what they mean,
a troubled tale or trophied turn,
within my heart they'd only burn
'til the echoes on the acetate
reveal what we can all relate,
then freely we can share our pain
& know that we are not insane
or at least a frenzy we can own.
it's enough for me I'm not alone . . .
(Chorus)
(Bridge)
I stumble to the floor until I realize that I'm climbing.
I can fall right up a staircase
just as easily as down . . .
'Cause hope can flip the building on its end and in the timing
needs a friend
or else it lands
within the sand
without a sound

A chance again to double-down,
perhaps a way of standing ground
for any sin that took a toll by every rescue of my soul.
Each choice I made to turn to you,
a thing I had to learn to do,
so grateful I could see it through
almost as if you always knew . . .
I choose again to share anew . . .
as if compulsively on cue,
more karma for we happy few,
whose destiny's the devil's due
(and yet I'm thanking god for you . . .)
(Chorus)
(Searching for the dawn until it's we who are both shining . . .)

AFTERWORD

*To My Darling Daughter, Eloise,
on the Eve of Her Birth*

November 20, 2015, 1:00ish a.m. PST

Hello Weezy!

Wow, this is kind of the first thing I'm ever saying to you in a very real way. In fact, I initially wanted this entire Afterword to be the Foreword so it would be the first thing you read, but we all felt that it would make more sense to the other readers if this appeared after they got to know me a little bit. Hopefully you won't have that problem. If I've done my job as a father, this will only be the most recent thing you are hearing from me. And hopefully not the last.

So first of all, I love you! Here and now from the year 2015. I am excited as I sit here with your mother waiting for your labor to begin, well, really hers. (By the way, you kicked the crap out of her rib cage and you need to call her more. Buy her a lovely Bundt cake. Nothing garners forgiveness like a lovely Bundt cake.)

But the key here is that you know how much we both wanted you. You were a total surprise and, in my mind, ever more intended by some higher power to be here—perhaps to save the world, perhaps to become part of it—but, in any event, to thrive and certainly to save my life. And mind you, my life is saved by the hope you bring to me. You are more than the sun, moon, and stars because stars always ultimately fade, while hope goes on forever and feeds everything. I'm honored to get to tell you that you'll understand one day (I feel like I just joined that club).

I don't know when in your life you'll be reading this book or how old you'll be, but it must already seem weird to be hearing me dialogue with you in this tone before we've even met. I wonder if this is close to how we'll talk. It is 2015, as I was saying, the night before you are to be born, and though it's the 20th, which is the day before you're expected according to science, in the minds of your parents, grandparents, aunts, uncles, grandaunts, granduncles, cousins of all degrees, in-laws, outlaws, Facebook followers, and general populace of friends who are in some sense involved and awaiting your arrival, you are keeping us all waiting.

I expect that sort of pressure to occasionally bother you at times with this bunch, but that's your family—patience comes only painfully to such a collection of independent thinkers, but by far it's your mother who shines throughout all of this and who is awaiting you most deeply. I want to tell you about her. . . .

It was April of 2014. We were playing a festival, and these two beautiful women approached me for help getting side stage for the Allman Brothers. One of them, the shorter one, though still very attractive, seemed more relatable—at least she didn't scare me any. But it was her taller friend who struck me as a goddess, leaving me utterly if momentarily helpless for any semblance of "game" or smoothness. Normally, as I look back at my past rapport with intimidatingly attractive women, I will make all manner of jackass of myself or sometimes stumble into a smooth banter all to get the object of my affection to say "yes" to some extent or another. But there was something about this tall, beautiful, free-spirited blonde that was different, and all such thoughts in my head were gone and all I could say in my heart over and over to myself was "Yes . . . " And in that subtle difference, so slight yet so enduringly significant, I didn't need to find the words—they came of their own volition.

I don't recall any strategy because when you truly decide you want someone, your self is revealed and strategy becomes far too stagnant for something that rings throughout your core so truthfully. I said yes in my heart and began to talk to her, and before the night was over I would steal a kiss—a respectful kiss but a real passionate kiss because I wanted one from her, and that was simply that. I also made sure to get her contact info, and with each step of the process I would say yes.

We were both involved with other people and did our best to respect those relationships, but we were instantly drawn to each other, and as I said yes, as I came to know your mother, I came to see what an amazing and passionate mind and heart had befallen me. She was so much younger than me, and her innocence in some of life's adventures seemed to need me. But the innocence in me could immediately realize and value the wisdom she'd garnered at so tender an age.

She knew of hearts and of love's purpose as it spoke to me . . . and we were off and running. I truly feel that it was she who began to make my life matter to me again, even before that night in Atlanta when I was gigging with a local band and she, having seen us the night before in Alabama, really wanted to go see Willie Nelson play at the "enormo-dome" there. We knew Mickey (Willie's harp player), and he got her into the show. When she met back up at my gig afterward, she waited for me to finish, and we went back to our room and conceived you.

So an automatic take-away here is that should you ever get the opportunity to see the Red Headed Stranger, please bring contraception (because apparently it only takes one out of every couple). Actually, take several forms of contraception because your mom was on the pill and Shotgun Willie don't mess around!

So there we were, less than a year into our relationship and pregnant with you! Bear in mind, we had just decided to get a dog (Trigger), and you were a total surprise. Yes, we both freaked, but we very quickly knew we wanted you so bad, like the sun wants light! We were already becoming a family, and off we went. We said yes to you, and every yes we've said has saved us in this, our newest chapter of this life we are living.

So it certainly seems time to pen a book of my life before I met you or your mom, partly because I'm finally starting to get to an age when my memory is starting to fade and I want to recount as accurately as possible these events I befell, now that I no longer live them with the same daily determination. I am now dedicated to a very new priority, one I hope I can deserve. I also craft this little tome to help understand how I got here as well as perhaps gain any catharsis in the retrospect at their recounting.

A great deal of this book was taken from my journal entries that I kept dutifully from around 1990 to 1999. Then I would recall the tale through my current eyes to allow the forty-eight-year-old man to reconcile with the determined young lad in his twenties. I hope I was sincere in that attempt and not just burying bodies (metaphorically as far as you know).

Which reminds me: all recounts in this book are not to be taken as factual or legally binding. They are merely my interpretations and embellishments for entertainment value. I try to be fair, but my brain always makes shit up to tell a tale and sell a nifty book. Perhaps I just don't want you to judge me—and perhaps you will and I should be judged—but my intention is for you to have gotten to know me well enough to make up your own informed mind (the rest of the readership will have to risk this uninformed, but they are paying me, so . . .). I hope you can know what it felt like. I must say the hardest part of writing this book was finishing it.

I often found myself telling the same story or mentioning it to Dean, my co-author, as we'd go through his edits only to have the story in question appear in the next line. I think I just wanted to keep reliving it, as the first telling brought so much back. Dean was great at keeping track of my tangential ramblings to give them form, and he even kept my subject-changing and time-jumping through my various yarns as accurate as we could (without disintegrating into pure non sequitur, of course). We felt that there was value in that tactic of yarn-spinning.

Retrospect does really tend to offer insight, and Dean had a great gift throughout this whole project for letting me shine where I shone best, and this wouldn't be possible without him. I hope the reader can keep track. The *only* section of the book I did not go over with Dean Budnick and the process we came to rely on is this very dedication . . .

And it is at this point that I put down this rather longwinded dedication I've been working on for the past two days and drive your mother to the hospital to give birth to you. So to be continued and see you soon!

November 23, 2015, 11:15ish pm PST

Oh my god, we just had you!

Call your mother! Call your mother! Call your mother!

Eleven hours and no drugs the whole time, she was such a champ. I cut your little cord after I got you both to the hospital (an hour away) in only thirty-five minutes. That Mercedes still moves!

You are so beautiful! Pulling you from your mother's nether regions has to be one of the most significant moments of my life! Well done, kiddo!

Anyway, I will wrap this up, my darling daughter, by telling you three true things that every father would want his daughter to know:

First, I am an undefeated thumb wrestler—righty, lefty, doubles . . . it doesn't matter. Well, I have lost on a rare occasion or two, but in the no-holds-barred underworld atmosphere of freestyle full-on thumb wrestling, you can't count on fair rulings or equal footing—or, rather, thumbing—every time. But suffice it to say, I would roam the Earth searching for a warrior to best me and never could. Concert promoters would bet money on me, though I was in it for the love and grace of the sport. One night I beat both Goldberg and Hulk Hogan (though, to be fair, Goldberg had just "real" wrestled five guys and was rather tired, and Hulk just kinda didn't wanna be standing there anymore and gave me the win). The moral? If you choose a ridiculous enough thing to be great at, you can rule at it (see harmonicas).

Second, I have pulled many four-leaf clovers—and even a five-leafer when needed. I guess I only tell you that because I want you to know they are out there. So look for them whenever possible if it isn't too much of a stretch.

Finally, I hear music in my head all the time. Like a punch-drunk fighter, I can't tell if I have played too many gigs and it's stuck in my head or if it's the reason I've played so many, but if you notice your dear old dad seeming distracted or as though listening to something else, I can only tell you that life all around us has music in it, and once you learn to speak or hear it, it cannot be ignored. I only hope that has been a good thing as I have decided to see it—or, rather, hear it—and I thank you for any patience you might require. I also thank you for showing me that love is a breathing two-way communicative conduit that started instantly when I saw that confused face first emerge, and the instant we started that conversation, love became the most important thing.

We are embarking on a grand adventure, you and I. This book is what I was doing while waiting for you. Enjoy it!

ACKNOWLEDGMENTS

John Popper thanks: My family, parents, siblings, cousins, uncles, nieces and nephews (especially Petra and Jeff), Trigger, Blues Traveler (Brendan, Chan, Tad, Ben, and Bobby), Duskray Troubadours, Brothers Keeper, John Popper Project featuring DJ Logic band, the Zygote band, Wasabi, the Dogs, and Dean Budnick.

Management: Lani Sarem, Seth Yudof and everyone at UD Factory, Charles Attal, Mat Whittington, Dave Geller, Meghan Allen, Scott McGhee, Doc McGhee, Susan Banks, Dave Frey, Debi Burdick, Pete Malkin, Adam Schneider, Dave Graham, Bill Graham, Tom Gruber, Dave Precheur, Scott Patterson, Lance Matthews, and Chris Davies.

Agents: Jeffrey Hasson, Keith Sarkisian, and Chip Hooper.

Elliot Groffman and Janine Small, Scott Padell, Sharon Kimball, and everyone at Padell Business management,

Stu Fine, Al Cafaro, Al Marks, Patrick Clifford, Tim Lipsky, Pablo Pascal, and every record label I've ever belonged to and the people who have worked with me at those labels.

Producers: Mark Needham, Sam Hollander, Craig Street, Jono Manson, Dave Bianco, Jay Bennett, Don Gehman, Terry Manning, Trina Shoemaker, Matt Wallace, Mike Barbiero, Steve Thompson, James Leroy Wilson, Rich Vink, Dave Swanson, Jim Gaines, and Justin Niebank

Teachers: Arne Lawrence, Chico Hamilton, Bernard Purdie, Anthony Biancosino, Marylou Huchet, Joan Katz, Linda Smith. Larry Manceer, Jeff Hooker, Mr. Sutherland, Mr. Deeks, Mrs. Lesson, Mrs. Miles, Dr. Kimberly, Father Coleman, and all other teachers who have helped me despite myself.

Oscar Arrandondo, Raul Flores, Marty Sheridan, Daryl David Pearsall, Jodie Platz, and any other security I've had the honor to work with over the years.

All bands I've had the pleasure of serving with on the various H.O.R.D.E. tours and the other package tours we've done.

Larry Bloch, Pete Shapiro, Adolph Dutell, Tom Hosier, Jason Rosen, and Daniel Kellison.

David Letterman, Howard Stern, Conan O'Brien, Jimmy Fallon, Jimmy Kimmel, Adam Carolla, Jay Leno, Dennis Miller, Jon Stewart, and every cast and crew of Saturday Night Live.

Greg Perloff, Nick Clainos, the Barsotti Brothers, Nigel and Kaaran James, every single member of every crew I've ever worked with from day one (even the shitty ones)—there are too many of you to name, and you and I both know what I've put you through, I couldn't ask for more.

Everyone in the Air Force Reserve, USO, and all branches of military who I had the honor of serving with in my various adventures overseas.

Literary agent Zach Schisgal, Ben Schafer, and everyone at Da Capo.

All friends, exes, and impactful characters—if you mattered to me, you mattered in this book and I want to thank you. And if the editors yanked you out of this book, you may still matter to me, so feel free to confer if you have questions.

And last but not least, all fans and audience members. I'm blown away by your interest, and you have all my love and faith.

Dean Budnick thanks: First and foremost, Mr. John Popper. During our final session John explained that he was getting tired of hearing himself share anecdotes. I never did. Those calls from the road and at home were quality entertainment no matter how ragged the voice on the other end of the line might have sounded.

Jordan Popper, for her steady presence and welcome perspective, and Eloise Popper, the ruler of the roost.

While charting the story of John and Jordan's romance and marriage, I celebrated my own twentieth wedding anniversary, so I salute Leanne Barrett for her good taste and good humor.

My children maintained interest and tolerance throughout the process. I am ever amazed by Caroline, who squirms a bit at the title, and Quinn (be sure to download Penguin Zoom and the latest games from Eleet Studios).

My parents have always been supportive, as they were once again, even providing some cover guidance over Thanksgiving dinner.

Speaking of that cover, it was a scramble to land the perfect image, so I extend my gratitude to Amanda Peacock for delivering the photo John envisioned. Deepest appreciation to the effort put in by many photographers and interested parties, including Eric Brodsky, AJ Genovesi, Andrew Schuman, Stewart O'Shields, Patrick Stevens, Danny Clinch, Jay Blakesberg, Stuart Levine, Michael Weintrob, Dino Perrucci, John Patrick Gatta, Vernon Webb, Marc Millman, Andrew Blackstein, Erik Kabik, and Dave Precheur.

Thanks as well to everyone at Relix, from publisher and friend Peter Shapiro on through Mike Greenhaus, Rachel Seiden Baron, Rob Slater, Matt Inman, Sam D'Arcangelo, Brian Stollery, Brad Tucker, Chris Mocharla, Kristen DeTroia, Amy Jacques, Lilli Friedman, Olivia Millman, Colby Casoria, Angela Ribbler, Jonny Pepperman, Nikki Wiesenberg, Steve Grybowski, Wayan Zoey, Andy Turnbull, Deb Schuler, and the crew.

I am thrilled that Zach Schisgal served as our agent on this book and that he sold it to Ben Schafer at Da Capo, where I had once hoped *Ticket Masters* would land. Lori Hobkirk, Josephine Moore, Lissa Warren, and Fred Francis have aided and abetted.

The process of looking back to the late 1980s, when I first saw John and Blues Traveler, sparked me to revisit that era of the Grateful Dead and led to my novel *Might as Well* (due out right around now). Thanks to Paul Lucas for connecting me with Tyson Cornell and Rare Bird Lit during the process of completing this book.

All of which brings me back around to John Popper, the man so nice I thanked him twice. Hail fellow well met (and in overalls, no less).

INDEX

attends Grammy Awards, 190,
  191
and Blues Traveler repertoire,
  69–70
death of, 203–204, 205, 207–208
finding replacement for,
  218–219
following death of Bill Graham,
  83
goes to Crobar, 172
and human fly musical suit guy,
  163–164
influence of, on Blues Traveler
  music, 221–222
joins Blues Traveler, 36
life in New York, 48–49
musical education of, 37–38
Popper's relationship with,
  103–104
role in Blues Traveler, 52
supports Popper's solo
  endeavors, 199
terrorizes Tom Cruise,
  57–58
and "The Mountains Win
  Again," 160–161
shotgun, 14–15
Showalter, Michael, 275
Shriver, Bobby, 308
Shriver, Eunice, 289, 290
Shriver, Sarge, 290
Silverstone, Alicia, 174, 250
Simon, Paul, 192
Simoyi, András, 9
Simpsons, The, 50–51

singing, 69–70
Sister Hazel, 177–178
Smashing Pumpkins, 140
Smith, Anna Nicole, 180–181
smoking, 214–215
social media, 277–280
social music, 52–53
songwriting, 34–36, 156, 168–169,
  242–243
Sousa, John Philip, 266
South Dakota, 107, 108
Southern Ground Music & Food
  Festival, 308–309
Spin Doctors, 45, 46, 88, 123, 125,
  126, 162
sponsorship, 133
Springsteen, Bruce, 25
stalker, 247–248
Stamford Catholic High School, 7
Stamos, John, 308
Stanley, Owsley (Bear), 68–69
"Star-Spangled Banner," 185–189
Stax, 150
Stefani, Gwen, 289
Stern, Howard, 224–231
steroids, 269
Stewart, Jon, 180
Sting, 289–290
Stone, Emma, 306
Straight on till Morning (Blues
  Traveler), 197–198
streaming music, 266
Street, Craig, 259
Streisand, Barbra, 256
sumo wrestler movie, 148–149